Safe Passage

Safe Passage

The Civilian Evacuation From Hawaii After Pearl Harbor

James F. Lee

A Finch Press Book

The Finch Press
c/o Diana Finch Literary Agency
116 West 23rd St, Suite 500
New York, NY 10011

917-544-4470
diana.fnch@verizon.net

Cover photo courtesy of the *Salem (Mass.) Evening News*.
This personal photo, taken in Hawaii of Lee's mother with his sister and some other children, was originally published in the *Salem Evening News* to accompany an article about Lee's mother's Pearl Harbor experience. Lee found the photo in the *Evening News* archives at the Salem Public Library while researching this book.

To my mother, Doris Lee, and my sister, Andrea Tonne,

And to my brother, Bob, who didn't live to see this book completed.

Also by James F. Lee
The Lady Footballers: Struggling to Play in Victorian England *(Rutgers 2008) Finalist, 2008 Lord Aberdare Literary Prize, British Society of Sports History*

When we arrived in dear ole Hawaii we were greeted
with aloha and leis
But the Japs attacked Pearl Harbor and made us
evacuees.
But now it is very heart breaking as our Dad is out on
the seas,
He won't be there to say aloha or send us away with leis.

Jay Buford, age 10
Honolulu Advertiser, March 1942.

"... they were part of this new fierce breed of Americans – united, brave, baptized by fire and madder than blazes!" – *San Francisco Chronicle*, December 26, 1941

We are on our way to the U.S.A.
From the shores of Waikiki
Everyone [sic] of us an evacuee
We are making history

We're the Army and the Navy
And staunch civilians too!
With our kids and trunks and canvas bunks
We are launching o'er the blue
On the docks we sit and smoke and talk
There is nothing else to do
While 500 children fight and squawk
To the fury of the crew!

We're the Army and the Navy
And we're staunch civilians too!
And we heard 10,000 rumors
So we're always in a stew
We've had orders from the captain
Not to throw things overboard
So the pails are lined along the rails
And what misses them is flooded [?]

We're the Army and the Navy
And we're staunch civilians too!
And the children scream each ice cream
Appears on the menu
When we land in port, we'll get a snort
And we'll clink a hearty toast
To the Navy and the Matson line
For getting us to the coast!

—Written aboard the *Lurline* in February 1942

Table of Contents

Acknowledgments

The following people, organizations, offices, libraries and archives provided the essential information that made this book possible.

American Red Cross
Ancestry.com
Archdiocese of Boston, Robert Johnson-Lally, Archivist
Archidocèse de Sherbrooke, Archives
Lee Anne Auerhan
Bertrand Library, Bucknell University
Beverly, Massachusetts Public Library
Beverly, Massachusetts Public School District, Diane Lewey
Boston National Historical Park, Phil Hunt
Boston Public Library
Bucknell University, Office of the Provost
Bureau of Medicine and Surgery, U.S. Navy, Andre Sobocinski
California State Archives, Sacramento
Anne Chewning
City of Beverly, Massachusetts, City Clerk
City of Haverhill, Massachusetts, City Clerk
City of Salem, Massachusetts, City Clerk
Commonwealth of Massachusetts, Probate and Family Court Department

Commonwealth of Pennsylvania, Dept. of Health, Division of Vital Records
Diocese of Manchester, New Hampshire, Judith Fosher
Haverhill, Massachusetts Public School District, Anne Jarzobski
Haverhill, Massachusetts Public Library
Hawaii Navy News, Karen Spangler
Hawaii State Archive
Kamehameha Schools, Honolulu
B.Z. Leonard
Lewis L. Manderino Library, California University of Pennsylvania
Library of Congress, Newspaper Archive
Lisbon, New Hampshire, Public Library
Lisbon, New Hampshire, Town Clerk
Michael McFayden
Ben Morris
Paul Musgrove
National Archives, College Park, San Francisco and Washington, D.C.
National Memorial Cemetery of the Pacific
National Park Service, Boston, Phil Hunt
National Personnel Records Center
Naval Historical Center, Washington, D.C.
Nazareth, Sister Theresa Marie O'Leary
New Hampshire Bureau of Vital Statistics
North Platte (Neb.) Telegraph
Office of Senator Daniel K. Inouye
Public Libraries in Beverly, Haverhill, Lynn and Salem, Massachusetts
Franklin D. Roosevelt Library
Reverebeach.com, Bob Upton
Salem, Massachusetts Public Library

Anthony P. Sammarco
San Diego Historical Society, Julia Cagle
San Francisco Maritime National Historical Park, Edward LeBlanc, Ted Miles and William Kooiman
Sons and Daughters of Pearl Harbor Survivors
St. James (Haverhill) Rectory
St. James Church (Salem)
Sisters of St. Joseph (CSJ), Boston, Therezon Sheerin, Archivist
Survivors of Pearl Harbor
United States Military History Institute, Carlisle, Pennsylvania
University of Hawaii, Hawaii War Resource Depository
University of Massachusetts, Lowell, Center for Lowell History
U.S. Army Human Resources Command
USS Arizona Memorial Archive, Everett Hyland, Stan Melman and Scott Pawlowski
USS Pennsylvania
Willamette University, University Archives and Special Collections, Mary McKay

Prologue

Four ships entered San Francisco harbor in a cold drizzle on Christmas morning 1941, while overhead a squadron of planes provided an escort. Two were warships, the light cruiser *Detroit* and destroyer *Cummings*, but the eyes of people lining the shore were drawn to the other vessels, painted a dull gray like the Navy ships: the passenger liner *President Coolidge* and the Army Transport *Hugh L. Scott*, bringing home the first casualties of the war in the Pacific. Rosalie Hutchison, completing her trans-Pacific voyage from the Philippines, and Nurse Ruth Erickson, still tending the wounded, were aboard the *Coolidge*, as were the Willamette University football team, American missionaries, British and Russian diplomats, Filipino businessmen, and two baby giant Pandas bound for the Bronx Zoo, gifts from Madame Chiang Kai-shek and her sister H.H. Kung to the American people in gratitude for their relief efforts in war-torn China.[1] In the cramped spaces of the ships were also families of servicemen, some widowed or having lost fathers a little over two weeks before, and other civilians uprooted by the Japanese bombing, dazed, cold, and seasick, finding themselves back on the mainland on a dreary winter day.[2]

A school photo of Doris Huntress, the author's mother. She later married Andrew Marze. (Courtesy of Phyllis Hansel)

Introduction
My mother's life turned upside down

Anyone at Pearl Harbor on December 7, 1941 has a story to tell – if he or she is willing to talk about it, that is. My mother, Doris Marze, was living in Naval Housing on the Pearl Harbor Navy Base at 520 10th Street, not far from the dry dock where the USS *Pennsylvania* was undergoing repairs. At 7:55 that Sunday morning, she and her husband, Andrew Marze, and their daughter Andrea, 2, were having breakfast, when they heard the roar of airplane engines and the thunder of explosions. Looking out at the sky, they saw low-flying torpedo bombers heading for the harbor. Overhead, dive bombers were attacking the Navy Base, just a few blocks from their house, releasing their payload with devastating effect, while fighter planes strafed adjacent Hickam Field. Andrew pointed out to Doris the torpedoes clearly visible underneath the planes. A bomb fell nearby, shaking their little cottage, cracking the glass frame of a photograph of her husband, a memento Doris would later treasure. Exclaiming, "This is no picnic!" Andrew rushed out to report to his ship, the USS Dobbin, which was lying at anchor in the East Loch of Pearl Harbor.[3]

Most survivors say that their first impression was that the Navy was practicing at war games, exercises that had become increasingly frequent and realistic. Planes and machineguns shattering the early-morning calm on Oahu was nothing new; that it was Sunday was both unusual and an annoyance. The realization that an attack was underway didn't register at first. Some said it was when they saw the red suns on the wings of the Japanese planes, others said that it was the shell casings dropping on their property; for others it was the view of the harbor and the flames and smoke coming from Battleship Row. The instant they figured it out, men like Marze scrambled to report to duty stations, some running, some driving, others commandeering taxis, as Japanese planes screamed across the sky; it was chaos.

In a matter of minutes, the United States was transformed. With the same swiftness, individual lives were utterly changed. On that morning before the bombing, my mother was living in the paradise that Hawaii must have seemed to a young woman who had never had a stable family, whose father had left years before, leaving his wife and four children with never enough money for clothes or furniture, with little hope for the future. Hawaii, even given the limited offerings of enlisted men's housing, represented a stability she had never known. Within a month of that awful morning, she and my sister Andrea, early evacuees from the attack, were back in a Massachusetts winter, back to the old life. Such a great change either kills us or we learn to bear it. My mother bore it stoically, never talking about it, burying it, leaving it unsaid, unspoken, in the past. Because I wanted to tell her story and the stories of the thousands like her, I set out to learn all that I could about the events and decisions that led her from Massachusetts to Hawaii before the war. What I didn't know was that uncovering that story, starting out three years after her death in 1998, turned out to be a ten-year journey for me and a discovery of deeply hidden family secrets.

People hide the truth, sometimes by lying, but just as often by silence. In my family's case, it wasn't by outright lying, but rather by half-truths – and a large dose of silence. This profound silence was finally broken when I was nearly 50 and found out that when she was seventeen years old and unmarried, my mother had given birth to a baby boy, something none of my siblings, all older than I, had known. I found this out by accident while trying to piece together the facts of my mother's gypsy early life. I wrote to the high school in one of the towns where she lived growing up to see if she ever attended. The school sent me a copy of her high school record, which ended in the twelfth grade with this notation: "Last membership [in school] Oct. 1. She became a mother in 1934. Sept. 28, 1934."

I found out more details from my mother's elder sister, whom I had not met until I was 48. I knew that my mother had an older sister, but after trying unsuccessfully for a year to locate her, I had assumed Elsie had died years before. I found Elsie after my father had mentioned in passing that he had received a Christmas card from her a few months earlier. I took the address, contacted her and had a delightful visit about a year before she passed away. Silence on the part of my father almost kept me from knowing my aunt. Elsie knew of my mother's pregnancy – although Elsie, 19 at the time, was living with her father, while my mother and her two brothers were living with their mother. Elsie told me the baby was a boy and was put up for adoption.

The uncovering of this secret led to more discoveries. My mother's youngest brother, my Uncle Ronnie, was a disturbed young man who spent time in mental hospitals. I remember my brother telling me that Ronnie vowed he would never live past thirty; true to his word he committed suicide while in a state mental hospital in Massachusetts in 1963. As the news of my mother's illegitimate first child hit me with a physical force as if I were punched in the stomach, I was struck with a new revelation: it's Ronnie. The baby had to be Ronnie. Was my uncle really my brother?

The numbers added up. Ronnie was born in July 1934. The birth certificate lists my grandmother Agnes Huntress as mother and her husband Llewellyn as father. But that didn't make sense because by 1934 her husband was long gone, separated since 1925, living in Haverhill, Massachusetts with his "other wife" Gracie. In 1926, eight years before Ronnie was born, Agnes sued her estranged husband for support of their four children ages 11, 8, 3 and 18 months. Conversations with Elsie and with another aunt confirmed that Llewellyn could not be Ronnie's father. The truth was my mother and her mother were both pregnant at roughly the same time with illegitimate babies! I never learned the identity of either father.

All of this family information was hidden from me, ferreted out decades after it had all happened; yet my mother's Pearl Harbor story was never hidden, it was just never discussed – at least not with me. I was born in 1952, the youngest of four children, fully eleven years after my mother's war-time ordeal, so even if it was a topic with my elder siblings, when I came along time had faded the immediacy of December 7, 1941 – although even I knew that time couldn't fade the memories of those who were there.

I never once dared ask my mother what it was like –the fear, the uncertainty, the pain, even the excitement. I knew somehow that I couldn't tread there, that a door was closed. It wasn't just her Pearl Harbor experience; I never really talked much to my mother about anything – we were not a talking family – but this one area was more especially so, or so it seemed to me. And even if as an adult I had wanted to ask my mother those questions, I was unable to. By the time I was twenty-five, my mother suffered the first of a series of strokes of increasing severity that at first left her bewildered and confused. I remember one painful scene visiting her in her hospital room when she begged me to help her escape. She led me into a lounge area, pleading to me to just open the door to let her out, whispering to me like a conspirator in some elaborate plan. It went on for about half an hour – her pleading, wheedling, me stupidly trying to reason with her. Finally, she gave me a withering look that suddenly melded into knowledge – she was defeated. Slumping her shoulders, she docilely followed me back to her room, like a child. That look of defeat broke my heart. These strokes would eventually leave her semi-comatose, languishing in hospital and nursing-home beds for nearly twenty years, unable to speak, unable to walk, unable to communicate in any way, until her death in 1998 at the age of 81.

So questions were never asked when they could have been answered –although I expect the answers would have been unsatisfactory.

About ten years before my mother's death and during a stage in my life when I was trying to make it as a full-time freelance writer, I told my eldest brother that I wanted to write a story about Pearl Harbor and especially about Ma's role in it. I thought it would coincide nicely with the 50th anniversary. His advice in 1989: "You better hurry up." He meant that the principals would all be dead soon, not that I should hurry to meet the anniversary deadline. I should have taken his advice, but other things got in the way, including a teaching career that left less and less time for writing. I put the idea out of my head.

I took up another project, a book. On June 1, 2001 I sent a final draft to the publisher. When I got back to my office after mailing the draft, I sat down and without a moment's reflection started on this book. Evidently it had just been waiting for the right time to come bursting out. By that afternoon I was well underway. For three months I buried myself in December 1941, immersed in the Pearl Harbor story. During that week of September 11, 2001 I felt as if I was living the historical trauma of Pearl Harbor simultaneously with the unfolding contemporary horror of the terrorist attacks. On Friday of that week I came across several photographs on microfilm from my hometown newspaper that accompanied a story about my mother, taking the local-girl-at-Pearl-Harbor angle. The three photos included shots of my mother, Andrew Marze and two-year-old Andrea. I had never seen a picture of my mother that young, looking so healthy, so vibrant and happy as she oversaw my sister's birthday party. I had never seen a picture of my sister as a young child. And I had never seen an image of any sort of Andrew Marze. I was on an emotional roller coaster, conflating two national tragedies, one occurring that very week and one 60 years before.

This book attempts to tell the story of people like my mother: the thousands of civilians, many of them military and naval dependents, who were evacuated from Hawaii in the months after the Japanese attack. In the few months after December 7th, a pervasive fear of another attack, or even an invasion, prompted the military government to remove any civilians it could from Hawaii, and to encourage evacuation for those it could not force to leave. There were some who needed no prompting, who clamored to be free of oppressive military rule, to be away from the war zone, or to be back with loved ones on the mainland. The military government on Hawaii controlled almost every aspect of the daily lives of everybody on the Islands, including the rationing of food. Simply put, the governor's office wanted to reduce the number of mouths it had to feed.

The evacuation required considerable cooperation among the Navy, Army, federal government, territorial government, and civilian officials, cooperation that often was lacking. Bureaucratic turf wars, personal animosities, and organizational complexities marred the effectiveness of the authorities on Hawaii to coordinate the evacuation smoothly. Moreover, because of the information blackout concerning the departure and arrival of convoys and the general censorship the military government exerted over the press and radio, there was no effective means of communicating with the public about evacuation protocol. Evacuation hierarchy and procedure confused people on the Islands: who had to go and who could stay? If you wanted to go, how did you go about registering for it? Questions of this nature plagued the evacuation throughout the entire process.

On the mainland, the returning evacuees were often treated as celebrities or heroes. Newspapers around the country played the local angle with the thousands of evacuees arriving from the war zone, using their stories to rally the public and urge greater sacrifice on the home front. Local newspapers were quick to point out that war heroes weren't just military men, but wives, widows, and mothers, too. According to the *Boston Daily Globe*, reporting a story of Martha Toner, a local Army wife and her infant daughter returning from the Hawaii evacuation: "Army wives and daughters have traditions to maintain and they're doing it in the traditional 'chins up' Army fashion ... If the Army's morale is one-half as good as that of the Toners, there need be no further worrying on that score at all."[4]

The material for this book derives from several sources: archival material, newspaper accounts, memoirs, histories, and interviews with survivors of the attack and evacuation. It is the first time that an entire book has been devoted to the evacuation in a comprehensive way. While there have been lots of individual survivor stories appearing in books and magazines, those have been focused on stories about survivors' experiences in Hawaii during the days leading up to and just after the attack, and not on what was involved in getting them off the Islands. And while the evacuation itself was not a secret operation (how could moving over 40,000 people over a six month period be kept a secret?), it has largely escaped the attention of historians. The ordeal of the civilian evacuees illustrates the danger they faced and the stoicism most of them exemplified at that time; indeed, if readers of today are to understand the sacrifices of that earlier generation, the evacuation story provides much insight.

Andrew Marze in Navy uniform
(Courtesy of Phyllis Hansel)

Chapter 1
"This Is No Picnic!"

Complete Surprise

The Japanese First Air Fleet, carrying 20,000 men aboard 33 ships including six aircraft carriers, had departed Hitokappu Bay on the island of Etorofu north of Hokkaido on November 26th, and crossed nearly 4,000 miles of ocean undetected, roughly following the 42nd parallel.[5] This route had been chosen because it was away from traditional shipping lanes. The passage was fraught with danger, not only from detection by American planes and submarines or by passing vessels, but also because of the necessity of refueling on the rough seas of the north Pacific, a tricky process even in calm seas. Progressing in utter secrecy and drawing ever closer to Oahu, the Japanese fleet maintained radio silence and nighttime blackout; even garbage was kept onboard to avoid the telltale signs of the passage of a huge armada.[6]

In the pre-dawn darkness of December 7th, the critical moment came to launch the attack, as the fleet lurked about 235 miles north of Oahu. Two waves of fighters and bombers were launched in succession, the first to strike military and naval installations with the element of surprise, the second to finish off the U.S. fleet and to inflict as much damage as possible to the island's air defense. The attack planners in the Japanese fleet fretted over the weather that morning; they worried about the low cloud ceiling interfering with the pilots' ability to find their targets. It was possible that the pilots might fly by Oahu entirely, unable to see the island because of the cloud cover, ironic considering that the Japanese fleet had already crossed thousands of miles of open ocean. Yet, despite the almost total darkness and rough seas, the Japanese launched 183 aircraft from six aircraft carriers in only 15 minutes. By 6:40 a.m., all the planes of this first wave were aloft, heading south towards Oahu.[7] About a half hour later the second wave was airborne. The planners needn't have worried. When the dawn broke, sunlight shone through the 5,000-foot ceiling of cloud formations, billowing edges starkly contrasted in shadow and light; the, sky, ocean, and cloud were streaked in shades of red, pink, and blue. The pilots would not overfly the island.

The attack force consisted of aircraft of several types well-known to American intelligence and dubbed with nicknames to identify them: Mitsubishi "Zeroes," one-man, long-range fighters; Aichi "Val" dive bombers, distinguishable by their fixed-landing gear and 500-pound bomb under the fuselage; and Nakajima "Kate" bombers, doing double duty, some operating as high-altitude bombers, each armed with a one-ton bomb, and some performing as low-flying torpedo bombers.[8]

Listening to radio broadcasts from Honolulu, the pilots heard only routine music, no warnings, no alarms, no calls to take cover. Kazuo Muranaka, listening to a radio broadcast from Oahu, heard the lovely voice of a young girl singing a Japanese song. Knowing that in just a matter of minutes those listening to her, many probably children like herself, would experience a devastating attack, he quickly turned off his listening device.[9]

What Muranaka didn't know was that while he was listening to the girl's song, Americans on the ground in Oahu were "listening" to him.

By the time Oahu was in sight, the Japanese planes veered westward and then split into several formations, attacking targets from the north, south, and west. By 7:55 a.m., the torpedo bombers struck first, coming in low from the south and west, their primary targets the ships in the harbor. Slow and unwieldy, the bombers were tempting targets themselves, and relied on surprise to be effective. Attacking in groups of three, as they approached their targets some of the more daring pilots were only 65 feet above the water, practically skimming the battleships' towers.[10] Their torpedoes were equipped with fins and propellers that traced lines in the water before the impact against the hulls of the ships lined like sitting ducks in the water.

Dive-bombers made a run down the mountainous spine of the island, some attacking Wheeler Field and others heading due south for Pearl Harbor, where they swooped over the Navy Base. Fighters provided cover for the attacking planes and strafed designated targets. The surprise was complete. People like the Marzes could only look upward astonished.

Within minutes the waters of the Pearl Harbor Naval Base erupted into a diorama of chaos: with the battleships *Oklahoma* capsized and the *Maryland* billowing black smoke; the *Arizona's* bottom damaged by a torpedo; the *California* and *West Virginia* both listing to port, hit by multiple torpedoes in the opening minutes of the attack; and the cruisers *Helena* and *Oglala* both reeling from direct hits from torpedoes. Japanese torpedo planes were streaking across the harbor, their rear-gunners spraying machine-gun fire at the targets they just bombed; above them Mitsubishi Zero fighters drew anti-aircraft fire from the ships desperately trying to repel the invaders. And above the fighters loomed the high-level bombers, waiting to finish what the torpedo bombers had started.

After dropping their loads, the torpedo bombers headed home to the carrier force, leaving the high-level bombers to complete the job.[11] One of them scored a direct hit on the *Arizona,* hitting the powder magazine and igniting a fireball and tremendous explosion that killed over 1,000 sailors immediately. Japanese bomber pilots flying at 10,000 feet felt the blast.[12]

Most military and naval dependents lived in base housing at the Pearl Harbor Naval Base and adjacent Hickam Army Air Field in southern Oahu, thus hundreds of civilians found themselves in the eye of the storm. Both facilities, of course, were central to the Japanese attack strategy, but in fact the entire island of Oahu was under assault. During both waves of the attack, dive bombers and fighters struck with deadly accuracy at Wheeler Army Airfield in the mountains of central Oahu about 20 miles north of Honolulu. Ewa Marine Corps Air Station, 17 miles west of Pearl Harbor, suffered repeated attacks from fighters and dive-bombers. Of these latter installations, only Wheeler had significant civilian housing.

Women and children felt their homes shake as dive bombers in single file swooped down one at a time, screaming earthward to drop its bomb before pulling up with a deafening roar of its engines. Civilians could see the faces of their tormentors when the dive-bombers returned moments later to strafe the area with machine gun fire, flying just above the treetops.

Men on the ground and aboard ships fought back with whatever they could, manning anti-aircraft guns, grabbing rifles, even futilely shooting pistols. Pilots desperately searched for planes undamaged by the dive-bombers and withering fire from Japanese fighters. All around southern Oahu, from Navy Base housing, from officers' housing on Ford Island, and from Hickam Field, officers and men, as well as civilians, reported for duty any way they could: on foot, by taxi, by car, some even commandeering trucks in their frantic attempts to get to their duty stations. They came from the apartment hotels and bungalows of Waikiki, from Kapahulu, a small neighborhood tucked behind Waikiki and under the shoulder of Diamond Head, from the tidy homes shaded by banana and tangerine trees on Wilhelmina Drive in the eastern highlands of the city, from the steep drives of Mount Tantalus overlooking northern Honolulu, and from Pearl City, immediately north of Pearl Harbor. Nurses and doctors raced to the Naval Hospital, Hickam Hospital, and Tripler General, where the wounded were already filling the wards, many of them horribly burned. Mothers gathered their children and watched their husbands leave, not knowing they would wait days to find out their fate. In the moments after her husband left, Doris Marze didn't want to be alone. Gathering up Andrea, she and three other Navy wives and their children found shelter in another friend's house and huddled there for the rest of the raid. "The planes never stopped their machine guns during the attack," she later said.[13]

By about 8:35 a.m. the first attack was over.

Explosion Aboard the Pennsylvania

The lull lasted about 20 minutes. The second wave approached its targets from the east this time, dive bombers flying along the valleys of eastern Oahu and high-level bombers circling south of Honolulu to make their run over Pearl Harbor from south to north. No torpedo bombers participated, because with the element of surprise gone these slow-flying, vulnerable planes would be easy prey for American anti-aircraft fire and fighters.[14] In this attack, dive-bombers were used to complete the destruction of ships not sunk or disabled at Pearl Harbor, to attack the airfields in eastern Oahu, and to continue raids on Hickam Field. This time, American defenses were able to mount more resistance with anti-aircraft fire, while several American planes had managed to get aloft, the pilots exhibiting great courage in the face of overwhelming odds.

During the second attack that began shortly before 9:00 a.m., the destroyer *Shaw* in floating drydock took a direct hit, creating an enormous explosion that left the ship twisted wreckage, while Hickam Field suffered devastating damage, first from high-level bombers and then from dive bombers and fighters. Fighters and high-level bombers hit Kaneohe Naval Air Station and Bellows Army Airfield on the east coast of the island during the second wave. In the drydock area of the Navy Base, the destroyers *Downes* and *Cassin*, along with the battleship *Pennsylvania*, escaped relatively unscathed during the first wave, but received considerable attention during the second. A Japanese bomber hit the USS *Pennsylvania*, which valiantly fired all guns back at the attackers.[15] The explosion killed about 28 men. The time was 9:06.

By 9:55, the Japanese air attack was over and the force returned to the carrier fleet.

American losses totaled 21 ships sunk or damaged, 188 planes destroyed, over 2,400 dead and over 1,000 wounded.

The Japanese lost 29 planes.[16] The United States found itself in a World War and Hawaii became a war zone.

Everyone's lives had changed utterly.

Andrew and Doris Marze.
(Courtesy of Theresa Fichtor Marze)

Chapter 2
Living on "Easy Street:" Hawaii Before the War

Hawaii Calls

The very names Honolulu and Hawaii held a promise of eternal sunshine and escape for Depression-weary Americans, becoming a part of the popular culture. In 1933 "My Little Grass Shack" became a huge hit, reinforcing the image of Hawaii as a tropical paradise, where people could idle in the sun all day. On the radio, islanders and mainlanders alike listened to Webley Edwards' "Hawaii Calls," a program featuring popular "Hawaiian" music that blended Tin Pan Alley with images of exotic South Sea Islands, while at the movies, a slew of films with big-name stars appeared in the 1930s, including "Birds of Paradise" (1932) with Joel McCrea and Dolores Del Rio, "Waikiki Wedding" (1937) starring Bing Crosby, "Hawaii Calls" (1938) with Bobby Breen, and "Honolulu" (1939) with George Burns and Gracie Allen.[17] Of course the reality would sink in once newcomers got there: finding a place to live, making ends meet, living apart from husbands away at sea. But this was a far better option than many mainlanders had ever had before. To those young people, who grew up precariously with their struggling families during the Depression, joining the Navy and seeing the world presented possibilities like those in a dream.

The great ocean liners, such as the Matson Lines' *Matsonia* and *Lurline,* and the *President Coolidge* of the American President Lines, were instrumental in perpetuating the exotic image of the Islands. Brochures showed native women in grass skirts, sarong-clad men playing guitars under palm trees, as well as pagodas and sampans. Even ships' menus showed silhouette drawings of "native" women with slanted eyes who could be Hawaiian, or Japanese, but at any rate Oriental. The primarily Caucasian "Malihini," or newcomers, coming ashore from those ships docking at Honolulu, found a world unlike any other in the United States, especially in its racial makeup: the largest ethnic group, comprising one-third of the population on Hawaii, was Japanese. Even the concept of Caucasian was different from on the mainland. Whites, or "haoles," as a racial label applied to those Caucasian groups that did not originally come to Hawaii as plantation laborers, thus excluding the Portuguese, who arrived in the 1870s. The middle class was comprised primarily of people of Japanese and Chinese ancestry.[18] As temporary outsiders, military and naval families may not have understood the nuances of the racial dynamic in Hawaii, but understood that it was racially unlike any other place they had known before.

Disembarking from the great ocean liners arriving from Los Angeles and San Francisco, the mainlanders got their first taste of the Islands. Many recall with affection the scene when their ship docked at Honolulu harbor, a scene that reinforced the romantic image of Hawaii. "Boat Day," the arrival of a big ship like the *Lurline, Matsonia, Monterrey, or Aquitania,* names well known throughout the United States, was a big event; indeed, those ships were the lifeblood of Hawaii:

> *The stirrings and preparations began just before dawn. Lei sellers took favored spots in front of pier sheds and along lower Fort Street, there to sit and chat while stringing garlands chosen from boxes and buckets full of blossoms. The women looked like an arrangement by Gauguin and the thick strands of plumeria, gardenia, ginger, or carnation laced the morning cool with perfume. Then dock workers and a few cops arrived, to begin their bawdy bantering back and forth in Hawaiian. Cab drivers jockeyed for best positions, creating occasional arguments, and the Royal Hawaiian Band's truck unloaded its instruments and chairs. Reporters and photographers arrived to catch the pilot-boat that took them out to the liner for offshore interviews with celebrities. The bartender at the nearby Beaver Grill began polishing glasses at the first crack of light. And when later the crowds of greeters came, the dockside swirled with colors, literally jumped with anticipation.*
>
> *I can shut my eyes now and smell the flowers, hear the music, feel the lift of excitement as I watch, in memory, the grand white ship being nudged into the inner harbor. Diving boys, looking like seals, bobbed for coins. The air between the ship and pier was bridged with shouts of recognition, and when the ship's deep whistle blew, the concussion could be felt, a blast filling every corner, pronouncing that another journey was ended, that it was time now for greeting and aloha. ... To experience a Boat Day was like arriving for the first time.*[19]

Twelve-year-old Beverly Moglich's pre-war, five-day journey to Honolulu aboard the *Matsonia* still endures as a most pleasant memory:

> *In August of 1940, my mother, sister who was eight, and I were mailed tickets to sail on the* Matsonia *to Hawaii. This was such exciting news, not only to be together with my father, but we bought steamer trunks and were able to travel just like the 'rich people' and the movie stars. We left Los Angeles harbor and sailed to Honolulu. Friends took us to the ship and the send off was fun and confetti was thrown all over the passengers and docks. Our cabin was of generous size. Two beds and room for a roll away bed for my sister. My mother had a friend who was a friend of the captain. We were guests at the captains [sic] table one night and this was very special. Everyone was so well dressed. My sister and I loved the trip, it was a dream, after the seasickness disappeared. Five days at sea and then we arrived sailing around the point of Diamond Head. There was music played by a good band. Women in their mumus stringing leis of flowers sat on the pier. Boys diving off the pier to get the coins thrown into the water by the passengers. Then we saw my father down on the dock. It was a glorious celebration to be together again.*[20]

Joan Zuber's arrival at Honolulu aboard the *Lurline* in 1940 was similar to Beverly Moglich's and the journey across the ocean to Hawaii had a similar dreamlike quality, a journey that made her feel like Shirley Temple in "The Little Princess." Joan and her sister ate cakes and ice cream offered by friendly stewards, watched "horse races" (little wooden horses moved by poles after the players rolled dice), went to movies, and attended puppet shows. The only portent of their eventual return journey was the lifeboat drills.[21] The nine-year-old marveled at the strange trees and flowers and fruits she saw upon arrival. Jumping into the family's Pontiac as soon as it was unloaded from the hold of the

Lurline, they drove from Honolulu, "...a sleepy town as we drove through it..." to Pearl Harbor "on a two-lane country road that traversed fields of sugar cane."[22] She and her sister lived with their parents on Ford Island and attended the Kenneth Whiting School, where they took a daily nap on the screened lanai. They had the run of much of the island, roaming about barefoot with friends, riding bicycles, playing in an old gun emplacement, and swimming in the pool near the Officers' Club.

Hitting the Jack Pot

A tall austere figure, easily mistaken for an academic with his round glasses and dark wavy hair, disembarked from an Army transport at Honolulu on August 20, 1940 and looked around with pleasure at his new home as the traditional lei was placed over his head. Fifty-one-year-old Lt. Col. Thomas Green had arrived to assume his post in the adjutant general's office. While crossing the Panama Canal during his journey from the East Coast of the mainland to Hawaii, he noticed many ships laden with scrap and other war materiel. He assumed they were bound for Japan, a policy allowed by the Roosevelt administration, despite widespread public disapproval.[23] Like most observers, Green accepted the conventional wisdom that war with Japan was inevitable. Yet, despite this general belief and despite some strong Congressional disapproval, the United States continued to be a major supplier of such war materiel to Japan well into 1940.[24] Any reservation he may have felt over this policy that day in Panama was tempered by the fact that he was going to Hawaii rather than to The Philippines, where he reckoned the coming war would take place. Green, a career

Army officer, first served in the cavalry fighting in France in World War I; he later was assigned to the Judge Advocate General's Department. Other than France, his postings were not glamorous: Arizona and Wyoming, and many years in Washington, D.C. as well. He looked forward to the tropical climate and the relaxed atmosphere of Hawaii, at least relaxed in comparison to the competition and tensions of duty in Washington. When this plum posting was dangled before him, he snatched at it right away, as he wrote in his unpublished memoir, "... at long last, after twenty-three years' service, I had hit the jack pot."

Like many Caucasians coming to Hawaii from the mainland, Green was surprised by and uncomfortable with the preponderance of Asians in the Islands; and like many mainlanders, he worried about the loyalties of those of Japanese ancestry should war come between the United States and Japan. He admitted trying to understand the "oriental mind" and finding himself "completely at a loss." Once he settled into his work like "a cog in a well-organized administration," he took it upon himself to study the legal structures of the Territory of Hawaii, so that laws could be "streamlined," enabling authorities, civilian and military, to take immediate actions should an emergency occur. He presented his findings to Lt. General Walter Short, the commanding general of the Hawaiian Department, soon after Short's arrival in Hawaii in February 1941.[25]

In December 1940, four months after Green's arrival, Joe Lockard was glad to get his feet on solid ground. The young Army recruit was thoroughly sick of the USS *Hunter Liggett*, the Army troop transport carrying him and several hundred other soldiers to The Philippines. It was a long and eventful voyage from New York, hitting the tail end of a hurricane in the Caribbean, putting up for repairs in Panama, enduring blistering heat off the west coast of Mexico. Honolulu was just another stop along the way. A year before, back in Williamsport, Pennsylvania, hanging out at the local gas station, the restless high school senior's head had been filled with stories about soldiering in the exotic East. As soon as he was out of high school, Lockard and a couple of friends enlisted "all fired up to go to The Philippines." But the journey across the Pacific was impossibly long, for the reality of life aboard a troop transport was nothing like the fantasies heard in the gas station. Making matters worse, he was one of the few soldiers aboard not seasick, which meant he got kitchen duty, a hot, dirty duty indeed. "The galley of a ship is not exactly a fun place to work," he said later.[26]

When a recruiter came aboard the *Hunter Liggett* in Honolulu and asked for volunteers for the Signal Corps, the 19-year-old jumped at the opportunity.

He was taken by train to Fort Shafter in northern Honolulu, and then by truck to a wooden barracks on the Kole Kole Pass Road, a short walk from Schofield Barracks in central Oahu, where for six months he and his fellow soldiers bided their time learning about field communications and radio physics. Radar at that point was in its infancy, and while the United States intended to use the new technology in Hawaii as part of the air defense of the islands, neither Joe nor any of his comrades would ever see a radar unit until July, 1941, when six mobile units arrived in Hawaii to be deployed in locations around Oahu. At Schofield, there wasn't much to do beyond the class work and Joe spent lots of time at the base library. Sometimes soldiers, flush with their $21 monthly pay, would sneak over the fence and go to Hasby's Bar, run by a Japanese guy on the Kole Kole Road near Lualualei.

In November, Lockard was assigned to the Opana radar unit in northern Oahu, about 40 miles north of Honolulu. The dress code there was swim trunks, "no spit and polish." "I enjoyed it," he said, "because I am not a big fan of regulations." He grew a mustache, smoked a pipe and, when not on duty maintaining the equipment, spent many afternoons swimming, spear fishing or playing volleyball at Kawailoa Beach, where his six-man Opana unit was based.

Green's and Lockard's arrival in Hawaii was part of a larger movement that had been building for years. Throughout the 1920s and 1930s, the United States looked with a wary eye toward Japan, concluding that Japanese foreign policy was antithetical to American interests. In the 1930s, the focus of the United States was primarily on the Atlantic and Europe, but Japanese military aggression in Asia forced the Roosevelt administration to take action to meet the growing threat. In the spring of 1939, the Navy made a quick transfer of ships from the Atlantic to the Pacific as a show of commitment to counter Japanese intentions, although many of those ships were sent back to the Atlantic Fleet after war broke out in Europe. In April 1940 the Navy held war exercises in the waters off Hawaii. By the next month, Roosevelt, over the objection of Admiral James Richardson, the Commander in Chief of the U.S. fleet, and the War Department General Staff, ordered most of the West Coast-based Pacific fleet participating in the naval maneuvers to remain at Pearl Harbor indefinitely. This move was intended as a signal to the Japanese to refrain from attacking European colonies in Asia. Richardson, however, felt that Hawaii was too difficult to defend and supply. In February 1941, the U.S. fleet was divided into three portions, the Pacific, Atlantic and Asiatic. Admiral Husband Kimmel was named jointly as Commander in

Chief of the U.S. Fleet, now a largely ceremonial title, succeeding Richardson, and as Commander in Chief of the Pacific Fleet. Despite Richardson's protests, the Pacific Fleet was based at Pearl Harbor.[27]

The evidence of Japan's growing military threat, so plainly visible to Green during his voyage to Hawaii, finally led the Roosevelt Administration to take action. An embargo on scrap metal shipments to Japan was authorized after the Japanese signed the Tripartite Treaty with Germany and Italy in September 1940. Congress authorized a dramatic increase in the size of the Navy in 1940, and in October of that year passed the Selective Service and Training Act, through which 16 million men registered for the draft. Sensing the dangers and threats to the United States around the world, Roosevelt issued a Proclamation of Unlimited National Emergency on May 27, 1941, granting the president emergency powers that, among other things, allowed the Navy and Army to use civilian shipping for military purposes. On July 26, 1941, high-octane oil of a quality that could be upgraded to aviation use was embargoed from shipment to Japan.[28] The Navy, realizing that personnel fluent in Japanese language would be essential for the conduct of the coming war, created the highly successful Navy Language School in October 1941, replacing the previous program for naval officers that had netted only 36 qualified officers in the previous twenty years of operation.[29]

The effect of all this activity on Hawaii was profound. According to historian Samuel Eliot Morison, by June 1941, the civilian force at the Pearl Harbor Navy Yard "was more than doubled and the naval personnel augmented many times."

> *... hundreds of acres of land were purchased for enlargement; housing facilities for naval and civilian personnel*

> *were constructed; a new dry dock started; foundries were equipped to turn out castings of any size; and complete machine- and toolshops [sic] were set up, rendering the Yard almost independent of the mainland.*[30]

Much of the housing demand came from the families of officers and petty officers who could now accompany their husbands and fathers to Hawaii once the Navy officially recognized Pearl Harbor as the homeport to the fleet.[31]

A Navy Family

Andrew and Doris Marze and their two-year-old daughter, Andrea, were one such naval family living at Navy Base housing. Doris and Andrew had met each other in Revere, Massachusetts, at a roller skating rink on the Revere Beach boardwalk. She was a poor girl from nearby Salem. Doris had short brown hair, soft brown eyes; she was of medium height, but looked small next to Andrew, coming up only to his shoulders. She was 18 when they met. Andrew, with dark, brooding, deep-set eyes, a hooked nose, and a wide ingratiating grin, was 24, yet he was already a veteran of seven years in the Navy. Not really handsome, but big, strong and steady, a "tough egg," the good-natured favorite uncle who could always be counted on to bring presents when he came home to Pittsburgh on leave. He was the kind of guy other men instinctively liked; Doris' brother called him "a swell fellow."[32] When he met Doris he was a seaman first class aboard the USS *Phelps*, a brand new destroyer temporarily berthed at the Boston Navy Yard.[33] Like hundreds of sailors in the Boston area, when he got liberty he went to Revere

Beach, where he could ride on the roller coaster, go to the fun house, get something to eat – and check out the girls. Revere was neutral ground, an escape, a natural meeting place for a young person to meet other young people from not just the Boston area, but given all the soldiers and sailors hanging out there, from all around the country. A working-class city between Boston and Salem, Revere was famed for its beach and boardwalk running along the sweeping curve of Massachusetts Bay. Revere Beach Boulevard, lined with restaurants, carousels, roller-skating rinks, fun houses and rides like the Wild Mouse, promised a world as exotic as Salem was mundane. On hot afternoons, bathers covered the narrow beach, the salt smell of the ocean combining with the aroma of pepper steaks, hotdogs, cotton candy, and popcorn. Kids would go to the castle-like Blackbeard's Palace arcade, entering under the gigantic head of the pirate over the front door. At night the lights glittered through the elegant Moorish arches of the Spanish Gables, or under the huge dome of the Nautical Gardens, or at the hacienda-inspired Pirates Den, all ballrooms where you might dance to the Dorsey brothers or Guy Lombardo, who made Revere Beach a regular stop. And soaring over it all was the Cyclone, a white, wooden roller coaster famous for its 100-foot drop.[34]

The beach was easy to get to on the narrow-gauge trolley line connecting Revere to Boston and the North Shore. The cheap transportation was a major reason why Revere Beach was so popular with working-class people of eastern Massachusetts, as well as with servicemen who came from the Chelsea Naval Hospital, Fargo Naval Building in South Boston and Charlestown Navy Yard.[35]

Andrew and Doris married in Salem in February 1937, and by September the *Phelps* was assigned to a new homeport in San Diego. After a two-year stay in San Diego, the *Phelps* was assigned to Pearl Harbor in September 1939 as part of the growing American naval presence in the Pacific. Doris, eight months pregnant with Andrea, stayed behind in San Diego to have the baby, who was born in October. In January 1940, Doris arrived in Honolulu aboard the SS *Matsonia* with infant Andrea in tow.[36] Two months later, Andrew transferred to the *Dobbin*, also home-ported at Pearl Harbor, and by November, 1940 he was promoted to gunner's mate first class.[37]

The Marzes had to wait for base housing to become available, so throughout 1940 they lived off base in Honolulu, where they would have found a slower way of life than they were used to, and one more racially integrated than they would have experienced on the mainland.[38] And even on the base, where they moved sometime in early 1941, everything was different in so many ways from back home. Just five weeks before December 7th, Doris invited a bunch of the neighborhood kids to celebrate Andrea's second birthday; it was late October, yet the children wore dresses and shorts as Doris served them the three-tiered cake out in the back yard. Doris' best friend was Korean and her dentist Japanese.

More Arrivals

Among the early arrivals to Pearl Harbor was ten-year old Patsy Campbell, a Navy brat who had already seen much of the world, spending three years in Panama, where her father, a radioman, had been stationed previously. They lived in base housing two streets over from the Marzes in a single-story grey block duplex at 203 8th St., across the street from Hickam Field and two blocks from the main gate of the Navy Base.[39] This was Civilian Area III, one of five new neighborhoods adjacent to the base: 238 buildings scattered over 192 acres, a ready-made community with a laundry, two mess halls, a fire station, and four recreational buildings. The 1,000 housing units were described in a government publication as all "two-storey, wood and cinder-block structures," divided into units of one, two, and three bedrooms. Schools were located in nearby Civilian Area I. It was a barebones, new neighborhood carved from cane fields just the year before: there was no grass or trees, no garages and few cars.[40]

For working-class people, used to hardships and to the material deprivations of the Depression, it was a comfortable neighborhood, offering them everything they needed, and probably more than many of them ever had on the mainland. Patsy loved attending the Navy Housing School. And she and her friends were free to run about, to play jacks, play with dolls, ride their bikes, and stay out after dark without adults worrying about them. Sometimes she and her friends would run alongside the tracks near her house, shouting out to the workers returning by train from their day's work in the fields to throw them pineapples. It was a neighborhood of young couples and their children, thrown together from around the country, where it was easy to make friends, where there were always people around to give help when needed, to look out for each other's kids.

Yet, some chose to live away from the bases, perhaps in downtown Honolulu or in one of the suburbs. One such couple, Eugenia and Lt. J.G. Robert Mandelkorn, assigned to the battleship USS *California*, lived in a big, rambling house at the top of Mt. Tantalus, the lush mountain that rises within Honolulu. Eugenia considered herself lucky to be living there.[41] She and Robert could afford the rent only because they were willing to put up with the neighborhood's limited water supply, its great distance from Pearl Harbor, and the house's constant need of repair. Their reward was the visual delight that surrounded them, a tropical paradise of luxuriant plants, soft fragrances, and songbirds. Their yard had a sweeping lawn, lemon and orange trees, a terraced garden, and a nearby forest of papaya, avocado, bananas, and torch ginger. Looking out their dining room window they had a spectacular view to the sea, and in the valley below "the houses resembled a patchwork quilt, which at night sparkled with lights." Eugenia threw herself into life on the Islands, raising her son Philip, 3, taking hula lessons with friends, and entertaining officers from the ship at dinner parties.

Not all couples lived in such splendor off base. Another young Navy couple, Mary Jo and Jack Hammett, had married on the mainland in 1940, the young bride following her husband to Hawaii on April 1, 1941 aboard the *Matsonia*. As a petty officer third class, stationed at the Naval Hospital at Pearl Harbor, Jack didn't make much money and the best living they could find was a rented room in Kapahulu, near Waikiki, in a house they shared with a civilian guard at Oahu prison, and a sailor named Frenchy from the submarine base and their wives. It was crowded, exciting and fun. They lived in a 10-x-12-foot corner room with a shared bathroom and no kitchen facilities. Rent was $35 a month. Mary Jo, an industrious 17-year-old, bought a hot plate and cooked whole meals with it, making sure the landlord was not around. She lied about her age and found a job at Chapman's Chicken Coop on Kalakaua Avenue, where they served beer and waitresses were supposed to be 21. As the only haole (white) waitress she got good tips from the soldiers and sailors coming in. She made a dollar a day, plus tips.

She tried to cover her lack of experience with bravado, but Chapman's Japanese cook, Freddie, saw through her and took her under his wing, teaching her the ins and outs of waitressing. The best part, though, was that often Jack could eat there for free, allowing the frugal couple to stretch their money. Sometimes he would bring home ethyl alcohol from the hospital; mixing that with Coca-Cola was all they needed to have a party with Frenchy and his wife. For entertainment, they would go to the Kapahulu Theater near their house, where another friend would get them in for free. With the money they saved, they could afford to go dancing in nightclubs around Honolulu. Later, they bought a radio and Mary Jo took hula lessons. Mary Jo was having the time of her life, living on "easy street."[42]

The civilian work force expanded almost as dramatically as the military force did during the early 1940s. One such civilian worker was Ed Sheehan, a Massachusetts native who found himself a job in 1940 as a sheet metal worker at Pearl Harbor, one of hundreds of young men, skilled and semi-skilled, hired to repair and build the growing U.S. fleet based there. He lived near Waikiki, where the rent for bungalows and apartments was low.[43] Like many of those arriving, he was a working-class man with limited prospects. He described his experiences in ***Days of '41: Pearl Harbor Remembered*:**

> *We who were in our early twenties in 1940 had been teenagers during the Great Depression. Almost all of my contemporaries at Pearl Harbor had been reared in pinchpenny harshness, knowing the unending struggles of fathers, families and friends. My own background near Boston was typical: high school dropout, day-laborer, tree-trimmer, stock-broker's messenger and helping my father with sheet*

> *metal jobs when he could find work. My top pay had been $18 a week, and most of that went without question to help feed our family.*[44]

Sheehan worked at Dry Dock One at Pearl Harbor, first as a sheet metal helper and then as a ship fitter. By the time Sheehan arrived at Pearl Harbor, much of the pre-war building boom hadn't occurred yet. "The narrow road from Honolulu to Pearl Harbor in early 1941 ran a couple of miles through sugarcane fields," he wrote. "Along the route, travelers also went over the Keehi Lagoon marshes and passed a few rickety stores and houses near where Honolulu International Airport now stands." The main gate to the Navy base "was little more than an opening in the fence at the end of the road." And despite the constant hum of activity around the dry dock, everything on the base, except for Ford Island, was within walking distance; palm-lined Alii Drive "where the high-ranking officers lived" and the officers' club and tennis courts were side by side with the noise and smell of repair facilities. "Workers boiled tar and riveters ripped the air within a pebble's toss of the admirals' offices."[45]

Located between Waikiki and Pearl Harbor, Honolulu "was a charming collage of quiet town against a backdrop of valleys and mountains..." where the Aloha Tower at 184 feet was the territory's tallest building. The larger commercial buildings were clustered near the waterfront, and only a short distance away was a more Oriental Honolulu of Hawaiians, Chinese, Japanese, Koreans, and Filipinos. Evoking an achingly nostalgic memory of place, Sheehan described the bars, neighborhoods, dance halls, hotels, cafes, brothels, noodle shops, the Oahu Market on King Street, and the small houses hidden in the luxuriant vegetation. And he drew people in equal detail, dignified Hawaiian elders, winos on the beach, brocaded Chinese matriarchs, kids polefishing in shallows, and old men playing cards. This was an exotic world to those recently arriving from the mainland, "a revelation of bright beauty…a promise of freedom in perennial summer…," a romantic view that might have overlooked the workers on the plantations and the domestics serving tea and cleaning houses, an oversight perhaps forgivable in these young people because it was so unlike any world they had ever seen.[46]

Long Voyage from Manila to Honolulu

On the morning of November 27, 1941, just one day after the Japanese First Air Fleet left Hitokappu Bay, the *SS President Coolidge*, docked in Manila Harbor after a voyage from San Francisco via Honolulu. Working under a partly cloudy sky, stevedores were getting the last of the passenger baggage and mail aboard, while freight clerks were attending to the loading of gold specie. By 12:30 in the afternoon, the ship was securing for sea and just awaiting last-minute baggage. Shortly after 2:00 p.m., the lines were cast off and the ship moved ahead dead slow, and after picking up the harbor pilot, proceeded full ahead towards the North Channel and out into the South China Sea for the long voyage to San Francisco.[47]

The *Coolidge* was a majestic ship. Launched in 1931 by the Dollar Steamship Lines in Newport News, Virginia, at 22,000 tons it was one of the largest non-naval vessels ever built in the United States at the time, capable of carrying nearly 1,000 passengers and over 300 crew and considerable cargo in its seven holds. Easily recognizable by its sleek black sides with white upper decks and two smoke stacks, the ship could reach a speed of 20 knots, and broke speed records for the eastward and westward runs between San Francisco and Yokohama. By 1938 the Dollar Lines was dissolved and in its place the American President Lines (APL) was created. When the *Coolidge* took on passengers and cargo in Manila in November 1941, its two funnels bore the colors of APL: black with a red band and a white eagle and four stars in the middle. Since June, the Coolidge had become an Army troop transport ship by virtue of the emergency powers granted to President Roosevelt under the Proclamation of Unlimited National Emergency in May.[48]

One of the last families to board that day was the Hutchisons, a mother and her two children, leaving behind Mr. Hutchison, a mining engineer in Mambulao on the Pacific coast of Luzon in the province of Camarines Norte, where the family had lived for the past two years. Fifteen-year-old Rosalie, an intensely curious young girl who always asked lots of questions, was glad to get out. Her time in The Philippines had been insufferably boring with no school to attend, no children to play with, nothing but endless days to fill as best she could. One day a family friend had come from Manila to lonely Mambulao, telling her parents that things looked bad, that they should get out while they could. After that day, her life completely changed.

Rosalie was no stranger to long sea voyages and she was delighted to be aboard the famous *Coolidge*, so unlike freighters, her parents' preferred mode of travel. It was strange boarding the ship, though, not many people around the dock – not the usual hustle-bustle in the port. It was as if Manila Harbor was closing down. Some small freighters lingered around the harbor but there didn't seem to be anything else going on. At the dock they boarded by walking up a gangplank, and once aboard they did not go upstairs to 1st class or even to 2nd class, but below decks to a cabin with hardly room for her brother's crib. She slept on the upper bunk.

The *Coolidge* left Manila and headed due south, passing Fortune Island 2.7 miles to the starboard and Cape Santiago at the western head of Balayan Bay, 2.5 miles to port, and then into the Verde Island Passages between Luzon and Mindoro. Shortly after midnight the next day, off the island of Panay, the *Coolidge* sighted the U.S. Army Transport *Hugh L. Scott*, where the two ships fell into convoy formation and continued south into the Sulu Sea. Aboard the *Coolidge*, Rosalie made friends with Fathers Arthur Cuneen and Edward Murray, Catholic missionaries returning from China. Cuneen had a light and easy way about him and kept everybody calm. Father Murray, tall, lean, with sandy-colored hair and a slight Scots accent, took Rosalie under his wing, filled her hours, teaching her to swim in the ship's saltwater pool and taking her up to the First Class level to see the twin giant pandas on their way to Washington as a gift to President and Mrs. Roosevelt from the government of China.

On November 29th the *Scott* and the *Coolidge* linked up with the Navy cruiser U.S.S. *Louisville* in the Celebes Sea. Indicative of the unsettled times, with the threat of war with Japan looming on the horizon, the cruiser had escorted both ships on their outward voyage from San Francisco earlier in the month and would now escort them back. Both crossings were under complete blackout conditions.[49] Later that day, with the *Louisville* on the *Coolidge's* starboard and the *Scott* on the port quarter, the small convoy sailed through the Bankga Passage off the northeastern tip of Celebes Island, now Sulawesi, Indonesia. The convoy crossed the Equator from north to south and passed the port of Ambon and proceeded southeasterly through the Torres Strait between New Guinea and northern Australia, where the *Coolidge* stopped to pick up a pilot for the perilous journey through the rock-strewn strait. The pilot was dropped off at Port Moresby. The next day, December 5th (December 4th in the continental United States), the *Coolidge* held its first boat drill of the voyage, which for Rosalie meant at least a diversion from the boredom of the voyage. She spent most of her time on deck because the cabin far below deck was so stuffy; she would stand at the stern watching the wake of the ship as it made its relentless zigzag course, and while movies were shown every night, the selection was limited. Rosalie had already seen "Blood and Sand" more times than she cared to remember. Sometimes she would watch the Salsamendi family, well-known Filipino jai alai players, practice their sport on deck.

In the early morning on December 7th (although given the position of the ship it was still December 6th on the U.S. mainland), Mrs. Chin Chu Shee, a third-class passenger, gave birth to a baby girl. The mother and child were reported as healthy and doing well. At the moment of the child's birth, the convoy was near the island of Espiritu Santo in the Coral Sea, about 3,500 miles from Honolulu.

A College Football Game

On the evening of December 6th, the same day that Baby Chin was born at sea, the Willamette University football squad lost a game 20–6 to the University of Hawaii in front of 24,000 spectators at Honolulu Stadium. The Bearcats, from Salem, Oregon, had arrived in Honolulu to the usual

Boat Day fanfare three days earlier aboard the *SS Lurline.* Also arriving on the ship that day was Shirley McKay, a student at Willamette and her father, state senator (and later Oregon governor) Douglas McKay, a friend of Spec Keene, Willamette's football coach. Father and daughter, big Willamette supporters, were accompanying the college football team to Hawaii on its trip to play the University of Hawaii and also the visiting San Jose State football team. It was Willamette's reward for its 8–2 conference finish.

The 7th was to be a day of sightseeing for the Bearcats and fans.

Chapter 3
"Such a Day of Terror"

A Lonely Outpost

On the afternoon of December 6th, an Army truck traveling from Kawailoa Beach turned left off the two-lane road skirting the northern shore of Oahu. It drove towards the ocean along a narrow dirt road hemmed in on either side by rows of sugar cane and then zigzagged up the steep slope to Opana, a 500-foot rise overlooking Kawela Bay, offering an unobstructed view over miles of sea. Two men got out of the truck, which then returned the way it came. These two men, Army privates Joe Lockard and George Elliott of the Signal Company Aircraft Warning Hawaii unit, would spend the night at this remote outpost sleeping in a pup tent. Elliott, a new man in the unit, was learning the fundamentals of radar, a new technology introduced to Oahu just six months before. The six radar units scattered around Oahu operated only three hours a day to save wear and tear on the vacuum tubes, which were in short supply. They generally limited their operating time to the hours between 4:00 a.m. and 7:00 a.m., deemed the most likely for an attack. In anticipation of the next day's training session, Lockard, the senior man, brought along an alarm clock to make sure they got up on time.

At 4:00 a.m. on the 7th they fired up the portable SCR-270-B radar unit. Lockard operated the oscilloscope.[50] Elliott, the plotter, would remain in radio communication until 7:00 a.m. with the Information Center at Fort Shafter in Honolulu, reporting any unusual echo, or target, appearing on the oscilloscope. A plotter at Shafter would then mark the information on the big floor map of the Islands at the Information Center. Officers from the Army Air Corps and Navy, viewing the map from a balcony above, would determine whether a reported object was an intruder. Following routine, Elliott and Lockard made sure the equipment was working properly and tested their antennae, radio, and oscilloscope by picking up radar returns from known landmarks. They got strong echoes, reflected signals from their radio transmitter, from Kauai 90 miles northwest, from Molokai to the southeast, and from the peaks of Puu Kuki and Kaleakala on Maui over 100 miles away. To their north stretched 2,000 miles of ocean. The radar unit couldn't track anything closer than 20 miles out to sea because its antennae leaked pulses that reflected off the Koolau Range looming behind them above Opana rise, in effect, creating a 20-mile blind zone within which they could not track any objects.

Nothing much happened during the three hours of the scheduled training at Opana. Around quitting time they decided to keep operating so that Elliott could get more practice. The crew at Shafter promptly went off duty at 7:00. Moments later, the Opana crew saw a large echo on the oscilloscope coming from due north over the open sea. Lockard was astonished. He later said it was the largest thing he had ever tracked on radar. When he looked at the baseline running as a horizontal line across the scope, he saw the regular radio interference from known objects, like little spikes perpendicular to the baseline; they called these spikes grass. The target echo appeared taller than the grass, about an eighth of an inch thick and running all the way to the top of the screen. They knew it wasn't a ship or interference from one of their island checkpoints. And the target, about 137 miles due north, was moving right at them. Lockard had experience tracking planes on the screen; just a couple of months earlier he had participated in an exercise with the radar unit on Koko Head picking up aircraft as they left a carrier 80 miles off shore. His unit was able to spot the planes almost as soon as they left the vessel. This mystery echo was clearly aircraft, but how many they couldn't tell because the planes were coming directly at them, making it impossible for the radar to pick up individual craft. What they couldn't know was that they were looking into the teeth of a squadron of 183 Japanese planes.

Lockard started tracking the target at 7:02, calling out the coordinates to Elliott; and with each new plot, it was clear the target was getting closer. Using a rheostat, Lockard tried sweeping the radio antennae back and forth across the echo point's coordinates on the scope to try to get a sense of its size. Looking from Opana rise out over Kawela Bay he could see nothing with the naked eye. In the meantime, Elliott reestablished contact with Fort Shafter but there was no one to talk to. He asked the switchboard operator to find somebody. An Air Corps lieutenant got on the phone. Lockard told him about the strange sighting from Opana, stressing the target's size and direction. The lieutenant, thinking it was probably a flight of B-17s due in from the mainland that day, said it was nothing to worry about.

At 7:40, they lost contact with the target. By that time, it was within the 20-mile radar blind zone.

Later, the truck came to pick them up to take them back to their base camp at Kawailoa Beach. As they headed west on the road looking forward to their breakfast, an Army truck passed them going in the opposite direction, the soldiers on it gesticulating and shouting. Lockard wondered what the billowing black smoke was to the south.

"It's Just an Alert"

About twenty minutes after Lockard and Elliott lost contact with the target on their oscilloscope, ten-year-old Patsy Campbell watched more planes than she had ever seen before, flying right over her house on 8th Street at the Pearl Harbor Naval Base, two streets over from the Marzes. Just the night before at Bloch Arena, emcee Joe Fisher had spotted the blue-eyed beauty with thick blond hair and an impish smile and asked if anyone would be willing to dance with the little girl. A sailor from the audience said he would. The two young people won the trophy for the jitterbug contest that night. Now she cheerfully waved at the planes as they passed over, just as she always did whenever planes flew by. A man from a neighboring house came over to Patsy and told her to wake her father and tell him to turn on the radio. She dutifully did, but then ran back outside to continue waving. She must have thought the world had gone crazy when that same neighbor told her to lie down on the grass – these were Japanese planes, he said, they might shoot at her. Patsy obeyed, but soon got back up to wave. This was too exciting to miss, especially with the planes flying so low that she could see the pilots' faces. By now her father yelled at her from the house to get inside. She was still unaware of the significance of what was happening around her.[51]

In Kapahulu, about a mile from Waikiki, and 12 miles east of Pearl Harbor, a loud pounding on the door woke pharmacist's mate Jack Hammett and his wife, Mary Jo. In his undershorts, Jack got up to answer the door. Standing there was their Chinese landlord coming for the monthly rent. Jack shouted back to Mary Jo to get the money. She handed the $35 to her husband, an exorbitant sum for that tiny room in that cramped house. The Chinese landlord rented to sailors living "on the beach" with their wives, and he knew that at any time they could be called back to their ships or bases. After counting the money, he said in a matter-of-fact voice, "The Japs are attacking Pearl Harbor."[52]

North of Honolulu on the green slope of Mount Tantalus, Eugenia Mandelkorn and her husband, Bob were awakened early that morning by their three-year-old son, Phillip.[53] They were looking out the big picture window in their dining room at the spectacular view towards the city, when they heard the gunfire and explosions. Their house shook as it usually did when there was anti-aircraft practice at the Navy base, but Eugenia couldn't make out why there was so much black smoke in the sky. Her husband, the air defense officer on the USS *California*, wondered why he hadn't been informed of this apparently large-scale practice.

Then the phone rang.

It was the wife of another young officer from the *California*, calling with the shocking news that the Japanese were bombing Pearl Harbor. "Don't be silly," Eugenia told her, "it's just an alert." "Turn on the radio!" exclaimed her friend, and hung up abruptly.

By this time Lt. Mandelkorn was running out the door, pulling his clothes on over his pajamas. Eugenia wrote later that for the next three days he wore a very "non-reg uniform – sport jacket, slacks and a Navy cap." Driving off, he shouted to Eugenia to remain where she was. Mt. Tantalus was probably the safest place in Honolulu.

At 7:00 a.m., Lt. Col. Thomas Green, assigned to the adjutant general's office at Fort Shafter, looked forward to a relaxing Sunday.[54] The air was balmy with hardly a cloud in the sky, and although the sun was up, it was too early to feel the heat of the day. He lived with his wife in Waikiki at the Niumalu Hotel in one of the little cottages the hotel had right down by the water. From his door he could look out over the blue Pacific, calm that day, and see the waves breaking over the coral reef about a mile off shore. There was a slight haze on the horizon. Three small civilian aircraft droned over the ocean at about 1000 feet.

Like so many others that morning, he heard the explosions and roaring engines, and ran outside. Looking skyward, he knew this was no drill. He raced back inside, grabbed his gun, shouted goodbye to his wife, and then jumped into his 1940 Ford to report for duty at Fort Shafter about three miles away. Steaming with impatience at the congestion and chaos on the road, it was all he could do to avoid hitting sailors and servicemen scrambling to their duty stations. He swerved around a group of sailors running toward Pearl Harbor, only to be confronted by a petty officer pleading with him to stop. Green didn't want to hit the man, so he slammed the Ford's brakes and told him to jump in. The colonel made it clear that when they came to the fork in the road, one leading to Shafter and the other to Pearl, all the sailor could expect was that Green would slow the car down and he would have to take his chances and jump out. At the critical juncture the sailor leaped from the car. Green looked in his rear view mirror with relief when he saw the man pick himself up from the road and continue on towards the Navy base.

On Their Own

The soldiers and sailors living with their families, and those civilians working at the bases, faced the gut-wrenching decision of whether to report for duty or stay and protect their families. Duty compelled them to rush into the face of the attack to Wheeler, Shafter, Hickam, Pearl Harbor, or wherever they were stationed, by any means possible. As Lt. Col. Green had discovered, they found the roads clogged with cars, trucks, taxis, and men on foot, all easy targets for Japanese planes. Mary Jo Hammett saw her husband commandeer a truck, and watched helplessly as it headed towards the rising columns of black smoke she could clearly see the distance.[55]

Many women like Mary Jo and Eugenia found themselves alone and instinctively turned to friends and neighbors for support. Gertrude Carmine, a young Army wife from Pittsburgh living at Fort Shafter, was on her back porch cleaning her daughter's white shoes for church when she saw the planes going overhead. "I thought it was another maneuver," she said, "but then I looked towards the harbor [Pearl Harbor] and saw smoke." Bombs falling on nearby Hickam Field shook their house as fires started to break out. Her husband left to report for duty and told her to run for the nearby "cold storage tunnel" and get under cover. The exploding bombs and roaring planes were too much for her daughter, who froze in panic. Gertrude had to hit her daughter to get her to start running for the shelter. In the safety of the tunnel several neighbors were already huddled for protection from the bombs. They had to restrain a young woman from running out; she was desperate to get to her baby whom she had left at home, presumably with her husband, while she was at church. Her child was eventually brought to her in the tunnel. Later, a soldier came in with two small children pleading for someone to look after them while he reported for duty as his wife was in the hospital. Gertrude took pity on him and looked after them for the next three days. The women and children spent 24 hours in the tunnel before they were evacuated to other safe locations.[56]

The day started pleasantly enough for Mrs. J. Richard Watt, sleeping in on a lazy Sunday morning at her Wheeler Field home while her husband rose early to give their three-month-old daughter her bottle. Mrs. Watt woke to the roar of the planes followed by a terrific explosion that shook the house. After her husband reported for duty, she spent a frantic three hours hiding in a closest with the baby and her next-door neighbor. "Such a day of terror I have never spent and never hope to spend again," she said.[57]

Another Army wife at Wheeler, Martha Toner of West Roxbury, Mass., asked her husband, "Do you think this is the Navy?" "No, this is war," he replied. Rather than huddling in a corner, as she may have been tempted to, she kept a façade of calm, putting her four-month-old daughter in the linen closet for safety, and insisting on making her husband's breakfast. As Japanese planes skimmed the rooftops of the officers' quarters at Wheeler, she could see the dust rising from the machine gun bullets hitting the ground. She held her husband back at the door, pleading with him to wait until the attack let up, fearing that to run through the hail of bullets was certain death. Later, she was evacuated to a converted schoolhouse in

Honolulu with other wives and children of Wheeler officers and men.[58]

Feeling "marooned" after her husband's departure, as she described it later, Eugenia Mandelkorn quickly got dressed, grabbed Phillip, and ran over to the next-door neighbor's house, where several people already had begun to congregate. They all took turns looking through the neighbor's telescope from which they could see Hickam in flames. When the attack ended, a man in their group said "they'll be back and finish us off – all of us." Phillip wanted to go back home and read Winnie-the-Pooh. Who could blame him?

Patsy Campbell's mother told her to grab the trophy she won at the dance the night before, thinking that it might be a good idea for her daughter to have something tangible from her life before the attack. Then with brother Edward and dog Tinker in tow, the family ran next door to their neighbor Mrs. Dixon's house. Mr. Dixon had already left for the Navy Base with Patsy's father, and the men felt the two families would be better off staying together. Looking out the Dixon's second-floor window towards Hickam Field, Patsy saw smoke and flames as men scurried about setting up barricades and gun positions; out the back towards Pearl Harbor thick black smoke billowed in the air. She couldn't believe what she was seeing. Like everyone else, they had the radio on and when the National Anthem started to play, Patsy's mother cried. To the ten-year-old this was more frightening than the chaos around her because Patsy knew that if her mother was crying, then things were really dire.

Outside the Dixon's house soldiers were setting up sandbagged gun emplacements to shoot back at the attackers. Several of the men had minor injuries, so Patsy's mother and Mrs. Dixon provided first aid and let others in to wash their face and hands. Later, despite rumors of poisoned water, they made fried egg sandwiches and coffee for the soldiers outside. Patsy helped them take it to the soldiers.[59]

Margaret Bickell, the wife of a pilot, had a ringside seat to the American response to the second attack. She and her husband had heard the bombs falling that morning and after the first wave of the attack passed, they and another couple jumped into a small convertible to take her husband to his airbase. The car was strafed on its way there, bullets piercing the windshield, forcing them to continue on foot. At the base she watched her husband take off in his plane, and get shot down. He swam about 200 yards back to shore, where he got into another plane.[60]

In some instances that morning there were signs of humor and humanity. Standing on the edge of the Palolo Valley in the Wilhelmina Rise section of Honolulu in the hills north of Waikiki, eleven-year-old Gordon Lavering, and his thirteen-year-old sister Elaine, watched as a squadron of Aichi "Val" dive bombers roared past them just above the rim of the valley. Attached to each Val was a 500-pound bomb. From their vantage point 600 feet above the valley floor, the children were almost level with the planes. They waved as the bombers flew past from right to left, the wing tip of the nearest one less than 50 yards away. The last plane in the formation wiggled its wings in reply.

The children ran home two blocks away to tell their mother what they had seen. As they arrived, another group of Vals coming from the direction of Koko Head to the east flew directly overhead on their way to Pearl Harbor. Later that day, his mother gave Gordon money, telling him to run down to the Oriental store in Kaimuki to buy some food. The store was packed with neighbors buying whatever they could right off the shelves. Gordon eyed the big jar with dill pickles behind the counter and asked for one. He ate it as he ran back home with the food. It was his first dill pickle. And he neglected to tell his mother he bought it.[61]

Carmel Rothlin, a nurse at the Kapiolani Maternity Hospital located at Punahou and Bingham Streets in downtown Honolulu, worked her regular shift from 3:00 p.m. to 11:00 p.m. on December 6th and on the following morning was awakened by another nurse who lived next door at the nurses' residence, shouting "Turn on the radio!"[62] She ran across the lawn to the hospital, where just the night before triplets were born and during the 7th at least two more babies would be delivered.[63] The hospital was chaotic. Rothlin doesn't remember exactly what she did that day, writing in her diary that she "just tried to help here and there." By the time her regular shift started at 3:00 that afternoon, lack of sleep and tension were taking their toll. She saw the shadow of a man in a doorway, and she felt sure he had come to kill her. When she realized he was of Japanese descent, she thought he had come to kill all the patients as well. He turned out to be a member of the Hawaii Territorial Guard.[64] Even familiar people became sinister. At one point, Rothlin was so tired that she put her head down on a desk to sleep, thinking that if the young Japanese woman named Tanaka with whom she worked was going to kill her, "well then let her." Instead Tanaka approached her and said, "You are so tired Miss Carmel," and rubbed her back. Rothlin was stunned by her kindness.

Andrew Marze

In the midst of the attack, Andrew Marze had made his way to the waterfront a half-mile from his home, but he never reached his ship, the *Dobbin,* a destroyer-tender anchored in the East Loch of the harbor on the other side of Ford Island. Crossing the harbor, now covered with oil, debris, bodies, and fire, would have been a very dangerous thing to do. Vice Admiral L.S. Sabin recalled ordering a reluctant coxswain to take Sabin and another officer across that very water in a motor launch to the *Maryland*, "passing through a sheet of flaming oil."[65] According to Doris, Andrew Marze boarded a ship "tied to a dock." This ship was the *Pennsylvania*, the flagship of the fleet at that moment tied up in drydock. A sailor aboard the *Pennsylvania*, Everett Hyland, said Marze could have gone to any of those ships docked on the base side of the harbor, but for whatever reason he made his way to the *Pennsylvania* in Dry Dock No. 1. "Our gangway was probably the closest thing to him," Hyland said.[66]

Other sailors were making similar decisions. A radio operator stationed on Ford Island, after spending the previous night with friends in Honolulu, rushed to the Navy base in a cab as soon as the attack began. He couldn't get to Ford Island because "all hell was breaking lose," so he "just looked around to help in any way we could." He and his friends reported to the *Pennsylvania*.[67]

The decision to board the *Pennsylvania* was a fateful one: Marze was killed when a 500-pound bomb from a Japanese high-level bomber struck the ship. A marine wounded aboard the *Pennsylvania* describes how Andrew Marze likely died that day, assuming that as a gunner's mate he aided in anti-aircraft fire. "The Japanese used battleship shells, with fins attached, for bombing the ships. In the *Pennsylvania's* case, the bomb came through the boat deck's steel deck and hit the heavy base of the 5" .51-caliber broadside gun in No. 9 Casemate. It apparently rolled over on the casemate deck before exploding [killing] [S] ailors on the boat deck, main deck...it also killed and wounded some in officers' country."[68] The casualty list for the *Pennsylvania* lists Andrew as dying of "multiple wounds," and the list from the *Dobbin* says he was killed aboard the Pennsylvania "while assisting in effort to repel air attack of the enemy."[69]

The USS Pennsylvania (in the background) after the attack on Pearl Harbor. The ship was in drydock during the attack. Andrew Marze was killed when a 500-pound bomb struck the ship. (National Archives Photo no. 80–6-19943)

Photo # 80-G-19943 Wrecks of USS Downes & Cassin, 7 Dec. 1941

At about the time Marze was killed, the *Dobbin* took some fire and lost three crewmembers. Once the attack began, Fireman First Class Jeff Maner, who had just received his rating on December 1, secured the refrigeration plant then ran across the passageway to the armory, Marze's duty station, to get ammunition to carry to the gunners. Marze wasn't there to unlock the door, so the crew smashed its lock with a fire ax.[70]

After the Attack

Colonel Green, after dropping the petty officer off during the mad rush to report for duty, eventually made his way to Fort Shafter. He was excited and itching to fight. On his way to the office of General Short, the commanding general of the Hawaiian Department, Green suddenly stopped in the building's library, confronted with a crushing moment of crisis.[71] With crystal clarity he had a premonition of his future – and it was not one that he wanted, not at this moment of attack when his country was in mortal danger. He realized that he would not be put in a field command in the coming war. He was a lawyer now, no longer a field officer or a young man – and he knew more about the formation of a military government than any other person in Hawaii. In a gesture of despair, he grabbed a book from a shelf and hurled it across the room.

Green checked his anger and entered Short's office. The general and his staff looked stricken, but he was relieved to see they were meeting the crisis with a "cool detachment." Short nodded recognition to the colonel, but said nothing directly to him. Green then went over to the office of Col. W.C. Phillips, Short's chief of staff, to await orders. Phillips had gotten a call from Hickam Field, which at the moment was under attack, requesting a line officer to report immediately. Green pleaded with Phillips to send him. Phillips, not realizing that General Short had other plans for Green, quickly assented. As Green was rushing out the door to report to Hickam, he heard the imperious voice of his commanding officer shouting, "Come back here, Green, I have need of you here."

Around 10:00 a.m., with the second attack apparently over, Short took Green with him to visit Governor Poindexter at 'Iolani Palace to talk about martial law. Green brought along his file containing all the previous research into military government he undertook after his arrival on the Islands. The meeting was tense; the governor clearly worried about another Japanese attack and about the possibility of racial violence in the territory; in particular he worried about Filipinos seeking vengeance on the Japanese population. There was long-standing animosity between the two groups, and a Japanese attack on The Philippines could only make a bad situation much worse. At first the three men had to repeat themselves because of sporadic firing outside the palace. Then, after much discussion, the governor got up from his desk and walked out to the veranda outside his office, to all appearances lost in thought. When Green and Short rose to join him there, they saw that he was looking at some commotion down on the street, which was scarred by two bomb craters. Apparently this scene helped Poindexter to come to a conclusion, for a few minutes later back in his office he told Short in a solemn tone that he would declare martial law and asked Short if he agreed. Readily concurring, the general then returned to his office leaving Green behind to work out the details. Later that afternoon, Green, the governor, and the acting attorney general drafted a proclamation declaring martial law in the Territory of Hawaii.

The governor told Green, "You people are in charge now and you have my sympathy."

From that moment on, Green, moving his staff into the attorney general's office at 'Iolani Palace, plunged headlong into the daily running of the territory, controlling nearly every aspect of government.

Green's premonition held true – he would serve his country behind a desk.

Jittery Nights

Later that night in the darkness of the blackout, Patsy Campbell's mother and their neighbor turned over the front room furniture to make a shelter against the next attack, which they expected at any time. They heard guns firing throughout the night. It was the longest night the little girl had ever lived through.

Rumors spread throughout the civilian population. Mary Jo Hammett heard that the Japanese had landed on the other side of Oahu, pillaging and raping. Listening to the radio, Mary Jo and her friends, all civilian and military wives, anxiously talked about cutting their hair so that they would not appear attractive. Mary Jo said their hair length would make little difference in the eyes of a Japanese soldier, but that they should arm themselves, just in case. At night they would gather together, each armed with a knife, "the butcher knife brigade," to plan what to do if Japanese soldiers would come.[72]

On Mount Tantalus, Eugenia Mandelkorn lay under her bed eagerly listening to the radio, and with the aid of a flashlight wrote down the police calls as they came in. The calls were dramatic and often dead wrong: sounds of gunfire, suspicious persons signaling out to sea from the docks, flares and rockets lighting up the night.[73] Voices on the radio pleaded with their listeners to keep calm, which was difficult to do given the warnings to boil water, and false reports of Japanese troop landings. At one point she heard that Pearl Harbor was being bombed again. Eugenia poured herself a scotch and soda to calm her nerves.

In the darkness, she spilled it all over herself.

The *Coolidge* Transformed

After December 8th [Pacific Time] Rosalie Hutchison watched as the crew transformed the *Coolidge's* gleaming white upper decks to a dull gray and painted all the portholes black.[74] But even from the first moments boarding the ship, she sensed the tension aboard, occasional outbursts from the adults, a general unhappiness, everyone with "a doom and gloom look." Down at the saltwater showers she heard women complaining, "wringing their hands and moaning" about their uncertain situation. One night Rosalie was knocked out of her upper bunk by an explosion that shook the *Coolidge* so violently she fell onto her baby brother's crib. She found out later that the Louisville had set off depth charges against a suspected Japanese submarine.[75]

Rosalie doggedly asked her mother what was going on, but could not get a satisfactory answer, so the 15-year-old turned to Father Cuneen and Father Murray, yet even they couldn't explain to her satisfaction why they had to drill once a week, assembling at the lifeboat in their bulky life vests. She was assigned to Father Cuneen's lifeboat. The next day the ship's deck log made no mention of the attack on Pearl Harbor, but for the first time an entry stated "Sailors policing vessel to prevent smoking." The convoy crossed the 180° Meridian on December 9th near Funafuti Atoll in today's Tuvalu. And on December 13th it crossed the Equator again going north near Christmas (Kiritimati) Island.

The seas got rough during the final approach to Hawaii, causing the ship to pitch and labor in the heavy swell, taking spray on the weather side and forward. On the morning of the 16th, the *Louisville* left the convoy to look for the destroyer escort that would accompany them to Honolulu. Two destroyers, the *Reid* and *Cummings*, joined them at noon. By 4 o'clock that afternoon, and with little fanfare, the *Coolidge* entered Honolulu Harbor docking at Pier 11.

Rosalie saw the still smoldering fires from Pearl Harbor and now understood the tension on the Coolidge, the preoccupied adults, the boat drills. And it made her worry even more about her father left behind in The Philippines. She couldn't know it at the time, but he had been captured by the Japanese and would be held in various concentration camps around Manila. It would be four years before she saw him again.

Chapter 4
"The Military Are in Complete Control Here"

A New Day

Monday, December 8th dawned to a new era on Hawaii. For people in the military like Joe Lockard, gone were the leisurely three-hour trainings of pre-war Hawaii. Gone were quiet afternoons at the beach. The truck he and George Elliott had seen passing them earlier as they were on their way to breakfast was a relief crew heading to Opana to man the radar installation. In fact, all the radar units in Hawaii from that moment forward would operate around the clock. His unit would no longer be housed in tents at Kawailoa Beach five miles west of the Opana site; instead they took over plantation workers' shacks at Kawela Camp #2, within walking distance of Opana. The 'spit-and-polish' that Joe Lockard so disdained was back with a vengeance.

Civilians awoke wondering if new air attacks would come, or indeed if yesterday's raids were a precursor to an invasion. Wives, who last saw their husbands just 24 hours before rushing from their homes to report to duty, were frantic with worry, not knowing if their husbands were dead or wounded. All through that Monday, Eugenia

Mandelkorn waited desperately for word from her husband. It finally came on the 9th, when she received a phone message from someone her husband had asked to call. Robert was all right, but one of their close friends, a fellow officer from the *California*, had been killed in action. Eugenia was stunned. Hatred for the Japanese welled in her "and a kind of helpless anger at the whole world for letting wars happen." She was sick to her stomach.

And, of course, the families back home on the mainland were equally worried. On the Friday before the bombing, my grandmother, Agnes Huntress, received a box of Christmas gifts from my mother in Hawaii. Agnes was delighted to get word from her daughter, Doris, whom she hadn't seen in two years, and from her granddaughter, Andrea, whom she had never seen. She was even more delighted as she read the letter in which Doris informed her that not only were things going well in Hawaii, but that she and Andrea would be home for a visit in the spring.[76] It was as if Christmas came early for Agnes as well.

That all changed, of course, two days later when word of the attack reached the mainland. Agnes had no idea of the fate of Doris and her family. She sent a telegram to Doris on December 8th, but received no reply. Not hearing anything actually gave her hope, because word of dead and wounded trickled in to local newspapers around the country in the early days after the bombing, before the government placed restrictions on listing casualties. Neither Doris nor Andrew appeared on any early reports of casualties from Hawaii. In fact, Doris Marze didn't learn of her husband's death until December 12th, when the Pennsylvania's chaplain notified her, five full days of anxious dread after she last saw him leave their home.[77] On December 19th, Agnes finally learned the extent of her daughter's tragedy when she received a telegram stating, "Andy killed. Andrea and I returning soon."[78]

The fate of Eugenia Mandelkorn and Doris Marze and thousands of other military dependents, as well as the wounded and civilians not associated with the Navy or Army, was now in the hands of the military government. It wasn't intended to be that way. On October 3, 1941, sensing the inevitability of conflict, the territorial legislature passed the Hawaii Defense Act, granting extraordinary powers to the governor in the event of war. Under this act the governor could register and fingerprint the population, regulate prices, control employment, require people to perform public service, take over private utilities, and order evacuations. It did not suspend the writ of habeas corpus, nor did it allow executive control of the courts. One of the first things Governor Poindexter did once he signed the act was to create a territorial Office of Civilian Defense (OCD) to provide for public safety and to help the governor carry out his new powers, including evacuation of civilians from the territory. Yet, the provisions of the Act were rendered moot because the military decided to ignore them. Before the end of the day on December 7th, the governor reluctantly ceded any power he might have had, extraordinary or otherwise, by agreeing to martial law and the creation of a military government for Hawaii, under which the military governor had control of transportation and virtually every other facet of life on the islands, including the judiciary. Poindexter telegrammed President Roosevelt on December 7th, telling him he suspended the writ of habeas corpus, in effect, allowing the military government to detain indefinitely anybody in the Territory of Hawaii without due cause. The president responded approvingly on December 9th.[79]

The evacuation of civilians had been very much a part of the pre-war planning. The Red Cross and the United States Army discussed the possibility at least eight months before the Japanese attack, and the Navy and territorial government maintained an advisory board before the war to formulate policies regarding evacuation of civilians. The possibility of war and evacuation was so likely that the president of the Mutual Telephone Company in Honolulu wrote Admiral Kimmel on December 5th asking if his telephone operators, many of them Navy wives, would have to leave if a general evacuation were ordered.[80]

In September, the mayor's disaster council, a forerunner of Hawaii's OCD, surveyed homes in the "safe areas" of Honolulu to assess, in the event of war, how many evacuees could be accommodated there from parts of the city deemed as unsafe, primarily those areas near military and naval bases. The military had already designated a line separating the safe from the unsafe areas. All the pre-war planning paid off. In a matter of days after December 7th, the Red Cross, working with the mayor's office and the Evacuation Committee of the OCD, headed by Frank Midkiff, moved 3,000 civilians to temporary shelter, some to private homes provided by volunteers heeding the call of the Red Cross, and others to hotels or to the YWCA. Much of the Navy Base housing, for example, was deemed unsafe for families because of the proximity to so many prime targets should another attack occur. Besides, the military government needed those units to house the waves of civilian workers expected to come over to the Islands to assist the military and naval forces with the war effort. By December 11th, Doris Marze and Andrea were evacuated from their temporary housing at the YWCA and moved to 1917 Dayton Lane, off Liliha Street, in a "safe area" of Honolulu.[81]

Up on Mount Tantalus, Eugenia Mandelkorn called the Evacuation Committee and the Red Cross, offering her home as a sanctuary for those being evacuated from the danger areas near Pearl Harbor and the military bases. Soon she was housing eleven women and children; two of the women were pregnant. They devised their own rationing system with the food Eugenia was able to buy at her local market. The adults kept the children active during the day by taking them on long walks where they could augment their food supply with any fruit they could find. After one such outing, they came back in triumph laden with avocados, bananas, and papayas.

By mid-December, most of those temporarily evacuated were allowed to go back to their homes. Eugenia was sorry to see them go and saddened by the thought of living in her big house alone with Philip, so she invited another Navy wife and her five-year-old son to stay with her for their remaining time in Hawaii. Two days later, a big Army truck drove up to her house and unloaded several cases of food. It came from the Army officers whose wives Eugenia had sheltered in the days after the bombing. They wanted to thank her for her generosity – and to replace the rations their families had consumed.

Establishing Order

Much of the day-to-day running of the Territory of Hawaii fell into the hands of Col. Green, now Short's adjutant. Green's first task, assessing the food situation, led to the disheartening find that there was an eight-day supply of rice on the Islands and a 30-day supply of other food. Hawaii's food lifeline was the steady passage of ships to and from the mainland carrying the necessities for the Islands to thrive. For all he knew at the moment, the sea-lanes between Hawaii and the mainland might be controlled by the Japanese, or at the least, could be threatened by the likely presence of Japanese submarines. The food lifeline had to be restored if Hawaii were to survive.

But there were other worries Green had to deal with, crushing worries in their urgency and number. During those first three days, he and his staff of three officers and seven enlisted men worked at a feverish pace, virtually around the clock. In rapid succession, the Office of Military Governor issued a series of Orders establishing its control over the territory, some 31 Orders during the first ten days alone. Most of those Orders were already in draft form in Green's martial law file, written well before hostilities ever began; they included the shutting down of all alcohol-serving establishments, creating a Provost Court system, closing schools, rationing gasoline, confiscating weapons, regulating the press, and establishing a curfew. Green was putting his theory into practice.

Exhausted and hungry after three sleepless nights, Green left his office on the grounds of the Iolani Palace at 3:00 a.m. on the 10th and drove to his cottage at the Niumalu Hotel on the waterfront. How different that ride was compared to his chaotic dash just three days before. Instead of screaming dive-bombers, anti-aircraft fire, and exploding ships, a tense and uneasy calm had descended on Oahu, everyone, civilians and military alike, suffering from the jitters. By the time Green reached the hotel his car had been shot at three times by skittish sentries. Walking to his cottage along the palm-lined path, he noticed a sentry keeping within the shadows of the palms swaying in the night breeze. Not wanting to get shot at again, the colonel hid behind a large coconut tree until the sentry came within reach, whereupon he stuck his finger in the soldier's back to simulate a gun barrel and commanded the man not to move, then managed to convince the sentry that he was not a Japanese invader.[82]

Washington Responds

Resupplying and reinforcing the Islands was a priority for the federal government once war was declared on December 8th· as President Roosevelt made clear to Governor Poindexter in his phone conversation on the day before, when he promised ships with food and planes would be shortly on their way.[83] The president was as good as his word, for by December 9th "aircraft, ammunition, medical supplies, and troops" were in transit to the West Coast to re-supply Hawaii." Feeding the Islands, let alone defending them, was a daunting task, given that at the beginning of the war, even before the huge influx of military people and civilians assisting in the war effort, food supplies were low. The Federal Surplus Commodities Corporation (later the Commodity Credit Corporation), diverted food initially bound for England, and started loading it in San Francisco on December 20th.[84] Yet the 14th Naval District would report the following month that "Replenishment and augmentation of all critical items were immediately started after the outbreak of the war. Shipments of fresh and dry provisions, steel, clothing, lumber, cots, helmets, small arms, burlap sand bags, bedding, salvage gear, etc., were requested of the west coast (sic) yards and the navy department (sic)". "At the end of the first week [after the bombing], practically all of the business of the supply department had been returned to normal".[85] It was a remarkably quick turnaround to get the Islands' food stores, armaments and manpower replenished.

Washington was a whirr of activity in those early days as it geared up to fight a war. Hawaii obviously received considerable attention, but much of the federal government's action embraced a larger picture than revenge for Pearl Harbor. Federal control of transportation was an issue that transcended Hawaii, but had an immediate and important effect on the Islands. The day after the Japanese attack, President Roosevelt wrote to the Secretary of War creating a Strategic Shipping Board that would operate under the president's authority in order to develop policies on how best to use the merchant fleet for the war effort.[86] It was a stopgap measure that ultimately was not very effective, in part because of disagreements between the Army and Navy, and was eventually replaced by the newly created War Shipping Administration in February 1942.

Roosevelt issued Executive Order No. 8989 on December 18, 1942, establishing the Office of Defense Transportation, part of the executive branch within the Office of Emergency Management. This order allowed the federal government to take over, plan, and coordinate all "domestic transportation" in order to prosecute the war.[87] At a press conference on Dec. 23, 1941, Roosevelt made creation of ODT public:

> *...I have established the Office of Defense Transportation... in the Executive Office of the President. They are to coordinate all of the transportation policies and the activities of the several federal agencies and private transportation groups, compile and analyze estimates of the requirements of the future, and coordinate and direct domestic traffic movements.88*

Also on the 18th, the War Department ordered the evacuation of all dependents from the various war zones around the world, including Hawaii. A summary of the evacuation policy shows that, at least as it pertained to Army and Navy dependents, the evacuation was not voluntary: "Both services are requiring the evacuation of service families and dependents except in the case of exceptional circumstances involving valid basis for deferment."[89] In short order after the bombing of Pearl Harbor, military authorities had set in motion the mass evacuation of service dependents from around the world, and the federal government provided those authorities with a means of acquiring ships to remove them.

Change of Command

Thomas Kinkaid, a newly appointed rear admiral, flew into Pearl Harbor on December 12, 1941 to take command of Cruiser Division 6. He was the brother-in-law of Rear Admiral Husband Kimmel, whose days as Commander-in-Chief of the Pacific Fleet were numbered. Kinkaid later wrote in his personal narrative of the war, "If I had been shocked by the sight of Pearl Harbor from the air, I was doubly shocked by the appearance of the members of CincPac's (Commander in Chief of the Pacific Fleet) staff and of the senior officers of the Fleet whom I saw at headquarters. Each of them looked as though he had not had a wink of sleep in the five days which had elapsed since the Japanese attack."[90]

Kinkaid himself had an exhausting journey to the Islands. On December 7th, he and his wife were in Chicago in transit to San Francisco, where they were booked for the December 11th voyage of the *Lurline* to Honolulu. When

Admiral and Mrs. Kinkaid arrived in San Francisco by rail on the 10th, they found that the crossing was cancelled and the *Lurline* confined to port because of the Navy's conservative policy requiring naval escorts for convoys. Kinkaid was able to get passage on the Pan Am Clipper still flying its regular route to Honolulu, but booked solid by government officials. The flight left the Pan Am terminal on Treasure Island in San Francisco Bay at 9:00 on Thursday night the 11th. Mrs. Kinkaid returned to Washington. Admiral Kinkaid, however, was not too weary to see that, despite the defiant mood of the naval leadership at Pearl Harbor, none of the officers there had "a concrete plan as to how we would 'get those ________.'"

Five days later, Kimmel, adjudged by his superiors to have been unprepared for the Japanese attack and apparently not mounting an effective response, would be relieved of command and replaced by Admiral Chester Nimitz. On the same day, General Short, the Army's commanding general in Hawaii during the attack, was replaced by Lt. General Delos Emmons. Both dismissed officers had to face a commission appointed by the president to ferret out just what happened on December 7th and how the Army and Navy could have been caught unawares. Despite the ever-present threat of a possible Japanese invasion of the Islands, and only two weeks after the attack, the Roberts Commission began hearing witnesses in Hawaii on December 22nd. On January 23, 1942, the commission found both Short and Kimmel in dereliction of duty. Thus began, as historian Gordon Prange put it in his book *At Dawn We Slept: The Untold Story of Pearl Harbor*, "a frantic, years-long search to find a villain - some American or Americans who had failed or some dastardly conspirator who had deliberately engineered the attack."[91] Kimmel and Short were the early prime candidates. Later suspected villains would include President Roosevelt himself.

A Difference of Opinion

Evacuation of the wounded was an urgent concern on Hawaii, and on the mainland as well. The Commandant of the 11th Naval District, Rear Admiral Blakely, sent a message one day after the Japanese attack to his counterpart at the 14th, Rear Admiral Bloch, asking if Bloch planned to send any of the wounded to San Diego and if so, how many and when? At that point, Bloch and Admiral Kimmel had no ships to send anybody, wounded or evacuees, anywhere. The three most likely vessels, the Matson Lines' *Lurline, Matsonia,* and *Monterey*, fast ships capable of steaming at 20 knots and that had long served as a means of transport between the mainland and Hawaii, were being held at San Francisco until escorts could be found to convoy them to Honolulu. A message to Kimmel from Admiral Stark, the Chief of Naval Operations (CNO) in Washington, that same day assured him that the *Lurline* had been chartered (by the Navy) and would proceed at an "early date" to Honolulu.[92] But when? Kimmel, Bloch, and the military governor all had wounded servicemen and thousands of civilians on their hands who needed to be evacuated from the Islands. The CNO was as acutely aware as anybody of the urgency of evacuation. His daughter, Katherine, and her husband and two children were among those waiting to be evacuated.[93] Compounding everyone's fears was a message from Stark on December 10 that said more attacks on Hawaii were expected, including a *probable* invasion of islands other than Oahu (author's emphasis). Kimmel asked the CNO if the hospital ship *Solace*, then at Pearl Harbor, could be sent to the West Coast, and if he thought the Japanese would respect that humanitarian ship. The response: no ships could proceed without escort.[94]

The Army also had ships available under the control of the Army Transport Service (ATS). Most Army Transportation Service ships were ordered into port in the wake of the Pearl Harbor attack, including nine troop carriers and ten freighters. Four of those vessels, the *Etolin, President Johnson, Tasker Bliss,* and *President Garfield,* which would all figure prominently in the convoys between Hawaii and the West Coast, had just departed San Francisco and were quickly routed back into port on December 8th and 9th to take on supplies. Two army ships at sea at the time of the attack eventually formed the first convoy carrying civilians and wounded from Honolulu to the West Coast of the mainland. On December 7th, The USAT *Hugh L. Scott,* an Army transport, and the SS *President Coolidge,* an ocean liner owned and operated by the American President Lines and under contract with the Army, were carrying evacuees from Manila to Honolulu accompanied by a naval escort. The *Coolidge* and *Scott,* thus, were the logical choices as the first evacuation ships under wartime conditions. As early as July 15, 1941, the *Coolidge* had delivered troops to American bases in the Pacific and evacuated stranded civilians from The Philippines.[95]

The slowness of the Navy's response in providing ships to Hawaii produced a rift between the services, with the Army favoring immediate action. The massive federal supply effort on the mainland for the relief of Hawaii was in the capable hands of General Brehon Somervell, the new Assistant Chief of Staff for Supply (G-4) appointed just two weeks before the start of the war, part of General Marshall's newly organized War Department staff structure. Somervell was not a popular officer: urbane, witty and charming, yet ruthlessly ambitious, known for his fiery temper and profanity-laced outbursts of anger laced with sarcasm. One observer labeled him "dynamite in a Tiffany box." Yet, his dogged persistence in whatever task he undertook and his hatred for red tape made him just the man to oversee the intricacies of supplying a worldwide war effort. A motto on the wall of his office perhaps best summed his character: "We Do the Impossible Immediately. The Miraculous Takes a Little Longer."[96]

His desire to do the impossible immediately put him at odds with the Navy. Somervell and the Army Transportation Service wanted to load the *Lurline*, *Monterey*, and *Matsonia* sitting idle at San Francisco with as many men, airplanes, parts, and ammunition as possible and make a dash to Hawaii without naval escort. Given the speed of those ships they would have little to fear from Japanese submarines. The Navy insisted on delaying any convoys between Hawaii and the West Coast until sufficient destroyers and light cruisers could be rounded up to provide escort. For four days, from December 12th to the 16th, the three Matson Lines ships bided their time, and Somervell fumed, before the Navy was able to supply a destroyer escort.[97]

The *Coolidge* and *Scott* arrived in Honolulu, December 16th, on the same day the Navy escorts finally arrived at San Francisco to free the ships waiting there, and the very next day two convoys, totaling ten cargo and troop ships and ocean liners, left San Francisco for Honolulu. Before those convoys could arrive in Hawaii, though, the *Coolidge* and *Scott* would already be well on their way to the mainland.[98] The convoys of military and naval dependents to the mainland were finally underway.

On December 19th, not wanting to lose any more time preparing for the evacuation of the Hawaiian Islands, the Army Chief of the Transportation Branch, Col. C.P. Gross, a friend of General Somervell's from their days together at West Point, ordered port commanders to arm all Army transports and chartered vessels "giving priority to the ships used in the evacuation of dependents of men in overseas garrisons."[99] Somervell, Gross, and the Army tried their best to coordinate with the Navy despite their differences. On December 20th, the Quartermaster General requested the Army Transport Service in New York and San Francisco "to offer every assistance to the Navy dept."[100]

This inter-service convoy disagreement worried General Emmons, the new military governor in Hawaii. His concern was that the bottleneck created by port congestion on the West Coast, the general lack of available transports, and the Navy's insistence on providing escorts "slowed the flow of supplies to the Hawaiian area." He sent "a steady stream of complaints about the shipping situation to Washington." Eventually the improving security situation in the eastern Pacific led to the lifting of the unescorted vessel ban in late January 1942. The effect was immediate. In March 1942, 200,000 tons of Army cargo was shipped to Hawaii; double the total for January.[101]

The two branches of the service knew well before the war that they would have to cooperate in the event of hostilities and worked out a pre-war plan of cooperation: the Navy was charged with protecting sea routes, while it was expected that the Army would turn all of its vessels over to Navy control. This transfer never happened, in large part because the Navy didn't have enough men to furnish crews for the Army vessels. When it became evident that the Army would retain control over its ocean-going vessels, the Navy and Army worked out a compromise that Army gun crews would man the guns of its own ships, regardless of which branch of the service provided the armaments to those ships. Many vessels commandeered into military service had been civilian freighters and transports before the war started and had to be converted for wartime use, including installing armaments. Yet, on January 7, 1942, the Navy unilaterally decided to provide its own gun crews on Army ships that had Navy armaments aboard, confounding the earlier agreement and leaving some ships with mixed gun crews.[102]

On Hawaii, the Office of the Military Governor established the Cargo and Passenger Control agency in January 1942 as an attempt to increase cooperation between the two services. The agency was headed by a naval officer and included Army, Navy, and civilian representatives; it "controlled and allocated berthing space and longshoremen and coordinated all shipping in Honolulu Harbor." But the general rule in Hawaii was that Army and Navy operations were handled separately, each service using its own supplies and shipping.[103] This tension between the Army and Navy over evacuation and shipping policies in Hawaii would persist as long as Hawaii was under military control.

Hierarchy of Evacuees

At some point, whether following the Navy's cautious planning or the Army's bold call for action, ships would become available to convoy the wounded and civilians off of the Islands, and authorities would need to decide who should go. On December 12th, Admiral Stark assigned the following priority to evacuees: "wounded, tourists, army and navy personnel, general personnel. Space available on Army, Navy and commercial shipping will be pooled. Com14 [Commandant of the 14th Naval District] evacuation control." The message said that the Army Chief of Staff concurs.[104] By mid-December, the Navy revamped the criteria as follows:

(1) Naval personnel – hospitalization cases.
(2) Dependents, account illness – established by the District Medical Officer.
(3) Dependents, account distress – established by the District Chaplain.
(4) Officers under orders and their dependents.
(5) Dependents living in navy housing areas ordered cleared by the commandant.
(6) Dependents who are prepared and desire to leave.[105]

Using these criteria, the Navy in December registered 12,960 dependents and planned for their evacuation. Although these Navy criteria make no mention of civilians unaffiliated with the Army or Navy, unlike the original criteria from Stark, which considered "tourists," Naval authorities were acutely aware that many unaffiliated civilians needed and wanted evacuating. Among those unaffiliated tourists were the football teams and fans from Willamette University and San Jose State.

While the hierarchy of evacuees was being sorted out, neither the Navy nor the Army was waiting around for orders from Washington before starting the evacuation process. On the day after the bombing General Short's Chief of Staff, Colonel Walter C. Phillips, sent this telephone message to General Marshall's Office: "Desire authorization for evacuation of dependents at expense of government and for crating and shipping furniture." A memo from Admiral Bloch, the Commandant of the 12th Naval District headquartered at Pearl Harbor, to Admiral Kimmel on the 15th proposed "to immediately start to evacuate the dependents of Navy and Marine Corps personnel in Hawaii." And on December 16th, General Marshall wrote to his step son-in-law, serving in the Army in the Panama Canal Zone, that no decision had been made as yet about evacuating military dependents from Panama, but "We are of course starting the evacuation from Hawaii."[106]

Putting Theory to Practice

Early in the morning of Monday, December 15th, Colonel Green phoned Governor Poindexter and asked for a meeting. A few minutes later Green walked out to the veranda outside his office on the second floor of Iolani Palace and took the few steps to Poindexter's office, where he gently wrapped on the French doors. Because General Emmons, due to arrive the next day, would officially replace the disgraced General Short on the 17th, Green had a lot to discuss with the governor. Just the night before Green had held a long conference with the officers on his staff to go over what they felt needed to be done to ensure the security of the territory. They all assumed Emmons would bring his own men and they would all be replaced. Green felt it was his duty to present the incoming military governor with a viable plan of action and he wanted the civilian governor on board with his recommendations. Under the Organic Act of 1900 establishing the Territory of Hawaii, the President of the United States appointed the Governor of Hawaii. It was essential that Roosevelt's appointed governor be involved with the creation of the military government if for no other reason than to give the new government legitimacy in the eyes of the Hawaiian people.

Green liked Poindexter and placed great trust in him. He learned early on that the septuagenarian governor had a way of talking around a subject, but that by the end of a conversation between the two, amicable decisions were usually reached. At the moment, Green was particularly worried about the fate of the Japanese population in Hawaii. Green and his staff felt that mass deportations of Japanese and Americans of Japanese ancestry to other Hawaiian islands or to the mainland was a mistake. He knew this position was risky and might create resentment with non-Japanese civilians, particularly the Filipinos and Koreans in Hawaii, but he questioned both the legality and practicality of such measures. In his mind, only those Japanese of interest to the FBI should face any kind of special scrutiny. Besides, Green had already made it known that he completely disagreed with the policy of mass evacuations of West Coast Japanese that was being discussed at the time. Green's persuasive powers worked. Governor Poindexter agreed that the incoming military governor would continue to provide food and security for the people of Hawaii and that there should be no mass deportations of any racial group.

Ever cognizant of civilian sensibilities in this new military government, which after all was his own creation, Green would repeatedly engage in this "veranda diplomacy," that perhaps epitomized the very essence of Hawaii. The next day Green presented to the newly arrived General Emmons his plan organizing the military government of the Territory of Hawaii, which Emmons heartily approved in full. The two men sat alone in the Green's office. After an awkward silence that Green thought presaged his sacking,

Emmons said, "Well, have you anything else for me?" When Green replied no, the general rose and said, "Well, I'll be seeing you."[107]

Green would not be replaced.

Running the Show

Green met often with Emmons, usually their first meeting of the day, and they formed a very cordial relationship in which the general clearly appreciated Green's attention to the details of government, once telling Assistant Secretary of War McCloy that Green "ran the show." Green's office was the focal point in the military government around which Hawaiians' daily life revolved: rationing, price controls, transportation, evacuation, curfew, public health, censorship, traffic control, alcohol restrictions, criminal justice; literally every aspect of government flowed through his office with the exception of taxation. Green himself often inspected convoys late at night before they sailed, making sure that all safety measures had been undertaken and that evacuees conformed to the criteria established by the military government and the Navy. Both Emmons and Green were sensitive to their relationships with the civilian leadership, with Emmons' encouraging Green's growing closeness with Governor Poindexter. Green told his staff to avoid an "autocratic mode," easy enough given the military's "complete control" in Hawaii; "we can believe ourselves infallible" he said, but reminded his staff that they were indeed not that.[108]

Most of the coordinating responsibility between the branches of the service, the territorial government, and the federal government fell to Green. His daily calendar was filled with meetings of representatives from the civilian government and their military and naval counterparts, and with visitors from Washington. He also received many civilians in his office as well. Much of the coordination involved the evacuation, a collaborative effort between the Navy, Army, and civilian government.

Among Green's regular civilian visitors was Frank Midkiff, as noted previously, Chairman of the Evacuation Division of the Territorial OCD, created by Governor Poindexter in conjunction with the federal act establishing the national OCD. The military government had no political will to order civilians to evacuate, but encouraged them to in order to reduce the burden of defending and feeding Hawaii. As a result, thousands registered for evacuation. Midkiff's many responsibilities included planning and overseeing civilian evacuations to the mainland and away from the danger areas on the islands. He fought to keep his independence from the military governor's office, while cooperating with the authorities as much as he could. Green didn't like him, considering him unreliable and subject to local pressure, little more than a socialite, and they often clashed about evacuation lists. From Midkiff's point of view, the OCD predated the establishment of military rule and by virtue of the Hawaii Defense Act had a legal basis for its independence.[109] The Army and Navy did not share this view.

Midkiff's Evacuation Division reported to the Director of Civilian Defense, Frank Locey, who reported directly to Green on many matters including evacuation. Locey had a much more cordial relationship with Green, who considered Locey a friend. Midkiff had access to Green as well, but apparently that wasn't enough for him. In an attempt to get his way, Midkiff repeatedly went over the head of his boss, Locey, and appealed directly to General Emmons. Things got so bad that Locey complained to Green, asking him to order Midkiff to stay within the confines of the hierarchy. Green thought it wiser to have a quiet word with Emmons who likely would see things their way.[110]

On the Navy's side, a major player, at least in the early stages of the evacuation, was Captain Max Frucht, headquartered at the Castle and Cooke Building in downtown Honolulu, whose official title was U.S. Naval Representative for Evacuation.[111] Frucht, born in London, England in 1877, enlisted in the Navy in 1893, and served in the Spanish-American War and World War I. When he received his captain's commission in 1927, it marked the first time in the history of the Navy an enlisted man had ever achieved that rank; he retired for the first time in 1940. He was called back to active duty in July 1941 and assigned to the Maritime Commission in Honolulu. As the man charged with carrying out the Navy's evacuation policy after the war started, he assessed the official priorities and determined who should evacuate and when. Frucht's role encompassed more than Navy dependents. Much of his correspondence shows that he was a coordinator between the various branches of the services, civilian ship carriers, and those responsible for the civilian evacuation. Frucht reported to Admiral Bloch, the Commandant of the 14th Naval District at Pearl Harbor.

These were some of the players responsible for coordinating the evacuation of ultimately over 40,000 civilians, the men who prepared the ships, arranged the evacuation hierarchy, and notified those who had to leave. Theirs was a task unique in U.S. history: a large-scale evacuation by ship of Americans from one part of the United States to another in time of war. Their efforts would be plagued by bureaucratic infighting, inter-service rivalries, and the conflicting desires of those wanting to stay and those wanting to go.

Chapter 5
"Get Over That Sore Tooth Soon and Get to Work!"

Early Fears

Lurking in the minds of everyone in Hawaii was the fear of invasion; indeed the very restrictions in place were there because invasion was a possibility. Surely, if the Japanese could be so successful in launching an airborne attack from the mid-Pacific and causing so much damage to the American fleet, could an invasion be far off? Why else bomb Pearl Harbor in the first place? And all the while the news from the Pacific gave greater urgency to those invasion fears as Japanese success followed success at Manila, Wake Island, Guam, Hong Kong, and Singapore. Hawaii must have seemed like the next logical step. In the days after Manila fell on January 2, 1942, Honolulu newspapers ran headlines such as "Americans in Manila Report Harsh Treatment by Enemy," and "Threat of Hostage Deaths Held Over Manila. Firing Squad Ready for Unruly Citizens." By the end of the month, Hawaiians were reading "Battle of Singapore Begins As British Evacuate Malaya."[112] On February 22nd, a front-page story by Rear Admiral Yates Stirling about the likelihood of another Japanese attack drove the image home, stating bluntly, "The outlook in the coming weeks is such that we must again be concerned with the safety of Hawaii." The admiral warned that if Japanese luck held, they were in a position "to clean up their conquest of the South Pacific."[113] Fear of an invasion and especially fear of an occupation was real and it was understandable. Many civilians naturally wanted to leave the Islands for the safety of the mainland, inundating steamship line offices, particularly the American President Lines and the Matson Company, trying to get passage back to the West Coast, all the while those companies were powerless to make such decisions because their ships were being commandeered by military and naval authorities.

Life was harsher on the Islands once the war started. Navy Base workers toiled around the clock every day of the week repairing damage and maintaining the ships coming in from around the Pacific. Like everyone else, Governor Poindexter was fingerprinted, a reminder that no one was above military law in these extraordinary times. By mid-January every citizen was issued a gas mask with strict orders to carry it around wherever he went. Telephone calls and mail were censored. Many building projects were delayed because of shortages of material, especially cement.[114] Nobody went hungry, but food became a focus. The military government could control prices, yet with the general lack of available ships from the West Coast, keeping up supply was always a challenge. Shortages of canned goods and paper products left store shelves empty.[115] Alcohol was banned, and later a rationing system was established. Ellenmerle Heiges recalls the perfect irony of her tee-totaling mother standing in long lines in Hilo to pick up Mr. Heiges' daily ration of beer. Most difficult of all was the strictly enforced blackout every night, turning the once-glittering nightlife of Honolulu into a ghost town. The color and light drained from King, Hotel, and Beretania Streets, replaced by gray and khaki. Even Honolulu's familiar silver buses received a coat of camouflage. You could still go to the Moana Hotel to dance to phonograph records, play cards, and sip soft drinks, but you had to be prepared to stay the whole night because of the curfew and blackout. Honolulu had "become about as dull under martial law as a Tokyo broadcast.[116]

The bombing, of course, affected the children who witnessed it, but the aftermath created a whole new set of anxieties for young people: Would the Japanese come back? Would civilians have to leave the Islands? For the first time many children saw their parents truly afraid; they saw them cry, or lash out in impotent anger. And for the time being, there was enough happening around them to constantly remind them that the war was not far away. Blackouts, curfews, and air raid practices were daily facts of life. Children were fingerprinted, given identity cards and just like everyone else had to attend instructional classes on the proper use of gas masks. Child-size masks were slow in getting to the Islands, so at first children were free from carrying the cumbersome masks everywhere they went. Tear gas exercises were perhaps the worst: every child, and eventually even the youngest, had to carry a gas mask at all times, and sometimes children would be placed in a room filled with tear gas and told to open their masks briefly to experience what tear gas was like.[117] And schools near military and naval bases remained closed. In the case of Patsy Campbell, her parents received a notice on January 6th from Agnes Vance, the principal of the Navy Housing School, where Patsy was a fifth grader, informing them her school would remain closed permanently because of its proximity to the Navy Base. Some parents began to wonder which option posed the greater risk: remaining on the Islands or evacuating across the Pacific.[118]

Gail Moul, a six-year-old boy, was so traumatized by the bombing he developed a stammer that he didn't lose until he was 21. Still in his pajamas on that Sunday morning, he heard the warplanes, while his father tended the pepper plants outside. Looking up, he saw a fighter in the sky, a Rising Sun under its wing, banking over the cyclone fence behind their house separating Hickam Field from the Navy Base. Bullets and shrapnel shattered a window in his house. He screamed as a bomb exploded nearby. He and his mother piled into a car with several other families and drove to a home outside the danger area; it was packed with 25 or 30 people by the time they arrived. They stayed in that house until the 14th, and didn't get word his father was alive until the 21st.[119]

Even older children were left with searing memories. Fifteen-year-old Nancy Walbridge, a student at Roosevelt High School in the Makiki neighborhood in northeastern Honolulu, was a well-traveled, resilient teenager whose Army-major father was stationed at Fort Kamehameha, an Army Coastal Artillery Post near Hickam Field. Like many children of Army officers, she had seen much of the world as her family followed her father's postings, including Panama, the Philippines and Japan. Yet, her travels couldn't prepare her for the ordeal she faced on December 7th. During the second wave of the attack she and a friend were strafed by Japanese planes and dove into a trench to escape the fire. She witnessed the deaths of civilians and suffered from nightmares long after. "The terror of it is hard to describe – the noise, smell. "Have you ever been in a war? Well you can't imagine the screaming and the noise."[120]

Another child at the time of the bombing wrote later of the anxiety she felt hearing the words "Wake [Island] falling." "I was scared and confessed to God all my sins and prayed for Him to make me good, thinking somehow my confession and promise of goodness would help end the war; or at least bring word my Dad was alive and Mother would stop crying."[121] She and her younger brother in Pearl City had seen destroyed homes, flattened trucks, and cars with bullet holes.

Family life was affected in many ways by the bombing and especially by the demands of duty in the aftermath of the attack. Eleven-year-old Gordon Lavering, the boy who witnessed the squadron of Japanese dive bombers flying down the Palolo Valley, was sad to be losing his sister, his "best friend" as he described her later, when she was evacuated in early 1942. Their parents felt that Hawaii was unsafe for girls, but that Gordon could look after himself. Their father, like so many others, worked extended hours as part of the war effort, while their mother, a Red Cross nurse, worked nights. She would call him each morning to wake him up when he would make his own breakfast and take down the blackout curtains. He attended school in a safe area so it eventually reopened after the attack, but at reduced hours, so he attended only in the afternoon, coming home each day to an empty house. Like many children on the Islands after the bombing, he needed to be self-reliant.[122]

Sometimes parents' words belied their anxieties about their children. The mother of one six-year-old who witnessed the attack said, "Thank goodness the children didn't see more of war." The little girl would run inside the house for a few days after the bombing every time she heard an airplane approaching. "But it passed," her mother said. "She's perfectly all right now."[123]

But was she all right? The effects from the attack could linger and manifest themselves later in the most unlikely of circumstances. Shortly after Andrea Marze had returned to the mainland with her mother, she was playing in the basement of her grandmother's house, when she heard a loud noise. She started yelling, "The Japs are coming! The Japs are coming!"

Harsh Justice

Military rule placed a burden on the Islands' population unlike that of any part of the United States before or since. For the first time in United States history a legally constituted American civilian government was stripped of powers guaranteed by the Constitution and replaced by a military governor. A provost court that superseded the laws of the Territory of Hawaii and of the United States replaced trial by jury; the writ of habeas corpus was suspended. Provost courts tried criminal and civil cases ranging from capital offenses to the most trivial.

Thomas Hanley, owner of the Lido Café on Nuuanu Avenue, got a taste of how harsh and swift military justice could be when he faced Honolulu's provost court judge Lt. Col. Neal D. Franklin. Hanley bought the Lido a little over two weeks before December 7th. Despite the ban on liquor, he gave two of his employees each a bottle of whiskey on December 30th, one imagines to celebrate the new year, and later that day police officers found the liquor in a car they were searching and traced it back to Hanley, who was arrested. When a liquor commission inspector did an inventory of Hanley's stock after his arrest, the agent found a discrepancy with an earlier inventory of some seven to ten cases of whiskey and 39 cases of beer. For his illegal disposition of liquor and his incorrect inventory of stock, Hanley got five years at hard labor. Only four days passed from the offense to the sentencing! This wasn't an anomaly. Later that month Franklin sentenced another tavern owner to five years and a $5,000 fine for selling liquor and failing to correctly report his inventory, and a restaurant owner to four years and a $1000 fine for selling a case of liquor for $144. Provost court decisions were not subject to appeal.[124]

Franklin was one of the earliest provost judges appointed by the military government, but by presiding over the court in Honolulu he was perhaps the most visible, and he got lots of coverage in the Honolulu papers, which delighted in recounting his acerbic wit that he gave free reign to in court. A look at some of his decisions provide an insight into just how much power the military had over the lives of Hawaii's private citizens. Finding little sympathy for Arthur Madsen's excuse of a sore tooth as a reason for his loafing charge, he suspended Madsen's sentence but gave him a $10 fine for loafing. He admonished Madsen to "get over that sore tooth soon and get to work." A young man whose license was suspended, threw himself at the mercy of the court, complaining it would be a hardship for him to go to work without a car; he was told: "Walk, young man, it's a healthy exercise." One speeder told the court he was an aviator. Franklin deadpanned, "Hm, thought you were driving your plane, did you?" Another defendant, obviously unaware of what he was up against, told Franklin that he was arrested for speeding on his day off, a precious and rare privilege in the aftermath of December 7th. "A day off and with all the time you had on your hands you had to speed." Franklin was merciless. "Why, I'll cure you of the habit. I am going to give you 10 days off in the city jail and I am sure you will do no more speeding. All you will have to do will be hard labor."[125]

Although the provost courts violated the Constitution, and placed a burden on the population of Hawaii not shared by the rest of the country, they were non-discriminatory insofar as they provided a venue where all participants before the court were treated equally. Young Daniel Inouye, a senior at McKinley High School on South King Street in downtown Honolulu, and a writer for the school paper, said "Although it was startling to see a person in military uniform with a .45-caliber sidearm attached to his belt presiding at court, it was generally accepted." Inouye, who would later serve with distinction with the 442nd Regimental Combat Team and represent Hawaii in the United States Senate, said, "I do not recall anyone complaining of unfairness regarding the type of justice that was rendered."[126] Inouye's remembrances do suggest that an overall fairness prevailed and the coverage provided in the press confirms this. For example, while reporting on the previous day's morning and afternoon sessions in Honolulu, *The Honolulu Advertiser* reported that there were 50 convictions for speeding and other traffic offenses. Among the convicted were "business executives, army and navy officers and enlisted men, defense workers, taxi drivers, and young and elderly women ..." Men in uniform received no special consideration. Franklin admonished one young naval officer: "The only speed I will permit you to do is to have you catch up and destroy enemy airplanes or submarines." Even a physician was fined $10 for speeding to attend to a patient. Franklin and his colleagues were so enthusiastic in administering their brand of rough justice that Sheriff Duke Kahanamoku complained the city-county jail was filled beyond capacity. "I don't know what we are going to do if the provost court continues to send us new guests at the present rate," the sheriff said. "Maybe people will be more careful if they know they may have to sleep on the floor at my institution."[127]

Hawaiians chafed under strict rationing, loss of civil rights, and the ever-present fear of invasion (at least until May of 1942). Those on the mainland, of course, endured rationing, but not to the same extent as people on Hawaii did, and while mainlanders faced the draft, they weren't subjected to nightly blackouts, they still had the right of due process, and they lived under an elected government. Islanders saw that life went on for the rest of the country with some degree of normalcy and they resented it. Hawaiians could read in their newspapers, for instance, that Joe DiMaggio was threatening a holdout in 1942 unless he got the salary he thought he deserved. The Yankees offered $37,000, his 1941 salary, but DiMaggio insisted that he was worth more, especially after leading the Yankees to win the World Series that year.[128]

A letter signed by 'The Texas Boys' appearing in many newspapers, including *The Honolulu Advertiser*, captured the mood around the country, but especially in Hawaii:

> *Would appreciate your convoying (sic) the following to Joe DiMaggio in the event the Yankees don't pay more than $37,000: 'We cordially invite you to try out with the 143rd Infantry, 36*th *Division. The pay is only $21 a month but that's better than nothing. Please advise. P.S. Why settle for yesterday's salary?'*[129]

Many felt another baseball star was also getting preferential treatment. Hawaii residents learned that Ted Williams was 'hiding' in a Chicago hotel as speculation swirled about whether he would play the 1942 season or would enlist.

Williams denied that he sought to get reclassified from I-A (available and fit for service) to III-A (men with dependents not engaged in work essential to national defense) because his mother was dependent upon his income, but asked that he be allowed one more season before he enlisted. Williams' status was front-page news in the Boston papers, which perhaps had not yet soured on the young left fielder at this point in his career, for the Boston press seemed to bend over backwards sticking up for Williams.[130]

Some of the pressure was taken off stars like DiMaggio, Williams, and Luke Appling of the Chicago White Sox the next day, when President Roosevelt said at a news conference that athletic events and other forms of recreation are necessary even during wartime to relieve the strains of war and work. And no less a star than Sgt. Hank Greenberg, former first baseman of the Detroit Tigers, came to the defense of Williams in the spring of 1942 as reported in *The Advertiser* by sports columnist Red McQueen. Greenberg pointed out that Uncle Sam called his number just as surely as he did not call Williams'. "I'm here [in the army] because Uncle Sam said this is my place... Uncle Sam has told Ted he doesn't want him right now. He's put him in 3-A. Nobody can tell me that Uncle Sam doesn't know what he's doing." Perhaps as a dig to DiMaggio, McQueen couldn't resist identifying Greenberg as "... a fellow who had a $45,000 a year contract taken away from him and in return for which he got a $21 a month contract."[131]

College Athletes Do Their Bit

In the darkness of her room in the completely blacked out Manoa Hotel on Waikiki, Shirley McKay would strike a match, risking the wrath of the blackout warden. She had to light it so she could see where the cockroaches were. The thought of stepping on one was more than she could stand, blackout restrictions or no.[132] The Willamette University sophomore was stranded – if you can call staying at the Manoa Hotel on Waikiki with 27 football players stranded.

Her father, Douglas McKay was a firm believer in "Busy Hands are Happy Hands," as Shirley put it later, and he was worried about what to do with the football team, idled by the restrictions placed on the civilian population. Because the students were officially tourists, they had nothing to do. He and Willamette's football coach Roy "Spec" Keene arranged to have the team stand guard duty at the Punahou School in the high ground overlooking Waikiki, not far from the Manoa Hotel. The boys from Willamette, along with the San Jose State players, took shifts guarding the perimeter of the school and sleeping on mats when off duty. Willamette quarterback Ken Jacobson thinks that ammunition might have been stored there, which is why the school needed guarding.[133] He also thinks it is a wonder nobody got killed or injured because the college boys were given old-fashioned bolt-action rifles even though many of them had never held a gun before.

Shirley wasn't idle either. She and the other women with the Willamette group volunteered at Tripler General Hospital at Fort Shafter to help washing dishes, rolling bandages, anything to help the nurses, freeing their time to attend to the wounded servicemen. Shirley's job was working with children wounded during the attack or who had become separated from their parents in the chaos after the bombing. She would read to the kids and keep them occupied. Although she didn't deal with them at the time, Tripler was the hospital where many of the burn cases from the attack were taken, something she would be acutely aware of the in coming days.

"A Stand-up Strike"

One of the immediate effects after the bombing was the scattering of prostitutes to houses all over Honolulu. Prior to the war, the Honolulu Police Vice Squad kept control over Hawaii's prostitutes in a way that bordered on serfdom. The brothels were limited to an area near Chinatown bordered by River, Beretania, Nuuanu, and Hotel Streets. Prostitutes were not allowed to visit Waikiki Beach, could not own property or automobiles, could not attend dances, ride in the front seat of a taxicab, wire money to the mainland, or be out after 10:30 at night. Those violating the rules could expect a beating or removal from the Islands. Further, the madams encouraged the women to take drugs as a way of keeping them docile and indebted to the house. In exchange for looking the other way, the police were paid off as much as $30 per woman per month.[134] The war changed all that.

On December 20th, Police Commissioner V.S.K. Houston sent Colonel Green a report listing those known houses of prostitution, which were allowed to remain open "notwithstanding that it is a violation of the law," and recommended that they all be shut down because their very existence "tends to weaken respect for law and order." He ended his report with a quote from a Captain Stephenson of the Navy's Bureau of Medicine and Surgery (and which clearly places the blame for prostitution on the prostitutes):

> *... easy access to recognized prostitution entices men who in normal circumstances would not frequent houses of*

prostitution. The soldiers and sailors of today are the citizens of tomorrow, (Houston's emphasis) and they must be protected.[135]

Green hated prostitution, considering it "ten times worse than slavery," and he disapproved of the wink-and-nod attitude of many of the local people towards the practice, but he was loath to impose any outside morality on a local situation. "Who are we, the Army, to preach morals?" he wrote. Chief of Police William Gabrielson of the Honolulu Police Department told Green on January 14th that prostitution was getting out of hand. "Whose hand?" Green entered in the diary. Later that day, Colonel Craig at Fort Shafter acknowledged the monthly take from the prostitution racket could be as high as $1 million. If that is so, Green wrote, "We are in for headaches..."[136]

Green was worried about Gabrielson's treatment of prostitutes. The police chief, unlike the police commissioner, was content with prostitution the way it always had been, and wanted to continue confining them to their "cribs," which Green opposed, saying they were free to come and go as they pleased. Moreover, the colonel insisted that if any prostitute violated the law she was to be brought before the provost court, not beaten up by the police. A delegation from the Police Commission came to Green's office asking that the Chief be allowed to handle the prostitution problem in his own way, but to his credit Green was skeptical, realizing that the police in effect, were trying to keep the lid on the old racket that was threatened by new realities brought on by the war. The clumsy attempts by the police to convince the military government that they were operating in the best interests of the women, convinced Green that they were on the take. "The police would beat up a prostitute, drag her out of her residence and throw her into the crib from which she had escaped," he noted in his diary. From Green's point of view, the entire operation in Honolulu was "Oriental philosophy," unfathomable to a Westerner, but was emphatic that "I'm damned if I am going to permit the police to abuse and beat up these women."[137]

Throughout the spring and summer of 1942, Gabrielson and the police kept up the pressure to forcibly confine the prostitutes to certain areas of town. Green suspected "skull-duggery" when he was told the mayor of Honolulu had complained that a prostitute was living next door to the mayor's house. Green said he didn't think the mayor would be interested. This was followed by a meeting a week later in which the provost marshal reported to Green that prostitution was rampant all over the city. Green ordered the marshal to investigate and found that the report was false; moreover an investigation of the mayor's neighbor revealed that she was indeed a prostitute, but contrary to the rules in effect at the time, had lived next door to that august gentleman for a year and never gave any trouble, and besides she worked downtown. Green suspected a concerted plan to force the military government to allow the police to behave as they saw fit regarding the prostitutes, and he believed Gabrielson, "an efficient cop, but devious," was behind it. At one point the colonel was so fed up with the whole tug-of-war that he confided to his diary "Corregador (sic) has fallen and we here are dealing with trifles."[138]

By September, the prostitutes had had enough. They hated Gabrielson, and if Green's diary is any indication, with good reason. Shortly after Green returned from a visit to the mainland, the prostitutes struck, driven they said not by overwork or low wages, but by a desire to be treated "as any other citizen or tax payer." They wanted to live wherever they chose, not where they were forced to live. In a long letter to Green they complained of their ill treatment, pointing out that they were patriotic Americans, many of whom helped the war effort by volunteering in hospitals, donating blood, and buying defense bonds. Nearly 100 prostitutes signed the letter and listed their place of business, which conformed pretty closely with the houses mentioned in Houston's letter to Green. The colonel joked that it was "a stand up strike – the first in history."[139] Undaunted, the prostitutes picketed for three weeks in front of the police headquarters. Finally, Emmons worked out a compromise with Gabrielson allowing the women the right to go where they pleased in the city and to live outside the brothels if they so desired; further the military government would oversee the health checkups of the prostitutes and the sanitary condition of the houses. The police for their part could still enforce all the laws that applied to the prostitutes.[140]

"Can Hawaii Take It?"

On April 11, an extraordinary meeting took place at the YWCA in Honolulu, where a regional conference of social workers took the pulse of Hawaii four months into the war.[141] The keynote speaker during luncheon was the director of civilian morale from the military governor's office, whose address was entitled 'Can Hawaii Take it?' and who, as might be expected, answered that Hawaii indeed could, but the afternoon sessions provided some unfiltered discussions that gave a straightforward appraisal of the well-being of the people. The Rev. Galen Weaver said that if people feel they are sharing in a common cause they would cheerfully sacrifice and endure hardships. He emphasized, among other things, constructive criticism and truth telling, two rather remarkable concepts during war, as a way to keep people engaged and willing to endure. Dr. Edwin McNeil confronted the problem of fear, saying that it is normal for people to be fearful and concerned over their security, and that the demand for services at his psychiatric clinic showed a marked increase. His patients were frustrated, McNeil said, because they were unable to do what they wanted or to leave the Islands when they wanted. They disliked the restrictions on their liberties and were suspicious of the information given out by the government.

Margaret Ottman from the department of public welfare said that since December 7th, her office received fewer applications to take children into foster care because, she speculated, people were afraid of taking on such a responsibility in the face of food and milk shortages and the ever-present possibility of evacuation. Mrs. Ottman presumably referred to both the possibility of evacuation from Honolulu to the interior of Oahu as well as from the Islands to the mainland. Other speakers looked at the positives remarking that crime was down, and now that most schools were re-opened, teachers were meeting the challenge of keeping children occupied after school hours.

Dr. Philip Platt noted that the community as a whole showed a great spirit of cooperation in building air raid shelters and in preparing for the possible evacuation into the interior, but added that "the real headache ... was the handling of Mainland evacuation." Platt's voice wasn't the only one criticizing the evacuation to the mainland. Two months earlier, columnist Laselle Gilman noted that while many people objected to the evacuation hierarchy (elderly over children, for example), the most significant problem was that the military government "remains silent on the advisability of evacuation for ordinary citizens." He implied that not knowing whether one would have to go or not added unnecessary stress to people's lives. "If wholesale evacuation is advisable, let those in authority say so; if not, an equally clear statement would be welcome," he wrote.[142]

But it is clear from the social workers' observations that evacuation was on the minds of the people and that evacuation fears cut both ways. Many civilians wanted to stay no matter what, especially those with no family to go to on the mainland. They worried that they would be evacuated against their will. And many others wanted to go as quickly as possible. These conflicting interests, against a backdrop of fear, gave birth to rumors that would plague the authorities for the first six months of the war: the water supply sabotaged; the Japanese population planning an uprising; an invasion fleet just off shore; everybody to be evacuated; nobody to be evacuated.

Chapter 6
"We Put the Turkey in the Bag and Left"

"Well, We Got a Ride Home"- The First Convoy Forms

Once the *Coolidge* docked at Pier 11 in Honolulu on December 16th, all passengers, even the San Francisco-bound passengers, were ordered off the ship. Customs guards patrolled the dock and the gangway of the *Coolidge.* The ship's quartermaster maintained vigil at the gangway as well, while junior officers patrolled the decks throughout the night. A complete blackout was maintained. The next day stevedores and crew began unloading the Honolulu-bound passengers' baggage and mail from the holds. Throughout the day on the 18th the new cargo was loaded and the work commenced converting sections of the ship into hospital quarters for the 125 critically wounded servicemen needing long-term care they could only get on the mainland.

Sometime during the afternoon of the 18th, Ruth Erickson, a nurse at the Naval Hospital, boarded the ship and began preparations to receive the wounded. Just the evening before, she had been ordered to pack a bag, wear her white nurse's uniform, and be ready for a new assignment the next day. She had no inkling where she was going. She and two other nurses were picked up by car at their quarters wearing their white ward uniforms, capes, blue felt hats, and blue sweaters, and still with no idea of their destination. In the car, they learned they were heading for the SS *Coolidge* tied at the dock in Honolulu and to prepare for a 10-day voyage.[143]

That same afternoon, Douglas McKay announced to his daughter in a loud voice, "Well, we got a ride home." McKay and Coach Spec Keene had gotten word, most likely from the Honolulu police, that two ships, the *Coolidge* and *Scott*, were about to depart taking wounded back to the mainland. It wasn't difficult getting steerage passage for the football players and coaches, but they pulled every string they could to get three 3rd-class cabins for the female fans accompanying the team. Steerage was dormitory-like space below the main deck at the extreme aft end of the ship, below the water line and near the propellers; it was dark, noisy, and stuffy. The metal bunks were movable so that cargo could be stored there if needed. Compared to these steerage accommodations, 3rd-class, with cabins on the upper deck containing six to eight metal berths and a lavatory with hot and cold water, must have seemed luxurious.[144] Up at Punahou School, the Willamette football players were told to be on board the ship the next day for the voyage home. Some balked at the idea, but Douglas McKay pointed out that it was either now or April. Spec wanted them to all return or stay together. They boarded the next morning, each person allowed only one suitcase.

On Friday, December 19th, the activity and bustle aboard the *Coolidge* picked up. San Francisco-bound passengers were allowed back on board, as were civilian evacuees;

last minute baggage, mail, and stores were loaded in the holds, and the wounded servicemen were secured. A pilot stood at the helm, the gangway was cleared and the last line hauled in. The tugs *Clayton* and *Miki Miki* helped turn the huge vessel and by 11:34 that morning the ship swung out, and eight minutes later the pilot was dropped off. At 11:44 the *Coolidge* and *Scott* departed Honolulu carrying well over 900 people home to safety.[145] Off Diamond Head, the two ships rendezvoused with their escort, the destroyers USS *Detroit, Cummings,* and *Reid,* thus forming the first convoy (#4024) from Hawaii to the mainland carrying war wounded, refugees, and evacuees.[146] Watching the two evacuation ships from the deck of the *Detroit,* Signalman John McGoran found himself thinking about the wounded aboard and felt great sympathy for them.[147]

Aboard the *Coolidge,* the three nurses and several corpsmen had spent the previous night sorting and stocking supplies brought over from the Naval Hospital. Nurse Erickson saw that many of the *Coolidge*'s wounded were very badly burned and probably shouldn't be moved, but her superiors had made the decision that cases requiring more than three months of treatment should be sent to the mainland immediately. She and her two fellow nurses, Catherine Richardson and Lauretta Eno, divided their time into shifts in order to provide the patients with around the clock coverage, Richardson from 8 a.m. to 4 p.m., Erickson from 4 p.m. to midnight and Eno from midnight until 8 a.m. In addition to the ship's surgeon, William Wildman, who had accompanied the vessel from Manila, two Navy doctors traveling as passengers were placed on temporary duty. Aboard the *Scott,* eight volunteer nurses from the Queens Hospital in Honolulu tended 55 wounded servicemen.

Everyone onboard was apprehensive about the comfort and well being of the patients and about the threat from Japanese submarines; rumors swirled about the likelihood of attack, especially when they neared the mainland. Many of the portholes were sealed when the ship was converted to a war footing during the earlier stage of the voyage from Manila. Because of the close quarters and the lack of ventilation, the smell from the wounds and medicines was overwhelming. Erickson, who never experienced seasickness, took some getting used to the conditions before her stomach settled down. Even 70 years later, the memory of the odor of the burns, the dressings, and the medicine was nauseating to Ken Jacobson, the Willamette quarterback, who with his teammates helped care for the wounded when they were told. Ken saw some disturbing things. Once he helped carry a wounded patient in a stretcher to surgery where, he said, doctors later amputated the man's leg. And he saw one burn case with an apparatus rigged over the bed so blankets wouldn't touch him – he was in pretty bad shape, Ken recalled years later.

Still the Willamette players were glad to pitch in, and welcomed the opportunity to get away from their quarters in steerage, down where the "coolies" normally slept, as Ken put it, and where the noise from the propeller shaft was overwhelming. Besides, if the ship got torpedoed, he didn't want to be below the waterline. When not helping with the wounded, Ken and his friends chose to spend most of their time listening to the radio in the ship's lounge or staying out on deck. They even slept in the lounge.

Shirley McKay helped with the wounded as well. It was quite an education for her. Prior to this voyage she had had little to worry about regarding her own health, let alone having to deal with young men facing excruciating pain, disfigurement, and a long convalescence. She was asked to take the temperature of severely burned men and amputees, to read to them, to help feed them, to help them in any way she could. This was different from reading to the children at Tripler Hospital or worrying about cockroaches in her hotel room. The smell of the wounds and the medicine made her feel ill, but she willed herself to help these young men so dreadfully wounded. One kept saying, "My dad won't want me now. I don't have my pitching arm." She tried to re-assure him, telling him that they would be thankful he was alive – but what could she really say? These young men, many her age, were despondent about the severity of their wounds.

For Rosalie Hutchison, the crossing from Honolulu to the mainland differed markedly from her journey from Manila. She was spared the trauma of dealing with the wounded, but if anything, this leg of the voyage was even more tedious than the first one because she was forced to spend more time in her cabin. Many of the decks were off limits because the wounded were now berthed there. She lost her access to the deck, the freedom and fresh air, her precious escape from the claustrophobic cabin and from the unbearable whining of the worried adults. No more swims with Father Murray, no more watching the jai alai team practicing on deck.

Rough seas plagued the convoy from Honolulu, adding to the discomfort of those aboard; the *Coolidge* pitched and rolled moderately and took on spray forward. All of the ships maintained a zigzag course to evade Japanese submarines. Despite the weather, the *Coolidge* held a lifeboat drill on the first day out. On the 21st, the USS *Reid* left the convoy, and later that day the sea calmed down.

At 4:30 p.m. on the 24th, Christmas Eve, during Nurse Erickson's watch, one of the wounded sailors, who had been extensively burned during the attack, died from his injuries. Dr. Wildman reported that Bosun's Mate Elvin Albert Dvorak died from toxemia and hypostatic congestion of the lungs. In her notes, Nurse Erickson recorded that Dvorak had been losing intravenous fluids faster than they could be replaced. The next day the convoy entered San Francisco Bay.

A Second Convoy Forms

The SS *Matsonia*, another Matson liner, had been requisitioned by the Navy in November 1941, pursuant to the Proclamation of Unlimited National Emergency, and converted into a troop transport. On December 5th, the ship left San Francisco carrying troops to The Philippines. After the Japanese attack on Hawaii, the ship was ordered back to San Francisco to take on war material and additional troops – and to await an escort.[148] The *Matsonia's* sister ship, the *Lurline,* not yet commandeered by the government, was also at sea on December 7th· traveling from Honolulu to San Francisco, when passengers were awakened by crew members armed with paint brushes and buckets blacking out port holes and windows. On December 9th, the *Lurline* officially started its new career as a chartered transport zig-zagging back to the mainland under forced steam, arriving eight hours ahead of schedule on December 10th.[149] Gordon Lavering's Aunt Alice, returning to San Francisco after a two-week visit with family members in Hawaii, was aboard the *Lurline.* Lavering was the boy, who along with his sister, had witnessed the squadron of Japanese dive bombers flying along the Palolo Valley on its way to Pearl Harbor. He recalled his aunt saying years later that the *Lurline* arrived at noon on December 9th at the Farrallon Islands, about 30 miles off the California coast, and spent the rest of the day circling the rocky islands. At midnight on December 9th, under blackout conditions, the *Lurline* gathered up steam and made a run for the coast, shooting under the Golden Gate. According to Alice, the US Navy was worried that the ship might be torpedoed by Japanese submarines at the mouth of San Francisco harbor, a concern that was shared by evacuees on the *Coolidge* sixteen days later.[150] The *Lurline* and the *Matsonia*, along with the SS *Monterrey*, bided their time in San Francisco awaiting Navy ships to convoy them back to Honolulu.

That escort finally came on December 16th in the form of the light cruiser USS *St. Louis*, and the destroyers *Preston* and *Smith*. During the attack on December 7th, the *St. Louis* had been berthed in the Navy Yard at Pearl Harbor and managed to get to sea relatively unscathed. On December 13th, the vessel was detached from Destroyer Division 10 and temporarily assigned to Task Force 15 and ordered to San Francisco to escort transport ships back to Pearl Harbor. When the *St. Louis* arrived at San Francisco Bay at nine o'clock on the morning of the16th to refuel and take on supplies, crewmember John O'Neil leaned on the lifeline and took in the beautiful view of the bay and city. "Our stay in San Francisco was unreal," he recalled later. "After nine months in Hawaii and over the Pacific to the Philippines, it was hard after those few hours in San Francisco Bay to sail back under the Golden Gate Bridge and on to that war without ever setting foot on the beach of San Francisco."[151] The *St Louis* left San Francisco at 4:30 the same day, spending only seven and a half hours in port!

The convoy was back in Honolulu on December 21st to pick up evacuees and wounded. On that day, nine-year-old Joan Zuber, who lived on Ford Island where her father was the commander of the Marine barracks, watched the three Matson liners approaching the harbor, surprised they were painted gray, not the gleaming white that she remembered so vividly from her arrival on the *Lurline* just the year before. Even the giant Matson "M"s emblazoned on the two smokestacks were painted over. Unlike the previous Boat Day, this time there would be no bands, no hula dancers greeting the ship, no boys diving for coins thrown from the side. She had no inkling of the transformation that the *Lurline* and its sister ships had undergone in recent days. Had she been able to watch the gray ships dock, she would have seen that instead of discharging happy travelers, they now unloaded troop reinforcements, war correspondents, and workmen to help with the salvaging and rebuilding of the Pacific Fleet.[152]

During the next five days, Army and Navy officers worked around the clock to get the three liners ready to carry evacuees on the second convoy back to the mainland. The *Matsonia*, for example, arrived without any beds, blankets, or mattresses to accommodate the anticipated civilian passengers. Two days before boarding was to begin, the Army managed to get 900 mattresses delivered to the *Matsonia* from Fort Armstrong, located on Honolulu Harbor across from Sand Island. The Navy informed the steamship agents Castle & Cooke on the 24th that there was space for 976 civilians aboard the ship and issued instructions to start boarding passengers at Pier 28 between 1:00 and 4:00 p.m. on December 25th.[153]

Many of those who would evacuate on the *Matsonia* or its sister ships wouldn't be notified until Christmas morning to be ready to depart that day. As a Navy wife, Eugenia

Mandelkorn knew it was only a matter of time before she and Philip would be evacuated. In anticipation of that event, she had gone shopping on the morning of December 23rd for warm clothing for herself and her son. Supplies of warm clothing were scarce in Hawaii in the best of times, and with the looming evacuations of thousands of people she knew she had to act fast before supplies were completely exhausted. When she returned home that day the phone rang with her instructions: be ready to leave in 48 hours. Christmas Day! She had hoped it wouldn't be so soon, but there was nothing she could do now. Joan Zuber, staying with family friends, received a phone call on Christmas Day telling her to get ready along with her sister to leave on the convoy about to depart for the West Coast. Their mother was already aboard the *Lurline* awaiting them.[154] Dwight Agnew, a ten-year-old evacuee on the *Lurline*, said when describing his family's departure that day, "We put the turkey in the bag and left."[155]

Eugenia Mandelkorn dreaded giving up the splendid view from her house down the side of Mt. Tantalus; she inhaled the lovely fragrances around her, wishing she could stay in this place that was a paradise for her. She arranged to see her husband at the Officers' Club at Pearl Harbor to say goodbye on the day of her departure – but after that, when would she see him again? Her only consolation was that she would be traveling aboard the *Lurline* with one of her close friends who had a child about Philip's age.[156]

On departure day, Joan Zuber recalled the "dark gray ship, funereal in color" where she and her sister were taken "down to our cabin on D deck, in the bowels of the ship. Three walls of the room were lined with triple layer bunks, nine bunks in a room." They were among the early arrivals on the ship and "Over the next two hours the *Lurline* began to receive her passengers: women, children and the wounded. Bodies on stretchers were gently brought up the gangplank and taken below deck."[157]

> *And then slowly, sorrowfully, the Lurline left the dock. There were no streamers to throw to friends on the shore. There were no leis, no parting songs. I knew we might never come back. There is a legend that if you drop a lei off the ship and it floats back to the islands, you will return. We were not allowed to throw a scrap of paper off the ship. A submarine might find it and sink us.*[158]

The second convoy (#4032), departing from Honolulu at 9:29 on the morning of December 26th, was much larger than the first, comprising three naval escorts and three ocean liners, the *Lurline*, *Matsonia*, and *Monterrey*, carrying over 2,800 evacuees and wounded. That it departed a full week after the first convoy was squarely because of the Navy's insistence, mentioned earlier, that all convoys between Hawaii and the mainland have escorts.

Once at sea the *St. Louis* led the way, 1,000 yards in front of the *Lurline* followed by the *Matsonia* and then the *Monterey*. The *Preston* and the *Smith* formed a screen off the port and starboard bow respectively of the *Lurline*. If Doris Marze, who was aboard the Lurline with Andrea during this convoy, went up on deck and looked out from the stern, she would have seen the *Matsonia*, the ship that had carried her and Andrea to the Islands just two years before. What a difference between those two voyages, the young mother and daughter arriving to be reunited with their family, now the two of them together leaving Andrew behind forever. All of the ships maintained a zigzag course and conducted anti-aircraft drills during the crossing. The evacuees knew they were headed to the mainland, but they did not know to which port; rumors circulated about Seattle, Long Beach, and San Francisco.

The *Lurline* was stripped of all luxuries, even hot water. Everyone had to wear life jackets at all times, drill for emergencies, and know their life boat location. Given the cramped conditions, evacuees ate in three shifts, and bathed in what some evacuees sarcastically called "soup bowls" filled with water. Adding to the discomfort was the zigzag course stretching the usual five-day crossing to seven with "...an ever-present fear that we might be torpedoed." Omnipresent seasickness only worsened the ordeal to such a degree that Joan Zuber found it difficult to avoid stepping in vomit because the heavy blackout curtains made it impossible to see where she was walking.[159] Even Eugenia Mandelkorn was uncharacteristically seasick.

On the first day out, the *Preston* reported submarine contact and commenced evasive maneuvers.[160] Aboard the *Lurline* a booming voice came over the loudspeaker: "Everyone! Everyone! All to the lifeboats. At once!" Word quickly spread that a Japanese submarine had been sighted. Eugenia Mandelkorn grabbed her son Philip and ran to her assigned lifeboat, but she and the others assigned to the boat were unable to lower the winch; it was stuck fast. She was frantic. A ship's officer came running to help and got the lift unstuck, however, by this time the alarm was over, the event proved to be a false sighting, perhaps by an overzealous lookout. But the ordeal left her, "completely undone," in her own words, thinking of how close Philip might have come to catastrophe.[161]

On December 29th, Joan Zuber turned ten while crossing the Pacific.[162]

"Information Regarding My Status"

Despite the extraordinary control that the military government exercised over the population, and despite the

Navy's and Army's power to commandeer ships and to control their own dependents, the entire evacuation process was mired in confusion. Navy dependents, for example, were ordered to register at one of three locations: Captain Frucht's office at Castle & Cooke in downtown Honolulu, or the Navy Housing Office, or the Defense Housing Overseas Transportation Office at Pearl Harbor. (See Appendix for sample Registration Form.) Non-dependent civilians and tourists wanting to evacuate were instructed to register at the Honolulu Gas Company; yet they flooded the offices of Castle & Cooke to such a degree that in order to relieve the pressure, Captain Frucht directed Navy dependents who hadn't registered yet, to do so at the offices of the American President Lines instead, where he had reserved office space for that purpose.[163]

On December 23rd, Admiral Bloch had ordered all dependents of Navy personnel to register for compulsory evacuation with only the following exceptions: those dependents permanently residing in Hawaii and those employed in defense work prior to December 7th. This order, although it applied only to military and naval dependents, left most civilians confused. Rumors still ran wild that all civilians would be forced to register, and eventually to evacuate against their will. Historian and author Gwenfread Allen believes that the confusion grew from the proliferation of government agencies often giving contradictory orders, compounded by human shortcomings such as petty animosities, personal feuds, and inexperienced officials.[164] Indeed, the array of offices having a role in the evacuation was bewildering. Whether you wanted to stay or go, who should you contact: the Navy, the Army Transportation Service, the Military Governor's Office, the Office of Civilian Defense, or Castle and Cooke? Complicating this bureaucratic muddle, the authorities were faced with a civilian population that had starkly conflicting desires about staying on or leaving Hawaii: some considered the territory their home, where their spouses, children, and parents were, while others feared a Japanese invasion, or desired to get back to family on the mainland, or resented the restrictions on their civil liberties.

Even the evacuating agencies, such as Castle & Cooke, one of the Big Five companies in the Territory of Hawaii, which owned significant stock in the Matson Navigation Company, were unsure of the status of civilian evacuees. A.J. Pessel, the Castle & Cooke agent, wrote to Frucht complaining that civilians, including tourists, residents, and visitors on islands other than Oahu, kept asking about their evacuation status. Pessel wanted to know what to tell them. Admiral Bloch replied for Frucht, writing, "...there is no plan for the compulsory evacuation of civilians residing in the Hawaiian area." Those civilians wishing to leave can do so voluntarily when space becomes available, Bloch wrote, but no one could predict when that would be.[165]

General Emmons heard the rumors, too, especially that the Army was going to require the evacuation of all women to the mainland. He wanted to quash this misinformation before it spread any further, and instructed Col. Green on December 30th to send a press release to set the public straight.[166] This was naïve on Emmons' part because the people weren't listening to what the government was saying about evacuation anyway, so why should a press release make a difference? But clearly the General was worried about the rumors. Moreover, by December 30th, two convoys had already departed and a third would leave the next day. Despite the secret nature of the convoys, the authorities could not hide from the public the fact that hundreds of their fellow citizens had been removed from the Islands.

Typical of those who wanted to stay and feared forced evacuation, was Mary Ella Butler, whose letter to the Navy's Overseas Transportation Office follows:

915 A-Alewa Dr.
Honolulu, T.H.
December 30, 1941

Commander J. A. (sic) Barrett
Overseas Transportation Office
Pearl Harbor, T.H.

Dear Commander Barrett:

If it would be at all possible to give me some information regarding my status as an evacuee I would be very grateful.

As my husband, Lt. j.g. (sic) K.L. Butler U.S.N.R. came on active duty from the mainland, his bona fide address is on the mainland: thus making it mine. However, I was raised here in Honolulu and my parents and family all make their homes here. Could you tell me what my chances are of remaining here with my family, which I would like very much to do.

Thank you.

Yours truly,
Mary Ella Butler
(Mrs. K.L. Butler)[167]

The Pan Am *Clipper*

There was another way to get off the Islands besides by ship, of course, and that was by air. Pan American offered weekly trans-Pacific service from the West Coast starting in October 1936 with its fleet of "flying boat" seaplanes, the famous Pan Am Clippers. The Clippers initially linked Honolulu with San Francisco, but eventually routes would connect to Manila, Canton, and Auckland, among other destinations, via specially designed long-distance seaplanes capable of traversing wide areas of open ocean with refueling stops along the way. These planes, such as the Martin M-130, with a wingspan of 130 feet and a 90-foot length, could make the 2400-mile San Francisco to Honolulu route in about 18 hours, but accommodated relatively few passengers; maximum capacity was 44, although often only as few as eight were possible because of space taken by fuel and cargo. Later, larger planes, such as the Boeing B-134 (wing span 152 feet and a length of 106 feet), carried a maximum of 74 passengers, and were built for trans-Pacific runs.

Each Clipper was named for its ultimate destination: *Hawaii Clipper* (Honolulu), *China Clipper* (Canton), *Philippine Clipper* (Manila, including also Hong Kong and later Singapore), and *Anzac Clipper* or sometimes *Pacific Clipper* (Auckland). A Clipper was luxurious with sumptuous meals served on china, and expensive, the *Hawaii Clipper* alone costing $720 round-trip (over $11,000 in today's dollars) for the 18-hour San Francisco-Honolulu leg. Passengers staying on for Manila or Canton after stopping at Honolulu, had refueling stops on the islands of Midway, Wake, and Guam.[168]

One of the most dramatic stories from the first months of the war was the around-the-world flight of the *Pacific Clipper.* After receiving word on December 7th of the Japanese attack while flying from New Caledonia to Auckland, Captain Robert Ford was instructed to continue on to Auckland. A week later he was ordered home, but not by the usual route via Honolulu to the West Coast, but rather to New York by flying westward on "the most practical route." By the time the Clipper landed at La Guardia, it had traveled 31,500 miles in 22 days touching on five continents, refueling at Sydney, Australia; Surabaya, in today's Indonesia; Trincomalee, in today's Sri Lanka; Karachi, in today's Pakistan; Bahrain; Khartoum, Sudan; Leopoldville, today's Kinshasa, Congo; Natal, Brazil; Trinidad; and New York City, where the unsuspecting flight control officer at La Guardia was greeted on the morning of January 6th, 1942 with Captain Ford saying on the radio, "*Pacific Clipper* inbound from Auckland, New Zealand." Along the way it barely avoided being shot down by suspicious RAF pilots and became the first commercial airplane to make an around-the-world flight.[169]

Because of expense and because so few passengers could be accommodated on these planes relative to ships, the Clippers played a minor role in the evacuation of civilians from Hawaii. But they played a role, nonetheless, especially during the immediate days after the Japanese attack. The *Anzac Clipper* was only an hour from Honolulu on a flight from San Francisco when hostilities broke out. It was diverted to Hilo, where it refueled and then flew back to the mainland.[170] The *Philippine Clipper* faced a more harrowing ordeal. On December 7th (December 8th Pacific time), the plane had just taken off from Wake Island heading for a stopover on Guam before its final destination of Singapore, when informed by radio that hostilities had broken out. With Captain J.H. Hamilton at the controls, the plane circled back to Wake and landed. While the Clipper was taking on fuel and rounding up Pan Am personnel for a flight back to Honolulu, two squadrons of Japanese planes bombed the island. The Clipper escaped bomb damage, but did have 16 bullet holes in it. On the approach to Midway Island, the refueling point between Wake and Honolulu, Japanese warships fired upon the Clipper. At Honolulu, the Pan Am people were dropped off, and the flight continued to San Francisco on December 9th, maintaining radio silence all the way. San Francisco newspapers reported the landing of the *Philippine Clipper* on December 11th with an unspecified number of passengers.[171]

Three days later, another Clipper landed in San Francisco from Honolulu, carrying 24 passengers and crew. The Navy wouldn't release the name of the Clipper to the press, but the *San Francisco Examiner* did list the passengers with some personal details included. The evacuees were mostly wives and families of servicemen or Pan Am employees.[172] One of them was Patricia Bellinger, 14, the daughter of Rear Admiral Patrick Bellinger, senior Naval Air Commander at Pearl Harbor. Admiral Bellinger's home on the northeastern end of Ford Island sat across from the *USS Arizona*, moored just off shore; the ship was so close that in a more peaceful time Ford Island residents could clearly hear movies played in the evenings on the after deck.[173] From the vantage point of her house, Patricia saw the *Arizona* explode, sending dozens of sailors' bodies through the air. The 14-year-old helped terribly burned seamen as they crawled from the water onto her sloped lawn into the shelter of the basement of her house, despite Japanese planes flying overhead.[174] The house was built over an old gun emplacement, and the basement was affectionately known as the dungeon.

Once the bombing started, people from the neighborhood, as well as a detachment of Marines, made their way to the dungeon. Among them was sixteen-year-old Mary Ann Ramsey, a neighbor of Patricia and the daughter of Admiral Bellinger's chief of staff, who also helped with the wounded, arriving now in greater numbers in ambulances, taking advantage of the relative safety of the dungeon. Her most vivid memory of that morning was the young man covered in "filthy black oil," with the skin hanging from him "like scarlet ribbons." His light blue eyes pale against the whites contrasted with the oil clinging to his face. All she could do was to help him to a mattress in the corridor out of harm's way.

On December 13, Patricia, her mother, and her younger sister were ordered to leave their home immediately. They grabbed whatever they could, then boarded Admiral Bellinger's gig, which took them to the waiting Pan Am Clipper. Joining them was Mary Ann Ramsey and her mother and several other families from Ford Island. As the boat made its way through the East Loch of Pearl Harbor to Pearl City, where the Clipper awaited for the flight that afternoon, the *Arizona* still poured smoke. Debris covered the water and patches of fire burned here and there fed by leaking fuel. She worried about her house and its roof damaged during the attack. Aboard the Clipper the windows were blacked out. The flight was terribly bumpy and most aboard were violently ill. After landing in San Francisco, Patricia and her family traveled to St. Louis to stay with relatives.

Another passenger aboard that flight, Mrs. Joanne Jones, was the wife of a naval officer killed at Pearl Harbor. The *Examiner* ran a story about her and her husband on December 21st, including a dramatic photo of her holding her late husband's sword and hat. Ensign Jones' funeral was held at St. Augustine's Chapel in Waikiki, presided over by the same chaplain who had married the young couple at that very church only six months before. Mrs. Jones was bravely smiling when she got off the plane and later told the Examiner, "... when I stepped from the plane I felt it best not to mention my own personal tragedy. I did not want any one (sic) to know I had been widowed by the disaster."[175]

Ensign H. C. Jones was killed aboard the USS *California*, leading a truly heroic action that would earn him a posthumous Medal of Honor. It was later determined that Ensign Jones rescued a sailor from a smoke-filled section of the ship, led the firing of an anti-aircraft battery, and organized a party to pass ammunition up to the guns until he was fatally wounded by a Japanese bomb. His Medal of Honor citation said that when sailors tried to move him from the raging fire he said, "Leave me alone! I am done for. Get out of here before the magazines go off."[176] Mrs. Jones was perhaps the first evacuee whose story was used to infuse a patriotic spirit with readers on the home front.

On December 12th, the Army and Navy took control of most of Pan Am's flying-boat fleet, and relied heavily on the planes throughout the war to carry government leaders, including President Roosevelt, military passengers, supplies, and mail; while the flying-boat fleet did carry some evacuees throughout the evacuation, that was a minor part of its wartime mission.

Chapter 7
Establishing Priorities

Oversight of the Lists

Turnaround speed and adaptability were essential in the formation of convoys. The vessels weren't all luxury vessels: they were a mixed bag of troop ships, tankers, cargo ships, as well as ocean liners, some under the control of the Army Transportation Service, some the Navy. Coordinating incoming and outgoing convoys was a daunting task and the responsibility of Cargo and Passenger Control, a section of the military government created jointly by General Emmons and Admiral Bloch that reported directly to Colonel Green. Its director was Commander E.C. Gray and his staff included an Army and a Navy representative. The Control was responsible for creating passenger lists of Army wounded and dependents as well as civilians, coordinating incoming and outgoing troop and passenger movements, and minimizing the turn-around time for ships in port.[177] The Navy was charged with caring for its wounded and dependents, and for providing convoy escorts, primarily destroyers from Destroyer Group 15 and some light cruisers.

By mid-December, Captain Frucht was trying to work out the lines of responsibility for civilian evacuation. Civilians (tourists) were to register at the Honolulu

Gas Company under the direction of Commander H.W. Boynton of the Navy, who was instructed to work with Castle & Cooke to determine the validity of civilian applications. Frucht and A.J. Pessel from Castle & Cooke agreed to a civilian, non-military-dependent fare of $125 plus tax for passage back to the mainland. Children under twelve were charged half fare plus tax.[178] This structure didn't work, in part because Admiral Bloch was dissatisfied with the pace of the evacuation of dependents, and unhappy with the work of Navy's "Officer-in-Charge," meaning Frucht or possibly Commander J.B. Barrett of the Navy's Overseas Transportation Office. The Military Governor's office was unhappy as well, announcing on February 13, 1942, that the Army Transport Service (ATS) would take full charge of civilian evacuation, including collection of passage money and assigning space. Castle & Cooke was instructed to turn over all its passenger files to the ATS, which would occupy the passenger office in the Castle & Cooke building. Civilians were now officially defined as "persons or dependents of persons who are not members of the army, navy, marine corps, federal civil service or other agencies of the federal government." The ATS prioritized civilian evacuees on the following basis: 1. pregnant women, 2. The aged, infirm and invalids, 3. Men and women in essential war industries on the Mainland, 4. Tourists, 5. Women with large numbers of children and infants, 6. Other women and children to go to school on the Mainland.[179] The military branches would continue to handle their own dependents.

Green's role in all this is unclear, but he certainly knew that a restructure of the evacuation process was under discussion on February 10th when he pointed out to Col. Throckmorten, the Army's evacuation officer, that the military government was not about to cede any of its authority to the ATS, particularly in regard to passenger lists. Green wrote in his diary: "They [ATS] furnish the ships but we have to handle the lists." Oversight of these lists was a high priority for Green, who only the day before admonished Frank Midkiff of the OCD for making unauthorized changes to the evacuation lists.[180]

Further complicating matters, on March 11, 1942, the War Department and the Chief of Naval Operations decided, without informing General Emmons, that the Navy, specifically the Commander-in- Chief of the Pacific Fleet, would have control of the evacuation. This decision was precipitated by a dispute between the Army and Navy over priorities for evacuation. The military governor maintained that civilian evacuees on convoys should be divided as equitably as possible between Army dependents, Navy dependents and general personnel (including tourists). The Navy's position in March was to evacuate the remaining Navy and Army dependents first (approximately 9,500 people) and then to evacuate the remaining 7,000 tourists and general personnel. Emmons was likely thinking of the radiogram of December 12th from the CNO listing the evacuation priority as wounded, tourists, Army and Navy personnel and general personnel, and to "pool the space available on Army, Navy and commercial shipping." That message also clearly labeled the Commandant of the 14th Naval District as controlling the evacuation.[181] Emmons said he never received word that the Navy was in charge. The Army could have been engaging in selective memory here, but it is important to note that General Emmons did not assume the military governorship until December 17th, a mere five days after the December 12th radiogram was sent. At any rate, the military government wanted to keep control of the evacuation a local matter.

Emmons, feeling the weight of his role as military governor of the entire territory, felt that morale would suffer if Army and Navy dependents were the only ones evacuated for the time being. He urged that the former practice remain in place, allocating roughly a third of the available space for each category of civilian. A compromise was reached, outlined in a memo from General Eisenhower, then a brigadier general and Assistant Chief of Staff in the War Department, on March 17th, in which control of the evacuation was placed firmly with CincPac, but that "due consideration" be given to Emmons' recommendations for tourists and other civilians.[182]

Midkiff's Plan

The changes in the evacuation policy worked out by the Army and Navy effectively isolated Frank Midkiff, head of the Evacuation Committee of the Hawaiian Office of Civilian Defense OCD. Midkiff's charge was to organize the evacuation of non-dependent civilians wanting to go to the mainland. From the outset of the war, the military and naval authorities ignored him. For example, on December 26th, when Captain Frucht ordered Castle & Cooke to start boarding tourists (civilians) on the *Matsonia* for the second evacuation convoy to the mainland, Midkiff wasn't copied on any correspondence.[183] Midkiff wrote to Frank Locey, his boss at OCD, complaining "I am responsible for the evacuation of [non-dependent] civilians," making it clear that this involved not only internal evacuation, but evacuation to the mainland as well. And he informed Green that "A very considerable portion of the responsibility" for evacuating non-dependent civilians to the mainland rests with the Evacuation Division of OCD. Green was not impressed, dismissing Midkiff as "a devious man." Undaunted, Midkiff fought for his role in the evacuation hierarchy by laying out a plan in January 1942 to create a consistent and logical hierarchy for civilian evacuees.[184] Midkiff suggested that when available, transportation be provided to:

1) Aged and/or sick and infirm;
2) Women (with their children) who have the largest number of infant and child dependents;
3) Persons who are needed for key mainland defense positions;
4) Women with their children who have been in Hawaii only short time, and who have no near relatives here. This includes dependents of Civilian Defense workers, as well as other persons.
5) Other civilian women and children.[185]

Midkiff was likely unaware of the brewing changes limiting civilian government's influence in the evacuation, when he wrote to Green that "Someone will have to establish priorities ... and arrangements will have to be made for registering them, arranging for their tickets ..." He suggested that experienced travel agencies, such as Castle & Cooke and the American President Lines, be designated as official agencies for registering non-dependent civilians, and that his proposal already had the approval of those agencies as well as the Red Cross and the Territorial Department of Public Welfare. Under Midkiff's proposal the Evacuation Division and the designated "experienced travel agencies" would register the applicants for evacuation, provide fare, funds and essentials for those with little or no money, arrange for the evacuees to be at the docks at the designated times (which was a military secret), and handle baggage and freight. It would require that the Army and Navy and civilian authorities work more closely together than ever to assess available space while maintaining strict secrecy.

Midkiff won a partial victory when General Emmons issued orders to the Army Transport Service on February 8th that incorporated many of the recommendations made by Midkiff, but clarified the lines of authority and responsibility. The ATS maintained responsibility for the evacuation of all civilians, including collecting passage money, assigning spaces, and all aspects of loading at the docks. The term "civilian" was defined and a hierarchy established, essentially the same as the one Midkiff proposed, except that pregnant women were given top priority. The Civilian Defense Committee was empowered to receive all requests from civilians, establish priorities, and notify evacuees of departure times. And further asserting the authority of the Army Transport Service, General Emmons made clear that the ATS would be *assisted* [author's emphasis] by the American Red Cross, Navy Relief, and the Evacuation Committee of OCD.[186]

And the plan worked. During the evacuation of about 4,000 people on February 14th, Midkiff wrote that "In one case, it was required to load 1,174 civilians onto one large ship, two-thirds of whom had to be arranged for within approximately 26 hours…something like a world's record for rapid handling of civilian passengers and their baggage was established." And endorsing the spirit of the Military Governor's evacuation orders, Midkiff wrote, "The Army Transport Service, with the assistance of augmented personnel from Castle & Cooke, Ltd., and the Evacuation Committee, handled the job efficiently and observed required priorities insofar as was possible. Approximately

1,600 of the most urgent civilian cases, as well as 1,200 other civilian evacuees were afforded transportation." On February 22nd, Midkiff wrote to General Emmons saying that the hierarchy plan had been put to the test and performed satisfactorily.[187]

Green by this time was apparently pleased with the routine of evacuation as well. On the day Midkiff was writing to General Emmons praising the new evacuation hierarchy plan, another large convoy was getting underway to the West Coast [#4057 – consisting of the *Aquitania, Lurline, Kitty Hawk, Wharton, U.S. Grant and President Garfield,* escorted by Destroyer Task Group 15.16: USS *Raleigh, Tucker and Conyngham].* As this passage shows, Green had a personal interest in this convoy:

> *By the end of February 1942, the project was well organized and the number of evacuees had materially increased. Ships were now coming in from the Mainland in larger numbers and none went back empty. One of the larger convoys which carried my wife was typical of the system used. That convoy began to get organized in the inner harbor at Honolulu on February 19th. That first group consisted of six transports of various sizes accompanied by a destroyer escort. From lists prepared beforehand, passengers were notified to repair to the dock when the ship was ready. When each successive ship was loaded it pulled out into the harbor and made ready to sail on short notice. In this convoy there were more than 3000 evacuees and once aboard the ships, there was no turning back for any reason and no visitors were permitted. Loading 3000 women and children is a tedious matter for all concerned but all made the best of it. The accommodations were crowded to the maximum. The evacuees were none too pleased at leaving their loved ones and few looked*

forward with pleasure to the voyage ahead. The ships lay in the Harbor for two days, which did not increase the morale of anyone. This enforced wait was due to the fact that the SS Acquitania[,] (sic) was coming from Australia with the first group of American wounded. During the second night the Acquitanian (sic) slipped into the harbor unannounced and all was ready. There was a patrolling of destroyers, submarines and aircraft preliminary to the departure of the convoy. At five o'clock on the afternoon of the 21st, the time of departure had arrived. It was planned so as to pass the dangerous Molokai Channel at night because the area was known to be a rendevous (sic) point for enemy submarines.

Suddenly, the Army transport, Grant, the flagship, came to life and began to pull out. She was loaded with sick and wounded, [and a few detainees and aliens.] [crossed out] The President Garfield swung into line behind the Grant. The Kitty Hawk, a former train boat which had plied between Cuba and Key West, came next. She was followed next in line by the luxury liner Lurline of the Hawaiian Steamship Line carrying 2000 evacuees. As the procession passed the beautiful Acquitania (sic) she suddenly came to life and took her position. She towered over the others and gave the appearance of a mother hen sheparding (sic) her chickens to safety. The Navy transport Wharton came from Pearl Harbor to complete the convoy. As soon as they cleared the harbor a hollow square was affected. This tight formation was maintained and they steamed ahead at about 300 yards apart. The whole armada was flanked by combat ships and an uneven zig zag course was adopted and maintained for the next twelve days until arrival in San Francisco.[188]

Chapter 8
"I've Got to Get on That Ship!

Subsequent Convoys

Colonel Green constantly worried about the welfare of evacuees and inspected many of the convoys before their departure to make sure conditions were as good as possible under the circumstances. He heard rumors about wealthy passengers being given superior accommodation during crossings and did his best to put a stop to the practice, often ordering changes of billeting on the spot if he found a family crammed into a cabin, while an individual had a cabin to himself. One night, while doing an unannounced inspection, he suspected that something was amiss when the officer accompanying him seemed hesitant to open the cabin door of the bridal suite. Green ordered him "to open the door without further delay." He shone his flashlight into the cabin and then quickly backed away. Inside were eight bunks, seven of them with two children each sleeping peacefully, one at the head and the other at the foot. In the other bunk slept a woman taking care of the children. He tiptoed out as quietly as he could.[189]

Some people were so desperate to leave the Islands that their desperation drove them to take drastic measures. Green attributed this desire to leave to a form of claustrophobia, exacerbated by the fear of future attack. One man in his thirties pleaded with Green to remove his wife from the evacuation list because of her bad character, and offered himself as her replacement on the ship. Green, appalled by the man's cowardice and disloyalty to his own wife, turned him down flat. The man fled Green's office screaming, "I've got to get on that ship!"

A few nights later, as Green was inspecting a ship about to convoy out the next day, he was astonished to see the man aboard; moreover the man brazenly approached him saying, "You see, I made it!" Green would have been well within his rights to throw the man in jail, but he felt that if the scoundrel remained in Hawaii he could poison civilian morale, a matter of vital concern to Green and Emmons, so the colonel allowed him to stay aboard, but only after making sure that his wife was aboard as well. Green said that the one thing of value he learned from the experience was that some people would even stow away to get aboard an evacuation ship.[190]

There was no escaping the fact that evacuation brought great anxiety to families who feared the crossing itself and dreaded separation from their loved ones. Irene R, Chilton, despite living on Oahu all her life, no longer felt that the Islands were safe for her children. The young mother was not a military dependent, but rather a civilian who, following the military government's call, opted to evacuate. She endured the long lines at the steamship office to register herself and her family. She soon received notice to report to the docks on February 18th. Of that day, she wrote, "We said our goodbyes and took a taxi to an army pier where the ship was docked. But as we drove away from Papa's house, I looked back and saw Mama and Papa sitting on the front porch, waving. I'll never forget that scene. That's the last time I saw Papa." She sailed on Convoy 4057PE aboard the S.S. *President Garfield*, leaving Honolulu on February 22nd.[191]

Lt. Joseph Leverton of the USS *Wasmuth* confided his fears to his diary. He yearned to have his wife Helen and two children, then living in Honolulu, safely on the mainland, yet he lamented, "I don't think much of having my family on the high seas at this time." His hope was that they would get a fast ship like the *Lurline*, and he even suggested to his wife to try to book passage on the Pan American Clipper. On the day of the attack, Leverton rushed to the *Wasmut*h, helping to get the ship out to sea, yet he still got to see his family with some regularity after December 7th·, whenever the ship came back into Pearl Harbor for refueling, and he could get liberty. Anticipating his time ashore with them, he constantly hoped that they still would be there, all the while knowing they would have to be evacuated at some point.

The interminable waiting created some sad ironies. On February 24th, as the *Wasmuth* provided escort for an outbound convoy, Leverton wondered if his family was aboard one of the ships. Late in March, with his family still in Hawaii, and while rumors were circulating that the *Wasmuth* soon would be sent to the West Coast, Leverton called the transportation office to check on their evacuation status and was told that there were many on the waiting list before Helen. His fear now was that Helen and the children would be left behind while he sailed to the mainland. On April 24th Leverton received a letter from Helen saying she and the children had sailed on the 22nd. He wrote in his diary on the 29th, "Have a couple of days in port. Sure was strange not to have a home to go to." His family reached

San Francisco on the next day. Leverton and the *Wasmuth* arrived there on June 10th.[192]

One of a child's worst fears was realized by Nancy (Walbridge) Herzog, the 15-year-old high school student mentioned in Chapter 5.[193] Without her knowledge, her father had arranged for a car to pick her up at the Army hospital where she did volunteer work, to take her to the docks for evacuation. Evidently, a family scheduled to leave on the currently forming convoy couldn't go because the children became ill, so space opened up for the Herzog family.

"The docks were chaotic," she said, "everyone going this way and that way... people would send you to one place and then you would have to go to another place." The man with the ship's passenger list told her which ship to go on, but it turned out to be the wrong one, and she ended up making the crossing by herself – with no money and no clothes. It was an old ship, very crowded –she thinks a converted cattle ship, not luxurious like the Matson Lines ships. She slept on a mattress in a corridor. Food wasn't bad – she ate during the second shift for meals. Most of the passengers were families, civilian evacuees. "I didn't know a soul," she says "... [but] people were really nice to me... one woman took me under her wing."

She arrived in San Francisco about a week later. The Red Cross put her on a train for Pittsburgh where her grandparents lived and pinned a sign on her with her name and destination, which she promptly took off when she got on the train because at 15 she felt she was too old for such things. How could people on the mainland even begin to imagine what she had been through already in her young life? Her grandparents met her in Pittsburgh and she stayed with them until her mother and brother arrived later.

Evacuees often complained about the short notice they received before boarding their ship. Rhoda Riddell, an officer's wife, for example, received a mysterious phone call at work telling her to pack and go to the Y in Honolulu, where she awaited a second call, which when it came said only: "Say nothing, but go to the dock tomorrow morning." But some evacuees were able to put off their day of departure. Peggy Ryan, the wife of a naval officer, knew a friendly clerk in the transportation office, who, whenever Ryan's name came up, moved it back to the bottom of the stack of evacuation cards. "Eventually, the stack grew too small to hide my name, and I received my call on 20 April," she wrote. Her convoy left two days later. In reminiscences of her time at Pearl Harbor as a child, Joan Martin Rodby noted, after registering for evacuation, "Our name came up twice and each time my mother decided that she couldn't do it."[194]

Despite the best efforts of Col. Green, some evacuees were more comfortable than others, especially if they were officers' families, or if they had some other connection. Jay Westin, the wife of Lt. Howard F. Westin, evacuating on the *Aquitania* with their one-year-old son, felt guilty that she and her son had their own cabin. When she visited other berths she saw that they each had three bunks with baby "buggies" in between. She said that because she was an officer's wife, and because her sister worked in the "purser's office" in Honolulu, she got preferential treatment. In one instance, though, all suffered equally aboard the *Aquitania*: there was no milk to give to the 500 children abroad the ship. Mrs. Westin fed her son ginger ale and crackers during the crossing.[195]

Another evacuee who experienced relative luxury during a crossing was Ginger, a 17-year-old girl whose father was an Army officer at Hickam Field. On December 29th,

Ginger and her family boarded a ship that sailed the next day, most likely the *President Garfield*, departing at 10:36 p.m. Ginger wrote in her diary that their evening sailing was under a brilliant waxing moon and they were served "super meals." Ginger wrote that the convoy consisted of four transports, four destroyers and a light cruiser, and that the two of the destroyers dropped off the next day. She was a keen observer, for according to CincPac War Diaries, the convoy (#4033) was comprised of four transports (the *President Garfield, Harris, Procyon* and *Tasker Bliss*) escorted by Task Group 15.7 (the light cruiser *Phoenix* and destroyers *Perkins* and *Aylwin*). Their quarters were a "suite with two bedrooms, a living room, and a bath ... on a private little deck with one other suite. [It] Has an outside door and one opening on our private stairs to the dining room." But like most children making the crossing home, she complained of boredom: "Have found life very dull on this boat compared to the trip over. No radios, movies, or other kinds of amusements except for books, and they wouldn't let me bring my camera with me, so I can't even amuse myself with that."[196]

Adolescents like Ginger did the best they could under the circumstances. Fourteen-year-old Peter Fullinwider, on the same convoy with Ginger, doesn't recall much about the December 30th crossing, but remembers his joy at being surrounded by his sister's sixteen-year-old girlfriends and talking with them for hours before the *Harris* got underway at Pearl Harbor. His sister Joan and her friends celebrated New Year's Eve on that crossing by listening to a Victrola in a hallway under blue lights while wearing their life vests. Bob Moritz, 11, was separated from his mother and sister as they boarded the Lurline on the December 25th crossing. They were assigned to a cabin on the main deck with four other women and their daughters; Bob was sent four decks below to a cabin that housed four other boys around his age and several Marine pilots' wives and their children. When not visiting his mother and sister, Bob recalls exploring the ship with his new friends. Their greatest find was the locker where the tennis balls were stored. "Most of those balls wound up in the drink," he said.[197]

Red Cross volunteer Edna Reese had her hands full aboard an evacuation ship, most likely the *Lurline*, during a late February crossing. Charged with entertaining approximately 150 high-school-age students on the ship, Reese needed to use all her ingenuity and creativity to keep them occupied. On this voyage some 2,000 passengers filled every space, with some of the decks "literally swarming with hundreds of passengers, all sitting on the floor, for the comforts of deck chairs and mattresses were unknown." Knowing teens love to dance, she found a cornet, a bass violin, and an accordion player among the passengers and then wrangled dance space for them in the purser's lounge by moving the chairs and the "old ladies" out of the room. However, she did complain that the young people "did not always behave in the most accepted manner." Evidently blackouts on deck were "a great temptation" for them, so that on the last night of the voyage she had the enclosed deck patrolled and off limits to everyone unless they had official reason to be there.[198]

Even during war, teenagers were still teenagers.

Voices of Children

Much of our first-hand knowledge of the evacuation crossings comes from the viewpoint of children, who are today adults recalling their childhood evacuation experiences. Patsy Campbell's three years in Hawaii came to an end on January 22, 1942, when she, her brother Edward, and their mother boarded the Navy transport USS *Wharton* for the long journey home. Her father remained in Hawaii. The *Wharton*, carrying women and children dependents and a cargo of Hawaiian pineapples, was part of a three-ship convoy along with the *President Garfield* and the troopship *Harris*.[199] They were escorted by two destroyers: the *Case* and the *Tucker*. The little convoy took over a week to reach the mainland because of the zigzag course it was forced to take to avoid Japanese submarines. Patsy remembers that when the Wharton's gun crews held gunnery practice each blast shook the ship so much the light fixtures fell out of the overheads, or ceilings. The worst part, though, was that the family's dog, Tinker, did not make the journey with them. One day, just before her ship was to sail, Patsy's mother took Tinker away. The brown mutt with a tail that curved back and looked like a doughnut, who had been with the family since their days in Panama, would be put to sleep rather than sent to an animal shelter. Her brother, Edward, said, "So many dogs and cats were getting sent to the animal shelter, [I] just couldn't give him away to anybody else."

Beverly A. Moglich, who celebrated her twelfth birthday a week before the bombing, lived with her parents and younger sister in Manalani Heights; her father was a chief warrant officer assigned to Ford Island. She was evacuated with her mother and sister aboard the *Lurline* on the February 22nd convoy (4057PE), the same convoy as Irene Chilton and her children, who were aboard the *President Garfield*. This is her experience during the crossing: (Note that early departures are a consistent theme in evacuation stories.)

> *The ships were scheduled to leave on February 23rd. but left in the evening of the 22nd [convoy records show a February 21st departure date] to confuse the Japanese in case they had spies working on the island. The layout of the cabins were for two beds, and when my mother, sister and I went to the islands in 1940 on the Matsonia a rollaway bed was put in the room for my sister. On this return trip twelve bunks were built, three deep. They had canvas laced on to the bunk. Not many coverings. Every passenger was given a 'Mae West' lifejacket to wear, including to bed at nights. We slept in our day time clothes. No night clothing was allowed. I was seasick and did not go to meals very often. I did eat candy bars which I loved anyway. They did give me energy. The weather was stormy and the seas were high at times, so many people were seasick.*
>
> *We were allowed out on deck during the day, sometimes. On one deck, one side was blacked out. I don't know why only this area, but that was the case. Since there were many times the normal passenger list we probably did not bathe as often. We certainly did not have any privacy. Screaming babies, arguments, on and on. My grandfather was in the lower decks which was for men only. He was able to come up to the upper decks during the day. He was the most wonderful man in the world and such a help to us for comfort. I walked round and round the decks for fun and exercise.*[200]

Carroll Robbins Jones characterized the evacuation as "a miserable event."' In fact, that is the title of a chapter in her 2001 book, *Hawaii Goes to War: The Aftermath of Pearl Harbor,* written with her husband Wilbur D. Jones, Jr. Carroll Jones' mother was a professional photographer and her father a naval officer serving on the USS *Shaw* at the time of the Japanese attack. One event during her August 1942 crossing was particularly memorable:

We kids were awakened late one night and told to quickly put on our life jackets. Since the convoy traveled in darkness at night, we had only little blue lights in the passageway on board, but could hear people hurriedly going by our room. The heavy doors to the rooms had been pulled open and secured and women with children had been given priority exit to the deck.

As we approached the stairs going up to the deck where we had many times practiced life boat drills, I remember clearly to this day the slow creaking of chains as the boats were lowered into the water. We had all been assigned a station and a boat number. It was pitch black, but as we became accustomed to the dark we could make out what was going on immediately around us and who was next to us. Those chains, creaking and groaning, was the most menacing sound I have ever heard… We were in the process of being lowered into the whaleboat, swinging side to side as we slowly dropped with the ominous creaking sound in pitch black, when suddenly everything stopped, and very quietly the word was passed that it was 'all clear.' Apparently a Japanese sub had been trailing us and got too close for comfort… I was too frightened to cry that night.[201]

Lockard Returns

Joe Lockard had become one of the early heroes of the war when it became known that he had tried to warn the Information Center about what turned out to be the first wave of Japanese planes attacking Pearl Harbor. He remained on duty in Oahu for a couple of months before he was called home to the Eastern Signal Corps Training

Center at Fort Monmouth in New Jersey for officer training. His champion was Representative Forest Harness (R-Ind.) of the House Military Affairs Committee, who took up Joe's cause after reading about him in the Roberts Commission Report in January. This commission appointed by President Roosevelt and headed by Associate Justice of the Supreme Court Owen Roberts, was the first of many inquiries into the disaster of Pearl Harbor. On February 21, 1942, Lockard found himself once more at sea aboard the USS *US Grant*, a Navy troop ship that was part of a convoy of six transports, evacuation ships, and cargo vessels escorted by three destroyers. For many years before the war, the *Grant* had functioned as an unarmed Army transport and later was transferred to the Navy and refitted with 3-inch guns. Now aboard the ship were about 1,000 Japanese prisoners, including Kazuo Sakamaki, better known as prisoner No. 1, the first Japanese prisoner of war, who was captured after abandoning his disabled two-man submarine off eastern Oahu on December 7th. Lockard said that the *Grant* was the slowest of the vessels in the convoy; it was certainly slower than the *Aquitania, Lurline, Wharton,* and *Kitty Hawk*, some of the other vessels in that convoy. And while there were some civilians aboard, most of the passengers, as he remembers it, were military people. He docked at San Francisco on March 1st. As luck would have it, Lockard would travel on the *Grant* again; the ship took him to his posting in Alaska later in the war.

Pets At Sea

On April 23rd, a convoy made up of a dozen ships arrived in the Bay area, most likely Convoy #4091 departing from

Honolulu and Hilo thirteen days before. One of the vessels docked at the Grove Street Pier in Oakland and unloaded 39 survivors (35 dogs, three cats and a canary) of the raid on Pearl Harbor. One of the survivors, named Steamboat, came with a sign attached to his cage that read, "My name is 'Steamboat.' Please be kind to me as I went through the blitz on December 7. I am a nervous pussie [sic] cat. Please see that I find my mistress, who loves me so." Steamboat's owner, Mrs. J.T. Scott, eagerly awaited her nervous cat at her home on Guerrero Street in San Francisco, where they were reunited.

Caring for these animals was Seaman Ralph Nesson from Long Beach, who exercised the animals on deck every day. His menagerie included Pomeranians, Dachshunds, terriers, Boston bulls, spaniels, police dogs, and collies. The *Oakland Tribune* described some as "just plain dogs." Nesson said that many of the dogs were skittish after their ordeal during the bombing, and that they trembled when the ship engaged in gunnery practice during the voyage to the mainland. Nesson was a good sport. As the ship was getting ready to leave Honolulu, a woman rushed up to him and handed him her dog's hairbrush, begging him to brush the dog's hair every day. He readily agreed, and carried out his charge faithfully.

During the crossing they were kept in cages lashed to the deck and covered with a tarp. Sadly, one of the dogs never made it to the mainland. It broke out of its cage and was swept overboard in heavy seas. Once the ship docked, the animals were turned over to the San Francisco S.P.C.A. and then shipped to their owners around the country.[202]

An April Crossing

Peggy Ryan, a young Navy wife, married to Lieutenant Paul Ryan, a submariner assigned to USS *Dolphin,* was not high on the initial priority list for evacuees so was able to put off evacuation until April 1942. Nevertheless, she remained in readiness for a sudden departure because, as she wrote, "We had been warned by military authorities that we would receive only twenty-four hours' notice of departure, so we lived from day to day out of suitcases, never sure when our call would come."[203] She received her notice on April 20th and was assigned to the *H.F. Alexander,* a transport manned by overage officers and a teenage crew from the British Isles. This was her experience in her own words:

> *My preparations were brief; our few household goods, mainly wedding presents, had been shipped several months before, and I had only to close my trunk and suitcases. The transportation office clerk informed me that the sailing was to be kept secret, but how does one conceal a departure with so much baggage in evidence? Friends drove me to the pier where the leave-taking was subdued. No bands, flower leis, and paper streamers – so customary in prewar years... By noon on 22 April, we got under way to join a convoy off the Pearl Harbor channel. Planes were circling overhead, and harbor craft patrolled around us as we were shepherded into formation...*
>
> *The stateroom, which I shared with two other women, was very small and made even more so by the installation of three tiers of wooden bunks. I chose a bottom berth, but found that it took some practice to even turn over because of the narrow clearance. My delicate condition [she was*

pregnant] and the uncomfortable rolling of the ship persuaded me to spend much of the eight-day voyage in my bunk.

My roommates were Army wives, and we made a congenial group... Shipboard life was austere. There were no recreational facilities such as shuffleboard, a lounge, movies, or card room. The meals were adequate if not appealing, the chefs relying heavily on mutton, beef, potatoes, cabbage, and turnips. The usual dessert was pudding or cake – both rubbery – or canned fruit. The bread was a type of hard roll which had been taken aboard in Australia, some weeks before...

In our convoy were ten ships – six naval vessels and four merchantmen. We were formed into two columns, the H.F. Alexander being the second ship in the port column. In the starboard column we recognized the damaged battleship Nevada, which had been patched up and was undoubtedly headed for one of the navy yards. The cruiser San Francisco steamed ahead of the convoy while the destroyers Case and Reid ranged back and forth on the flanks. We zigzagged constantly during the day and even at night when the moon was bright. The weather was usually very windy and squally, and quite rough.

We passed much of our time watching the naval ships perform maneuvers. Every morning the San Francisco would catapult a seaplane for antisubmarine patrol. Then, three hours later, a second plane was shot off, after which the first one would land alongside the cruiser to be hoisted aboard by a crane. Then there was the day when the Nevada and the transport Henderson held a firing practice with their 5-inch guns aiming at a target spar towed by the Pyro. When told that the Pyro was an ammunition ship, we could only hope that the aim of the gunners was accurate.

Our greatest concern was a submarine attack. Daily, when we awoke in the morning our first move was to look out the port to check the presence of our escorts. One night, we were nearly thrown out of our bunks as the ship made a sudden turn to port. We immediately surmised that a submarine was after us; not until morning did we learn that the Chaumont had fired a red flare signaling a submarine contact, later reported to be false. Incidents like this kept us a shipload of nervous women.

...Not only were we required to muster every day at our assigned lifeboats, but we were briefed on the location of the boat's water flasks and rations. We practiced wearing and adjusting our life jackets, which had to be within arm's reach at all times, no matter where we were. Every morning an officer made the rounds of the outboard cabins to dog down our porthole cover. But unfortunately, the room at once became stifling, so in defiance of safety regulations, we reopened the port with a sturdy coathanger (sic), first being sure to turn out all lights...

On the seventh day out, the purser announced that an entertainment would take place that evening in the dining room. After dinner, stewards pushed tables together to form a makeshift stage. Our master of ceremonies was a retired vaudevillian whose wife served as the pianist. By any standards, the show was a true amateur hour. But if the harmonica players, magicians, jugglers, and singers were undistinguished, the show also provided the most unforgettable incident of the voyage. It came when one of the very youngest of the crew began to sing old Irish ballads in a beautiful tenor. He evoked such a feeling of nostalgia that the entire audience became affected, and most of the women were teary-eyed. There was not one person listening who did not share his longing for home, whether it was faraway

Ireland or some special place each of us had left behind. We had been uprooted, and the young Irish boy had suddenly and poignantly made us realize it.

On the afternoon of 28 April, we suspected we were nearing the West Coast when a destroyer, the USS Laffey, came steaming over the horizon, and came alongside the Nevada to deliver a package. Promptly, the battleship left the formation and headed north in company with the Laffey. The next day, we sighted a scouting blimp on antisubmarine patrol. These next were anxious hours, for according to our rumor experts, enemy submarines always lurked off busy ship channels. Happily, there were no alerts and early in the morning of 30 April the sight of the Golden Gate generated a mass felling of relief at reaching safety in the beautiful city of San Francisco.[204]

Chapter 9
"We Aren't Allowed to Talk About Convoys"

Information from the Want Ads

Honolulu newspapers, unlike those on the mainland, barely mentioned convoy arrivals and departures in their pages because of enforced military secrecy. Occasionally some stories were published, but never with the detail provided in mainland publications, especially West Coast papers. A short piece on the front page of *The Honolulu Advertiser* on January 1, 1942, mentioned the second convoy, which had departed on December 26th, as having arrived in San Francisco, and distilled into two short paragraphs the good spirits of the wounded and their eagerness to get back to the fighting. In the last sentence of the story, civilians are identified as mostly families of Navy personnel in Hawaii. While Honolulu newspapers could not comment directly about evacuees and convoys, letter writers sometimes did. In the *Advertiser* on January 7th, Mrs. Rothe referred to the vital positions "vacated by persons returning to the Mainland." She complained that as a British citizen she was not allowed to work for the Army or Navy. And "A Navy Wife" complained that since she was notified to be ready to leave in a week or ten days with her three children, she noticed that civilian men were also leaving. "Are they afraid of the Japs?" she wrote. "Are they more important than women and children or is the one with the 'pull and the folding money' the one who knows how to beat the racket?"[205]

The classified sections of newspapers gave an inkling of how pervasive the impact of the ongoing evacuations was on life in Hawaii, with ads from people selling stoves, refrigerators and cars, identified as "Evacuating" or "Leaving." A home-grown industry of sorts developed with evacuees needing to sell appliances and cars quickly to a public looking for a bargain. The White Sewing Machine Agency advertised for evacuees to turn in their old sewing machines for "a liberal allowance" on a new one to be delivered on the mainland, while Sears advertised a clearance on "Evacuee" refrigerators, all "in practically new condition." Surprisingly, trans-Pacific business continued unabated. In mid-February, Hawaii Auto Sales ran a used-car sale "in order to make room for a large shipment of new cars," which could only be coming from the West Coast. And Hawaiian Freight Forwarders, Ltd. advertised freight to the mainland to firms and individuals.[206] The *Advertiser* even advertised itself, suggesting that evacuees already on the mainland would appreciate a subscription as a gift for only $1.50 a month:

> *Many Former Residents*
> *now on the Mainland*
> *will enjoy a subscription to*
> *The Honolulu Advertiser*
> *to keep up with the changes in*
> *HAWAII*

Real estate became a bargain for those who stayed. A heartfelt "I Must Sacrifice My Beautiful New Home," appeared in the Honolulu Advertiser Real Estate pages on February 20. On that same page another owner selling his home on Dole Street put clearly for all to see "Owner Being Evacuated," while still another seller "already evacuated on Mainland," offered his fully furnished Manoa home for $8,500. Alfred P. Fernandez, whose family lived in the Damon tract, remembers in 1942 that the haole population was moving back to the mainland and that their houses could be purchased cheaply. His parents bought a two-story, two bathroom, four bedroom home on fashionable Alewa Heights for only $11,000, a bargain price. Some evacuees were able to make a small profit. Then sixteen-year-old and soon-to-be-evacuated Willie Jarvis remembers his mother selling their house in Waikiki a hundred yards from the water for $1400 in 1942; she had bought the house two years earlier for $1200.[207]

Honolulu War Diary

Some of the most obvious references to the evacuation to the mainland came from Laselle Gilman's column in the *Advertiser*, "Honolulu War Diary." In the months after the Pearl Harbor bombing, Gilman devoted parts of several columns to the evacuation. Gilman told readers that evacuation of civilians was strictly a voluntary matter: "If you're a civilian and want to get the heck out of here, you can figure your chances from the priorities listing of the military governor," but acknowledged that "The Army announces the priorities but remains silent on the advisability of evacuation for ordinary citizens." Realizing that individuals lack vital information to make an informed decision, he admonished the government, "If wholesale evacuation is advisable, let those in authority say so; if not, an equally clear statement would be welcome."[208]

A wholesale evacuation never materialized, yet the substantial one that did was largely unreported by Gilman. In a piece in February, hinting at the two-way convoy traffic, he said, "We aren't allowed to talk about convoys, but the postmen have been very busy the last few days ... Also a number of local residents who were stranded on the Mainland by the Blitz [the Japanese attack] appear to be again in our midst." On the other hand "Evacuees are packing up once more, but their bunks are being rapidly filled by workers from the Mainland." In March, he described the evacuation to the West Coast "as yet a mere trickle ... chiefly the families of Service personnel, many of whom had no choice." A month later he wrote, "The wahine-keiki (woman-child) evacuation still continues, a slow trickle eastward to the Mainland." In a colorful piece the month before (see Appendix), not in a column but rather as a news story, Gilman, who covered Honolulu Harbor as a beat before the war, described the changes in the harbor as a result of the war, saying it remained a very busy place, still geared to the loading and unloading of cargo, but no longer the produce and passengers from around the Pacific, rather more likely now the materiel of war. "Travelers – evacuees, perhaps – leaving Hawaii," he wrote, "move in accord with grave military tactics and their safe journey is a military success. Travelers, thus, serve in silence, and so does everyone else remotely connected with shipping in Honolulu. Details of voyages are military secrets, the ships in convoy move as units in a military campaign, and no one sails without military approvals. Ships names and sailing dates are not discussed."[209]

Gilman had little patience for those evacuees who spread what he considered to be misinformation when they returned to the West Coast. A reader sent Gilman a clipping from a Dallas paper quoting an evacuee who was reported to have said that the Japanese in Honolulu were so sure that the Japanese attack would be successful that on the night of December 7th "many of them moved into homes evacuated by Americans. When the owners returned the Japanese occupants told them, 'This was your home, but it isn't anymore.' " Gilman added, "We have her name, but we'll save her hubby, still with the Navy here, embarrassment. This might be noted by prospective evacuees; if you must talk rot, don't talk to those nasty newspapermen, who will quote you." Another reader sent in a clipping from a mainland paper that said Hawaii, once a paradise is now the 'Purgatory of the Pacific' paying for its pre-December-7th sins through the current alcohol prohibition, blackout and martial law. "Gilman lamented that "It is probably only human for a traveler from Hawaii to lay it on thick when he or she reaches the Mainland, mainly for the splash such startlers will make." Gilman's point resonated with a reader who wrote a few days later, "About the Navy wife who talked in Dallas – I was quite glad you mentioned that…I understand quite a number of innocent bystanders were hurt because of her…babbling. There are still many thousands of us yet to be evacuated, so perhaps it wouldn't be amiss to give Service wives another lecture…"[210]

Secrecy was the order of the day, so much so that even Gilman, with his many contacts in the shipping companies, didn't know what was going on. In one column in February Gilman wrote about his pre-December-7th plans to talk with Howard Copple, a printer aboard the *Lurline* who printed the ship's newspaper, menus and programs, but that Copple hadn't returned to Hawaii since the bombing. A little over a week later Gilman reported that he received a note from Copple saying that he had been in Honolulu several times since the war started and would be back again. "The Japs with their phoney (sic) little subs and pop-guns didn't scare me off the high seas nor did it frighten my ship ... The only time we will part is if she goes down ... " From what we know of the *Lurline's* movements in the first few months of the war, Copple and his ship were constantly on the move.[211]

Copple ended his note with "A Slip of the Lip May Sink a Ship ... " And Gilman well knew, as did 'A Navy Wife' that any information about a ship's movements could wind up in enemy hands. Yet people needed some sort of outlet so that they could talk about their shared experience. Myths sprouted up, like this "latest bit of choice-and-juicy" relayed by Gilman:

> *It [the story] concerns a local lad who was riding on a Waikiki bus and noted across the way a woman who was talking loud and long to another woman. Behind this pair sat two more women who were also listening, though obviously not invited to the party.*
>
> *The garrulous number in front rattled on about her new furniture, new jewelry, new raiment, and life for her seemed pretty pleasant. But for the other two women the breaks, from the young fellow's observation, didn't seem quite so good. They looked a little grim as the gabbler in front went on boasting.*
>
> *"You know," the lad heard the woman in front continue, "I sort of wish this war would last five years – my husband is earning more money than ever in his whole life and it sure is swell."*

> *Shortly after that the talkative wahine (woman) got off the bus; so did the young man, and so did the grim women who had been listening.*
>
> *The bus pulled away and there were the four on the corner.*
>
> *And then, according to the young man, one of the young women who had been listening said to the gabbler: "So you want the war to last five years, do you? Well, here's something from my husband at Hickam field." And she handed the complacent one a right to the jaw.*
>
> *"Yes," said the other grim one, "and here's something from my husband at Pearl Harbor," Whereabout she implanted a lusty kick upon the traditional sector. And the wrathful pair departed.*[212]

A few days later a reader submitted two clippings of the same story with different locales, including Seattle. Gilman responded that "such stories become national property in surprisingly short time."[213]

Ironically, most of the writing Gilman did on the civilian evacuation was on the coverage the evacuees got in West Coast papers; in other words, he reported on the reporting, while practically ignoring the actual story, or at least the Hawaiian end of it. It could have been his way of getting around the censors in the military government. His entire piece of April 4th was devoted to covering *Los Angeles Times* columnist Tom Treanor's March 5th "The Home Front" column (see Appendix). In that piece Treanor gave detailed descriptions of the hardships endured by the evacuees during a crossing, but emphasized the upbeat demeanor of most of them. Gilman's column repeated those hardships to his readers, which perhaps was the first time many of them got an inkling of how serious and dangerous the evacuation could be.

Treanor also talked about the hardships of life in Hawaii, which of course, Gilman's readers were fully aware of, but in doing so talked about the changes in places like Honolulu: the beaches covered in barbed wire, the discomfort of a blackout in a warm climate, rising prices of food, and the evacuated houses along the beaches. As he relayed this to his readers, Gilman mentioned another West Coast writer, Chapin Hall, who pointed out the changes in Honolulu since the start of the war: "It obviously is not the Hawaii of yesterday," Hall wrote, "but the islands will come back, and so will the thousands of yearly visitors who once fell such willing victims to their charm."[214]

Chapter 10

"The docks are a madhouse of mothers and children."

The First Convoy Arrives on the Mainland

The first convoy carrying wounded servicemen and evacuees arrived in San Francisco on December 25, 1941. As the ships passed under the Golden Gate, Shirley McKay and her friends broke out singing "California Here We Come," thankful to be home and relieved that the rumors about a probable submarine attack as the convoy approached the mainland had turned out to be false. Rosalie Hutchison gazed up at the bridge and remembered her experience just two years before, when she passed under the "pretty Golden Gate" all lit up with lights. On this wartime Christmas Day, she said later, "nothing was light then, just grey and foggy."

Entering San Francisco Bay, with the *Cummings* leading the way and the *Detroit* taking up the rear, the *Coolidge* and *Scott* broke off from their escorts and docked at Pier 44 at about 8:00 a.m. Rosalie and Shirley and the other passengers had to wait while the wounded were unloaded to ambulances waiting at the dock to take them to area hospitals. Many of the Navy casualties were taken to Mare Island Naval Complex in San Pablo Bay by two waiting ferries. Hundreds of people, held back by armed soldiers and sailors, pressed against the barricades set up three blocks from the docks, hoping for a glimpse of those disembarking from the ships. They didn't know who was aboard, they didn't even know that the ships would be arriving that particular day, but they had heard rumors for several weeks that evacuees would be coming, and on this day the rumors came true, the news spreading by word of mouth along the shore of the bay into the heart of San Francisco. Some of them hoped that a son wounded at Pearl Harbor might be aboard, or a sister sent home safely away from the fighting. This was their first tangible sign of the reality of the war.

Standing in the persistent drizzle and within sight of the towering superstructures of the ships, they saw ambulances and taxis careening towards the docks. They pressed the sentries with questions: "Do you know whether Johnny Thompson is aboard. He was an aircraft gunner... or something." They were unable to see the wounded disembarking first, many carried on stretchers giving the thumbs up as they were loaded on to the ambulances, smiling and defiant; while others, more grievously injured, lay quiet, wrapped in bandages. A sailor on a later convoy, describing a similar scene, said, "Those boys with the burns – poor guys." A San Francisco police inspector was overwhelmed by what he saw that day. "I saw them. I saw what bomb blasts and shrapnel did," he said. "I saw what were once fine husky lads. And it hit me like a Joe Louis punch in the pit of the stomach."[215]

Hazel Holly, a reporter for *The San Francisco Examiner*, was there to see the civilians disembark:

> *THE LINES MOVED down the gangplanks and the piles of baggage, including tricycles, toys, baby buggies and dunnage bags spread farther and farther. Cars drove up,*

took on passengers, and were whisked away by the military police.

It was a motley crowd: there were women in fur coats with paper leis around their necks; there were hatless women in slacks; there was one young widow who carried a tiny baby – she didn't know where she was going.

THEY WERE ALL so very tired, so very glad to be safe ashore, and so appreciative that San Francisco women had come down to meet them, and to take them wherever they wanted to go.[216]

Because the departure and arrival dates for convoys were military secrets as were the number of ships and number of passengers aboard, the Red Cross in San Francisco and at other West Coast ports never knew when a convoy would arrive, or how large it would be, until the day of arrival; Red Cross volunteers and facilities would have to be at the ready constantly. In the weeks between December 7th and December 25th, the Red Cross Headquarters at 625 Sutter Street was transformed to "expedite the whirl of activity" anticipated, with the big front windows cleared of exhibits and replaced with desks and a big new telephone switchboard.[217] Columnist Ernie Pyle, who would later become famous for his reporting from the South Pacific, visited Red Cross headquarters in San Francisco and had nothing but praise for the job that organization was doing, and urged readers to make contributions.[218]

Over 300 volunteers from the Red Cross and other organizations gave up their Christmas Day to work at the docks and reception centers, and did so at a moment's notice.[219] When the first phone call came in to the Red Cross Chapter House at 8:30 on the morning of the 25th, volunteers around the city were alerted; they dropped what they were doing and rushed to predetermined assembly points for transportation to the docks. Some units, such as the Canteen Corps, were put on standby to await further orders. Mrs. Tadini Bacigalupi, in charge of the canteen, and her staff took only a half hour from the time they finally received their phone calls to set up canteens on two docks at noon. The Red Cross Motor Corps sprang into action, transporting food to the canteens, handing out warm clothing, and taking evacuees from the docks to the Women's City Club and to other shelters. And at Red Cross headquarters, volunteers contacted the destinations of the evacuees traveling beyond San Francisco, alerting authorities that refugees from Hawaii and the Pacific would be arriving soon and in need of help.

During the afternoon, a ship's surgeon pointed out that the wounded hadn't eaten in some time and requested that the Red Cross help. Under the circumstances, the best the Red Cross could do was to have the nurses dispense chocolate. When the wounded were carried from the ship across the pier to a river steamer that would take them to Mare Island Naval Hospital, it was discovered that the steamer did not have provisions to feed them and that the earliest they could be fed was 10:00 p.m., 14 hours after the ship had docked. The Canteen Corps scrambled to feed the men as quickly as possible and even placed provisions on the steamer before it left for Mare Island.[220] By 4:30 that afternoon, no evacuees were left on the docks.[221]

The December 25th convoy's arrival featured prominently in both of San Francisco's big newspapers, *The Examiner* and the *Chronicle*, and was reported on front pages throughout the country. The *Chronicle* published passenger lists of the returnees, while *The Examine*r did not shrink from describing the casualties of war:

> *They came back to the mainland yesterday, the maimed and the blinded – the first war casualties to arrive from Hawaii.*
>
> *Convoyed transports brought them. And brought to San Francisco and the Nation, the horror and full impact of Japan's treacherous Pearl Harbor attack.*
>
> *They jammed the ship (sic) hospitals, overflowed into staterooms.*
>
> *There were men hideously burned by explosions. There were fracture cases. There were sightless men. There were the bruised and bewildered children who had never thought much of an enemy before.*[222]

When their ships docked, the evacuees told their stories to reporters: being awakened on that Sunday morning, hearing the noise from the diving planes and exploding bombs, and thinking it was war games – complaining about their Sunday morning being disturbed. And then seeing the planes, recognizing the Red Suns, the "meatballs" in military slang. Mrs. M.R. Williams, disembarking with her three children, stoically told reporters, "My husband is fighting. He was alive when we left, but I don't know where he is now, or whether he's still alive." Sixty-five years later, all Mrs. Williams' youngest and only surviving child, Merle, could remember of that crossing was the dry-cork life vest he was forced to wear around the clock that made him roll with the ship when he was lying down. His mother had to stuff pillows and clothing in his bunk to keep the then three-year-old from rolling back and forth.[223] Reporters especially sought out children for their comments. "Daddy told us to run under a tree," said thirteen-year-old Eva Castle. "A bomb tore up some of our house." Thirteen-year-old Albert Boesenberg said, "Dad told us to be soldiers, but it was hard to be a soldier with all the noise and the kids yelling and the mothers screaming." Rosalie Kiddy, 3, said, "When the bombs fell I crawled under the bed. Mummy was there too, and my brother. But I didn't cry."[224]

The evacuees also told reporters about the crossing – a sad Christmas party, carols on Christmas Eve, blackout conditions and overcrowding, but also about dancing and movies to help morale. Most complained about the need to wear life vests constantly. Many women on the ships volunteered to help care for children aboard, especially for those children whose mothers were overwhelmed caring for infants. Others volunteered to make bandages and dressings for the wounded to whom many other passengers donated books, magazines, clothing, and cigarettes. A sense of dread pervaded the ships as passengers and crew scanned the ocean for periscopes.

All in all, the San Francisco Red Cross handled this first convoy of two ships, about 858 evacuees and 180 wounded, with great dispatch. In reality, it was prepared to handle much larger evacuations: for this Christmas Day arrival, the organization only needed to utilize two of its nine reception centers in the city to process and house the evacuees. Moreover, many of the passengers, including those expecting war and those on the crossing from Manila, had booked passage before hostilities started, so were well prepared to come home. Evacuees coming on later larger convoys, given only the shortest of notice to report aboard the ships, would require more assistance from the Red Cross when they arrived on the mainland, and the Red Cross' next and much harder test would come one week later.

Second and Third Convoys Arrive

When the second convoy arrived the next week, Red Cross volunteers were awakened by early morning phone calls that said "Nine-thirty," and nothing else; that was all they needed to know; the ships with refugees would be arriving at the Embarcadero at that time. Although this second convoy was much larger than the first, almost 2,900 evacuees, including 139 wounded, the scene was similar – the wounded rushed from the ship; the bewildered and dazed civilians - only the faces changed.

As the evacuees disembarked facing the "icy winds" of San Francisco on New Year's Day, some reacted like twenty-year-old Ruby Thompson, clutching the hand of her two-year-old son, and reluctantly answering reporters' questions. The young woman was bitter and angry. Her husband was dead, and her son would never know his father; she didn't want to say anything that could put another sailor's life in danger. Her major concern at that moment was finding out how to get a ticket back home to Atlanta.[225] What she wouldn't tell reporters, and what they wouldn't report even if she had, was that her husband had been killed aboard the USS *Arizona*.

Others arriving at the docks were not so tight lipped. William Hall, an evacuee in the first convoy, said he was "very gloomy" about the war the country now found itself fighting. "And I think you people here in San Francisco should be prepared to take some punches in the jaw and stomach," he said. He called San Francisco the "second line of defense" and said, "the Japs are stronger than we like to give them credit for." Hall, who represented American publishers in the Far East, had been in Japan only a few months before and made his way out of that country by going through Shanghai to Manila before boarding the *Coolidge*.[226] Such speculation annoyed people back in Hawaii, where gloomy language was virtually censored from the vocabulary, and likely perked up the ears of the censors on the mainland. Laselle Gilman, writing under military censorship constraints for the conservative *The Honolulu Advertiser*, which enthusiastically supported the military government, complained about loose-lipped evacuees and the newspapers in California that "have given them considerable prominence." Gilman felt great sympathy for the stoicism and discretion of women like Ruby Thompson, and of men like her husband "who volunteer, knowing they'll go where they're sent, and like it," when he wrote, "Dammit, the rest of us are mere spectators and the least we can do while the show is on is to keep our silly mouths shut."[227]

But the fact remained that the arrival of the evacuees provided mainland newspapers, where censorship was voluntary, with an outlet for information, at a time in which there was precious little, allowing them to report details from the war zone.[228] While the evacuees were a news story themselves, what they saw in Hawaii and on the ocean passage was quoted by reporters eager for facts. *The Examiner* and the *Chronicle* devoted much of their January 1st issue to the evacuees' arrival on the second convoy. Three large photos ran on page 10 in *The Examiner*, showing Mrs. Thompson and her son, six young wives sitting at the Civic Center after their arrival from Hawaii, and a row of Navy wounded on cots awaiting transfer to a Navy hospital. In addition to the main story on page one, *The Examiner* ran a story with lots of photos and quotes from evacuees entitled, "Evacuees Picture Horror in Hawaii." "If it can happen at Pearl Harbor, it can happen here," said one evacuee, who then went on to praise the Honolulu cabbies "as polyglot as the island itself," for loading military men into their cabs and driving "right into the inferno that was Pearl Harbor." Another told of Japanese pilots machine-gunning civilians, while a thirteen-year-old described two Japanese planes deliberately diving into airplane hangars "when they ran out of ammunition."[229] The *Chronicle*, in addition to its page-one coverage of the convoy's arrival, ran two full pages inside with generally upbeat evacuee stories, including the account of a Honolulu reporter who was aboard one of the ships, and photos of children disembarking and evacuees being processed at the Civic Auditorium.

By the time the third convoy arrived in San Francisco on January 6, 1942, the ships were composed primarily of evacuees and not of wounded servicemen.[230] *The Examiner* put that story and an accompanying story about evacuees from the same convoy arriving in San Diego, on page 3, but did run four large photographs. The *Oakland Tribune* gave it front-page coverage and added details that must have made the censors take notice: one of the passengers, Francis Jenkins, professor of physics at the University of California, was returning after a secret visit to Hawaii a week after the war started. He refused to discuss the nature of his visit.[231]

The experiences of evacuees in later voyages were no less stirring. Tom Treanor, the *Los Angeles Times* columnist, described the hardships faced by evacuees arriving in March 1942:

> *The trip back is an ordeal. When the last load came in, the mothers, some of them with three and four children, looked blank with fatigue, worry and confusion.*
>
> *A 13-year-old boy said: "There were more kids aboard than there were rivets." And he was just about right.*
>
> *It was miserably crowded. The weather was rotten. Nearly everybody was sick at the same time. There weren't enough stewards to clean things up promptly. Many people had colds.*

BECAUSE SALT WATER was used in the pipes it couldn't be heated to avoid corrosion. To get hot water the passengers had to fill a bucket and take it to a steam pipe. They would put the pipe in the bucket and the steam would squirt in and be absorbed, heating it up.

There was a milk shortage, even for the babies.

And yet – the workers generally agree on this – there were no complaints. The evacuees were tired and bewildered, but they were taking it as war.

They're not to be pitied. They're lucky. They've already made their adjustment to the long struggle ahead.[232]

Red Cross to the Rescue

The joy, or relief, or dread of reaching the mainland was tempered by the reality of biting winds – and even snow in the unseasonably cold Bay Area winter. Local County Medical Associations and Nurses' Associations had physicians and nurses on hand for any emergencies that needed tending to. From the docks evacuees were transported to Reception Centers, where their particular needs could be addressed: temporary shelter, medical attention, small loans, or transportation assistance to their homes, or at least temporary residences. Those leaving the point of debarkation quickly, and who didn't have pressing needs, were put up at local hotels for the night.[233] Those needing clothing were issued some right there. Although evacuees were given a limit of 1,000 pounds of personal property per family, many did not have winter clothing after spending time in tropical Hawaii, or even if they had such clothing didn't have time to pack it and ship it, given the extremely short notice of their departure.[234]

A letter from a Hawaii resident working on the docks in San Francisco provides a poignant description of how ill-prepared many of the evacuees were for the weather:

> *We are now called out to meet the ships of evacuees as they come in and the docks are a madhouse of mothers and children, some children making the trip alone and many Hawaii girls who have married soldiers coming to live with their husbands' people in mid-Western towns and farms. The latter class are (sic) terribly in need of protection as they don't even know how to get off the docks after they arrive, never having been here before. Most of them have hardly any money and all are insufficiently clad in silk dresses and little thin jackets. They would be better off to find a hideout in the hills of Hawaii than be submitted to the Southern color line and totally unfamiliar surroundings. Someone should tell them to stay at home if they are unprepared to come here…*[235]

Many evacuees' personal stories tell about the importance of the Red Cross being there when they got off the ships. At the dock in San Francisco on New Year's Day, Eugenia and Philip Mandelkorn and their friends were greeted by Red Cross volunteers, who found them hotel lodgings in adjoining rooms for the night. Considering that they had been without hot water for the previous week, the first thing they did in the hotel was to give the children baths, anticipating the luxury of their own baths later. Thin walls separated their bathrooms, so they could talk to each other as they soaked in their tubs, laughing at the simple joy of taking a bath. The next day they found a spot on a hillside where the weak January sun made it at least warm enough to sit comfortably outside, while the children played in the grass. Eugenia's friend said she loved San Francisco, and felt happier there than she had in a long while. She proposed that they reunite there with their husbands for the next year's New Year's Day.

Also arriving on January 1st, Joan Zuber's mother struggled to hold herself and her two girls together, and hadn't thought beyond their arrival on the mainland. The Red Cross secured a room for them at the Stewart Hotel, and later helped them find more permanent lodging in San Francisco as they awaited word of Major Zuber. The Red Cross also aided the Hutchison family, helping them to secure train tickets for the trip to Pasadena to her grandparents' house. Rosalie eagerly anticipated her reunion with her grandparents and great-grandmother, because from the time she was two years old until her departure for The Philippines two years earlier in 1939, Rosalie had lived with them while her mother and father were abroad. Tempering her joy was the anxiety of leaving her father back in The Philippines.

It was a cold day when a convoy carrying Patsy Campbell, her mother, and her brother Edward arrived in San Francisco on January 29th. This was Convoy 4051PE, the eighth to arrive on the West Coast during the evacuation. The Red Cross met the evacuees with blankets, sweaters, coats, and clothing of all types, as well as food when they disembarked. Edward admittedly didn't like cold weather and, still wearing his Island clothes, thought he was going to freeze to death. Someone got him a lady's coat to put on, but he stolidly declined to wear it, saying he would rather freeze. Eventually, the Red Cross found him something to wear less hurtful to his pride.

When Beverly Moglich arrived at the docks in San Francisco on March 1st aboard the *Lurline*, the Red Cross greeted her family with coffee, cocoa, sandwiches and warm clothing. "We waited for hours on end," she wrote later, "not knowing where we would be going at least for the night." They had only the clothes on their backs and a few suitcases. "At last our family was taken to a hotel right downtown."[236] Arriving in the same convoy aboard the *President Garfield*, Irene Chilton looked forlornly at her two children not knowing what to do, when a woman approached identifying herself as a Red Cross volunteer on her day off; the woman had brought her mother down to the dock to see the convoy arrive. She helped Mrs. Chilton to call relatives, to book a ferry ticket to the railroad terminal in Oakland, and then drove her and the children around seeing the sights of San Francisco before they caught their ferry. She even bought the children comic books and candy.[237]

Sometimes, if a case were particularly urgent, the Red Cross would take extraordinary measures to ensure that an evacuee got effective treatment. When Mary Winter, a stretcher-bound young woman suffering from cancer, was returning to her home in Michigan, the Hawaii Field Director radioed ahead to San Francisco to alert the people there to be on the lookout for her. She and her nurse arrived on a convoy on June 30th, where she was met by a representative from the railroad, who arranged her transportation home; a Red Cross ambulance took her to Children's Hospital until she was ready to depart. The Red Cross also restocked her dwindling supply of medicines, and telegraphed her mother in Michigan to tell her when she might expect her daughter.[238]

Chapter 11

"Is this a Red Cross Car?"

Dispute on the Docks

The nation's response to the attack on Pearl Harbor provided women with unprecedented opportunities to help with the war effort. In the San Francisco area, women's volunteer organizations stepped forward to provide aid to servicemen and relief to evacuees arriving in convoys from the Pacific war zone. The proliferation and rapid expansion of these organizations, identified by a bewildering array of acronyms, led to redundancy and overlapping of services, as might be expected, and yet with one glaring exception, they cooperated with each other under the leadership of the American Red Cross.

The National League for Women's Services (NLWS) provides an example of this spirit of cooperation. Operating at the Women's City Club at 465 Post Street, San Francisco, the NLWS ran a Defender's Club, serving both as a place where servicemen could come for relaxation, and as a receiving center for evacuees. A staff of fifty volunteers ran the center, providing temporary lodging, childcare, a playroom, medical care, shower facilities, clothing, and a cafeteria. An evacuee coming through the center might meet with a Red Cross nurse and a social worker; could make travel arrangements with Travelers' Aid; or get a ride to a hotel or to the rail station by drivers from the Red Cross and the American Women's Voluntary Service. A Red Cross official called it "the best equipped of all the evacuee centers [in San Francisco]."[239]

Despite a request by Secretary of the Navy Frank Knox that the American Red Cross take the lead in assisting evacuees from the war zone, on January 5th, the 12th Naval District, headquartered in San Francisco, designated several Navy-affiliated agencies to assist naval dependents arriving on convoys. By the time the third convoy arrived at San Francisco on January 6th, three Navy organizations, the Navy Wives' Emergency Service (NWES), Navy Mothers, and the C.C. Thomas Navy Post Auxiliary, greeted and assisted the naval evacuees.[240] Under the command of Lt. Comdr. Howard McKinley, these three agencies mirrored the efforts of other social agencies providing temporary shelter (at Hotel Powell), transportation, food, clothing, and travel assistance to evacuees arriving on Navy ships. Red Cross expertise was utilized, but only upon the Navy's specific request.

The 12th Naval District also named the American Women's Volunteer Service (AWVS), a national organization offering many services similar to those of the Red Cross, as the "official driving organization for the Navy in San Francisco," in effect making it the sole agency responsible for transporting Navy dependents from the docks to their temporary destinations in the Bay area. By "capturing," in a sense, the naval dependents, AWVS drivers could take the evacuees to AWVS-run facilities and bypass Red Cross facilities. In San Francisco, the AWVS ran classes in air raid protection, motor mechanics, map reading, first aid, and nutrition. Like the Red Cross, its members wore uniforms.

The AWVS was particularly interested in providing aid to evacuees, forming a canteen and motor corps detachment to assist evacuees at the docks, both of which were in service as early as the third convoy's arrival.[241]

Alice Throckmorton McLean, who modeled the organization after the British Women's Voluntary Service (WVS), founded the AWVS in 1940. McLean saw firsthand the service rendered by the WVS during the London Blitz and wanted women to be prepared to help in a similar manner in the United States should the war ever reach American shores. AWVS volunteers all received training for various tasks including ambulance driving, administering first aid, and operating canteens. Starting out in a basement antique shop in Manhattan, by the end of the year its national headquarters was in a mansion on East 51st Street. By mid-1941, it had 350,000 members across the country. In an interesting paradox, the organization was derided as a plaything for the rich – Mclean was an heiress, and among the volunteers were celebrities such as the actress Joan Crawford – yet it was open to all women regardless of race or income level. There were three AWVS units in Harlem alone, as well as integrated units in Atlanta, New Orleans, Tucson, Chicago and Pittsburgh. One of its mottos was "Cooperate, Not Duplicate."[242] Yet the AWVS did duplicate the efforts of other already-established organizations. In a sneering article deriding all women volunteers as ineffectual and out of their depth, *Time* magazine recognized that a problem with the AWVS was that it "sometimes overlapped the work of the Red Cross, sometimes duplicated the work of the OCD [Office of Civilian Defense]."[243]

This duplication of services between the Red Cross and the AWVS led to a confrontation of such intensity that it caught the attention of Washington. On January 21st, a windy, raw day in San Francisco, Convoy 4036, including the ships *President Taylor, President Johnson*, and six others, arrived at San Francisco with over 300 evacuees.[244] The Red Cross and AWVS were notified of the incoming convoy, leading each organization to dispatch its fleet of cars to pick up evacuees and set up canteens to greet them. When they arrived at the docks, the AWVS cars were waved through the Navy checkpoints, while the Red Cross was denied access. At one pier the row lasted several hours as volunteers and Navy personnel engaged in a standoff over who should get access to the docks. The *Examiner* describes an AWVS car pulling up to the entrance of a pier: "'Is this a Red Cross car?" the military policeman asked the driver. When she answered "No," he said, "That's OK. We've been told not to allow Red Cross cars on the dock.'" As the evacuees disembarked, they were given an information card by the Navy listing services available; number 1 on the list was the AWVS motor corps. In an apparent snub, the Red Cross was listed next to last as an agency for "continuing services." The scene on the dock was described as one of "wild confusion" and a "bitter row," although most of it was sorted out by the time the evacuees disembarked.[245]

Just two days before, on January 19th, the role of the Red Cross in the evacuation had been ironed out, or so it seemed, in a joint statement by the Office of Civilian Defense, Office of Defense Health and Welfare Services, and Red Cross (see Appendix). The Red Cross would provide nurses and social workers aboard vessels during the crossing, and take charge of reception, intake services, and interim care, the latter including the "provision of necessary food, shelter, clothing, medical aid and local transportation in cooperation with the Army and Navy." Further, "in dispersal of the evacuees the Red Cross will arrange for adequate transportation and will provide necessary assistance in transit."[246] The Red Cross naturally assumed it was responsible for the evacuees and would ask other agencies for help only as needed; local naval authorities either were unaware of this joint statement, or chose to ignore it.

The principals in the dispute appealed to Secretary Knox and even to Eleanor Roosevelt to intervene, but both declined to get involved. Washington wanted the matter settled in San Francisco. Locally, the *San Francisco Chronicle* gave its strong support to the Red Cross, imploring that "No other organization can put itself in conflict with this truly Federal agency."[247] After several days of tense and bitter meetings, Jack H. Helms, the regional director of the Office of Civilian Defense (OCD) hammered out a compromise with representatives of the Navy, Red Cross, AWVS, Office of Defense and Welfare Services, and OCD. As far as transportation was concerned, the Red Cross and AWVS would share equally in the supply of cars for evacuees, the total number needed for a particular convoy to be determined by a neutral dispatcher appointed by the OCD.[248]

The Red Cross initially appeared to have won victory in the dispute because the policy announced by the government agencies specifically named the Red Cross as being in charge of the evacuees from their arrival on West Coast docks until they were homeward bound. The government even granted the Red Cross greater participation in the entire evacuation process, permitting about 100 Red Cross nurses and social workers passage to Hawaii where they would work with evacuees before boarding the evacuation ships, accompany them on the ocean crossings, and work with their local chapters on the mainland to help them to get home.[249] Moreover, the AWVS was not mentioned by name. That omission was not an oversight, but rather reflected the fact that the Red Cross was a quasi-governmental organization with the President of the United States as its titular head. The Red Cross, for its part, said it still would cooperate with the AWVS.[250]

Despite the good intentions of the parties involved, Red Cross social worker Hazel Gill observed many problems, which she outlined in a report to the Honolulu Chapter detailing her experiences on a crossing from Honolulu to the West Coast in late February, most likely Convoy #4057, which departed from Honolulu on February 21, 1942.[251] Gill wrote there were 2,000 passengers aboard her ship, so it is likely she was aboard the *Lurline*, which was part of the convoy and one of the few ships capable of carrying so many evacuees. Upon landing in San Francisco, she reported that the docks were chaotic: there was no Red Cross dock captain and no central information desk to be found and she had no one to give records to pertaining to the needs of the evacuees. She also observed that Navy officials and Red Cross people were bickering. While she realized the volunteers at the docks in San Francisco were doing their best under trying circumstances, Gill urged greater cooperation between the parties and better planning. She pointed out that one cardiac patient nearly died waiting for attention on the dock before the quick action of one of the nurses saved him.[252]

Feuding between the Red Cross, AWVS, and the Navy continued throughout the spring. The San Francisco Red Cross was furious at the AWVS for getting in the way of its mission and at the Navy for its lack of cooperation. In a March 23rd letter to A.L. Schafer, the Manager of the Pacific Area for the Red Cross, Frederick J. Koster, of the San Francisco Chapter, complained bitterly about the situation in San Francisco. In a dig at the AWVS and the Navy he wrote, "Caring for evacuees does not mean merely receiving them at the docks with canteen service and motor transportation to wherever they may desire to be transported locally..." It also seems that some of the agencies looked at helping the evacuees as a contest. "The Navy Relief Society here designated an outside competitive organization as its auxiliary, which organization has carried on a competitive, and in effect, obstructive program ever since the Navy evacuees have been arriving."[253] There was no problem with Army dependents; in fact, Colonel Boone, the Army's contact in San Francisco for evacuees, called Mr. Schafer to praise the Red Cross' handling of the evacuees in the first convoy.[254] He was supported by Secretary of War Henry Stimson, who assured American Red Cross Chairman Norman Davis of the Army's full cooperation in handling evacuees, even promising to urge commanding officers abroad and at points of debarkation (San Francisco, San Diego, San Pedro, and Seattle) to utilize Red Cross services more fully.[255]

Schafer passed on Koster's complaints to Red Cross National Headquarters in Washington, and if anything, his report was even more emphatic in his description of the problem, citing two examples to show how bad things had gotten. He called the AWVS as "a very aggressive group" led by Mrs. Phyllis Tucker, chairman of the San Francisco chapter of AWVS. Mrs. Tucker was a daughter of Michael de Young, founder of the *San Francisco Chronicle*, and wife of Nion Tucker, a wealthy San Francisco banker and winner of the Gold Medal for bobsledding at the 1928 Olympics. She was a leading socialite and philanthropist in the Bay area, founder of San Francisco's Cotillion, a requirement for any young lady wishing to enter society. Her sister, Helen Cameron, was Chairman of the Motor Corps Service of the

Red Cross. According to Schafer, "... these two women are not on speaking terms and that they are using these two organizations to express their own personal hostility to each other."

Another problem identified by Schafer was the AWVS campaign in Oakland to raise money to supply supplies for evacuees, especially layettes, clothing and accessories for newborns. The AWVS requested assistance from the Oakland Chamber of Commerce, which notified the Oakland Chapter of the Red Cross, which in turn relayed the request to the Regional Red Cross Office. The Red Cross in San Francisco not only had a large store of clothing already on hand, but also 4,400 layettes available for incoming evacuee families. The AWVS was running in circles and wasting everyone's time.[256]

Schafer was not at all shy about placing the blame for the inter-agency imbroglio where he thought it belonged: the U.S. Navy. "The Navy itself has not been as cooperative as has the Army," he wrote. "As a matter of fact, I find now that the Navy were cognizant of and had encouraged the A.W.V.S. in Oakland to make available funds and materials for the purchase of layettes."[257] He offered no proof of how he knew this, but there is no question that the rift was a deep and bitter one. Still, things eventually improved. Eleanor C. Vincent, the assistant national director of military and naval welfare service, wrote in a letter describing her experience at the dock in San Francisco in May 1942:

> *Two ships were at this particular dock and passengers were disembarking from each. There were men, women and children all in manner [of] clothing and bearing little baggage. They flocked to the desks headed "Information, Telegraph Office, Baggage, Clothing, etc." The Red Cross appeared to*

be in charge of: canteen, clothing, a nursery, for the care of children and infants while mothers were attending to the baggage. Navy Relief women, with the assistance of several sailors, were taking care of baggage. Transportation appeared to be a joint project of the American Women's Volunteer Ass'n and the Red Cross. The latter seemed to be confined to station wagons and ambulance service.

Not all was perfect, for Vincent noted that evacuees were still bewildered by the confusion at the docks and by a lack of knowledge of just what services were available to them. She recommended that "one or more experienced Red Cross social workers should be present at the pier." She also advised that free telegraph service should be made available to all disembarking evacuees.[258]

Eventually the agencies sorted their differences out and managed to get along and do their jobs with as little interference from each other as possible. On June 29th, when a five-ship convoy arrived in San Francisco, Anne Carter of the Red Cross Disaster Service noted that a Red Cross caseworker was assigned to each of the four docks where Army personnel, dependents, wounded, or unattached civilians landed. Regarding the one ship containing naval personnel, Carter reported that no Red Cross caseworker was assigned to that pier because "AWVS were doing the work."[259] The Navy continued to take care of its own; the Red Cross took care of everyone else.

But the working relationship was certainly better. Carter said that on June 30th there was considerable cooperation between the various agencies as the *Mt. Vernon* docked on Pier 32 with 382 civilians and "a large number of Navy personnel." Red Cross Canteen, Clothing, Information-Welfare Services and Nurses Aid were operating on the pier "with [Red Cross] Motor Corps supplementing AWVS Motor Corps." AWVS, Navy Relief, Travelers Aid, and the Red Cross all worked together in harmony. "There was no friction with any of the groups, everyone assuming their responsibility and proceeding accordingly."[260] Even Schafer would write about the two large convoys arriving at the end of June 1942: "Reports to the contrary notwithstanding, there has been perfect cooperation between those elements which earlier in the year caused considerable trouble."[261]

Chapter 12
"No Warm Clothes Were Offered These Women"

A New Ordeal

Once she landed in California on New Year's Day, getting back to her hometown of Salem, Massachusetts would be as much of an ordeal for Doris Marze as the ocean crossing had been, and while there was no grave danger such as prowling Japanese submarines, she and other exhausted evacuees were faced with great discomfort: overcrowding, hunger, cold, and, in her case, theft (her purse was stolen during the journey). The Red Cross could meet evacuees on the docks and help arrange transportation home, but once they left San Francisco, there was little organized help available for them, and those early cross-country rail journeys were haphazardly arranged. Those traveling to the Northeast would have to change trains in Chicago for the five-day journey. Compounding the evacuees' misery, most of the nation was suffering from the worst cold spell in a decade. The relative cold that greeted the evacuees in San Francisco was replaced by the absolute cold of the Rockies and the Plains. The cold was so intense in the West that the United States Weather Bureau, which had been under censorship constraints from reporting weather conditions to keep that sensitive information from falling into enemy hands, relented and allowed broadcast and publication of the severe cold warnings so that farmers could take heed. All along the rail line from San Francisco to Chicago, towns were inundated with snow and suffered plummeting temperatures, difficult enough for the people used to such weather, but unbearable for the refugees on the trains uprooted from their lives in tropical Hawaii. Gail Moul, the six-year-old boy who developed a stutter after the Pearl Harbor bombing, remembers being cold on the train on his way home to Virginia with his mother. His train had to stop at one point because of deep snow, and people came to shovel off the tracks.[262]

People all across the country suffered from the deep freeze. On January 1st Los Angeles reported a measurable snowfall, its first in ten years. A New Year's Day blizzard left three feet of snow in Iowa and eastern Nebraska, forcing trains from the West Coast to arrive four hours late in Laramie, Wyoming on January 2nd. Reno, Nevada claimed lows of zero on January 5th, while in Ogden, Utah water connections froze on several railroad cars arriving from the East. The cold wave extended into the South with Atlanta reporting below freezing temperatures for the week of January 5th through 12th, including record snow and cold on the 8th, 9th, and 10th.[263]

Despite the well-planned operation of greeting evacuees at the docks, the Red Cross wasn't prepared to care for the hundreds of evacuees traveling cross-country, especially from the second convoy, which deposited over 2,700 evacuees in San Francisco on New Year's Day. Traveling with a trainload of evacuees from that convoy, Red Cross worker Mary B. Perry reported their suffering in a letter to her boss in Washington:

We first noticed the plight of the evacuees at the Ferry, where they started their trip [to their home destinations]. The Women's Motor Corps and others helped them to the gate but no further, which meant they carried baggage (as the Red Cap system was swamped), herded babies and themselves as best they could on and off the Ferry to the waiting train. The confusion meant we were almost an hour [late?] in leaving.

Due to the time of departure from Hawaii (the night of December 24th) and the fact that they were given two hours' notice of their departure, after dark they had not been able to pack properly or get hold of warm clothing. Many of them were inadequately clothed for the winter and had no chance to purchase things in San Francisco, due to arriving New Year's Eve and leaving New year's [sic] Day for the east [sic]. We reached Chicago in below-zero weather Sunday night. Apparently no warm clothes were offered these women.

With four extra Pullman coaches, and two or three extra tourist [non-military dependent civilians] trains as far as Ogden, full of evacuees, the supplies in the train were not adequate. This, of course, was further complicated by our being 10 hours late into Chicago. No additional service had been allowed so people waited hours for service in the one diner and some women with small babies who could not go to the diner waited three or four hours for service.

The one stewardess on the train was completely swamped getting formulas filled, babies fed, and the sick ones cared for. One person could not be expected to handle the situation, particularly as there were babies with dysentary [sic] as well as heavy colds. Two babies were so ill a doctor was called to meet the train at Ogden (even though there were two Army doctors on the train) and this doctor charged $5.00 a piece [sic] for the children he served.[264]

Perry, a Red Cross Regional Child Consultant to Richard N. Neustadt of the Office of Defense Health and Welfare Services, happened to be making a trip East and saw firsthand the situation on the docks in San Francisco and on the train to Chicago. She saw that the Motor Corps did take the evacuees to their hotels or hospitality houses, "but they had to spend hours on New Year's Day going from one office to another trying to get papers filled out and reservations made, leaving babies with older children or others." As her letter mentions, those evacuees leaving right away didn't have time to get settled before taking a ferry to get to the train station in Oakland. Once the train reached Chicago, it was greeted by many relatives of those whose train journey ended there, but by only one representative from Travelers' Aid. Perry wondered how the others going on beyond Chicago made their travel arrangements. Perry's main point in her letter was that if large groups were to be convoyed across the country, somebody had to provide adequate services for them. The irony was that "the evacuees with us were officers' wives and children, most of them had money, but the circumstances limited their ability to care for themselves. They did not want help but could not handle the situation because of the size of the group with which they found themselves."[265]

Canteens Aiding Evacuees

Evacuees traveling across the United States also received assistance from volunteers along the way as they journeyed to their hometowns. In many locations along the railway line, local groups formed canteen committees to provide food, cigarettes, and magazines to troops traveling through on trains, but they aided evacuees as well. Some of these canteen services were privately run and others were Red Cross operations. One of the most successful canteens was a private one in North Platte, Nebraska.

Two trains with evacuees passed through North Platte on January 2nd and were greeted with candy and fruit at the canteen housed in a former restaurant at the Union Pacific train station. They were described as refugees from the Hawaiian and Philippine Islands. Two days later the canteen served two (train) carloads of families that had stopped briefly at North Platte "headed east from the Hawaiian Islands." Among them was a family of refugees from Hawaii, a mother, grandmother, and four children traveling under the auspices of the Red Cross and "the Naval [sic] relief aid." The grandmother's husband had been killed during the Pearl Harbor bombing.[266]

The canteen in North Platte, the only one in the state of Nebraska, came about through the hard work of Rae Wilson and several other young women who wanted to do their part to help the war effort by providing treats and supplies to the trainloads of servicemen passing through North Platte. They solicited donations of food, magazines, games, and cigarettes from area businesses, and donations of volunteer time and money from such disparate groups as the Red Cross, the Navy Mothers, the Daughters of the American Revolution, and even the local Alamo Bar. At first, they opened the canteen in a shack near the railroad depot, but quickly outgrew that location, prompting Miss Wilson to write to the president of Union Pacific on December 18th asking permission to use the vacant space at the UP train station that formerly housed a restaurant. The canteen was very successful, serving over 4,700 soldiers the last week of December alone, and forcing the canteen committee to repeatedly ask for new donations, especially of food and magazines.[267] Civilian evacuees traveling eastward to their uncertain futures on the mainland benefitted from this civic kindness.

As the months passed, canteen services became less essential for civilian evacuees because the Red Cross assigned nurses and social workers to attend to the evacuees' needs aboard the trains. In early April, the Red Cross Pacific Area wired the El Paso Chapter asking that it send volunteers to meet a train containing evacuees when it pulled into El Paso. The local chapter complied and with only four hours' notice mobilized the canteen corps and motor corps to meet the evacuees. Only two passengers actually chose to leave the train during the ten-minute stop in El Paso. The Red Cross nurse and social worker aboard expressed surprise to the local chapter that they were called to meet the train when there was no real need. Other chapters apparently faced similar disappointments. Nurses and social workers, when asked what they thought, told Red Cross officials that local chapters didn't need to meet trains, but only that they be available in case a special request for services was needed.[268]

It was never entirely clear who was responsible for the costs of providing for the civilian evacuees. The Pacific Area Office of the Red Cross held discussions with the Federal Security Agency about submitting vouchers to them for payment on a case-by-case basis, and also explored the possibility of getting reimbursed for some expenses from the U.S. Public Health Service.[269] The joint statement of January 19, 1942 issued during the San Francisco dock imbroglio by the Office of Civilian Defense, the Office of Defense Health and Welfare Services, and the American Red Cross, presumably ironed out the role of the Red Cross in the evacuation, but was unclear about payment. Evacuation of civilians was labeled "a national responsibility." The Red Cross was clearly identified as being responsible for intake services and interim care of the evacuees, including food, shelter, medical care, transportation, and clothing, and was further authorized to call upon other organizations for help if needed. Late in 1942, the assistant port transportation officer in Wilmington, California, sent a letter erroneously saying that the Red Cross was responsible for supplying meals to Army enlisted men as well as civilians en route from Hawaii. Robert E. Bondy, the administrator of Services to the Armed Forces in Washington, D.C. made it clear in a letter to the Red Cross Pacific Area Office that the Army would provide for its own men, and that the Red Cross should stick to the provisions in joint statement. Feeding civilians, from Bondy's point of view, was a Red Cross responsibility and, one might assume, on the Red Cross' dime.[270]

Hometown Heroes

At midnight on January 6th during the coldest winter in years a sad reunion took place. Doris Marze, who had left Salem nearly four years before with her husband, Andrew, came home to her mother, on the second convoy of evacuees from Hawaii, back to the life of constant moving from tenement to tenement, living hand-to-mouth with limited hope for the future. She arrived in Salem after crossing the country by rail, getting off at the huge Salem station with its two enormous towers looking like a gothic cathedral. Her mother, Agnes Huntress, had never seen Andrea before, so the reunion was bittersweet.

Doris' arrival in Salem generated considerable interest. A front-page article ran in the *Salem Evening News* on December 11th with a photograph of her holding Andrea as an infant, the headline reading "Unheard from Honolulu." A little over a week later on December 20th, the Salem paper informed Salem readers, in another front-page story, the sad truth that Doris already knew that Andrew Marze had been killed in action. Three photographs accompanied the story, one showing Andrew in civilian clothes; another Doris laughing as she presided over Andrea's second birthday party in their backyard in Hawaii; and the third a family portrait, with Andrea being held by her proud father. The *Boston Herald* reported the death the same day. After her return to Salem, The *Salem News* ran another story and photo with the headline "Widow Returns to Live Here."[271]

Two days after her January 6th arrival in Salem, Doris' 21-year-old brother Louis, vowing revenge for the death of his brother-in-law, enlisted in the Army. On January 10th, a newspaper ran an inspirational story about Doris' experience coupled with her brother's enlistment. The piece features a large photo of Louis holding a picture of Andrew Marze as Andrea sits on her mother's lap while Doris and her younger brother Everett look on. The story encourages the public with several references to Andrew's heroism and this quote from Doris: "You don't know what you can take until you have to take it."[272] On the same day, the *Boston Daily Globe* ran a story about two-year-old Andrea Marze's early Christmas, when her father decided not to wait for the actual day, and brought home presents for his daughter three weeks early. In this story Doris speculated that her husband might have had a premonition of the war to come.[273]

Other returnees from around the country arriving back in their hometowns became local heroes of sorts, held up as examples of American fighting spirit in the face of catastrophe. The experience of children especially was compelling for local readers, and here newspapers could take advantage of reporting on the ordeals of the evacuees in a way that could support the war effort and extol the public to greater sacrifice. The *Kansas City Star* gave coverage to young Richard Kennedy, a student at the Ladd School in Kansas City, who addressed a school assembly recounting his adventures during the bombing and his subsequent evacuation to the mainland with his mother. In a piece entitled "He's a 'Veteran' at 10," Richard talked about the convoy of destroyers and a cruiser [probably the December 19th convoy] and 3-inch and 5-inch guns arming his ship. "Freckled-face Richard" saw the "stricken" Arizona and "overturned" Oklahoma, and heard that "Fifth columnists had passed on information as to the location of every ship..."[274]

The *Galveston Daily News* used the backdrop of a "salvage for victory" scrap heap in Galveston to tell the story of two young evacuees, thirteen-year-old Donald Forney and his sister, eleven-year-old Jean Forney, who witnessed the attack from their home near Hickam Field. Donald and Jean, along with their mother and older sister, were evacuated in March, while their father, a captain in the Army, remained in Hawaii. A photo with the cutline "Slapping the Japs" shows Donald and Jean donating to the scrap heap shrapnel they had collected during the bombing. The story took the angle of giving their own shrapnel back to the Japanese, and allowed the two children to talk about their own experiences and laud the courage of the Americans under fire. The family was strafed twice during the attack, once in their home and once in their car as they made their way to Honolulu, while Donald took photos with his camera. Donald described a chaotic scene as half-dressed men scrambled to get to their posts. Some of the scenes seem exaggerated: a machine gunner completely naked, his hands scalded by the hot barrel, downing a Japanese plane before his comrades drag him away from his gun. Another scene describes soldiers shooting down a Japanese plane with pistols and rifles. Only the briefest mention is given to their journey to the mainland. The *Daily News* added, "Donald's experience with treacherous Japanese methods has given him a war psychology far more realistic than that of the average American. He said he was 'amazed' at the half-hearted war attitude of the people in the United States and could not understand how both soldiers and civilians were grumbling about working 'overtime' in an emergency like this."[275]

One actual hero also received considerable attention when he arrived home from Hawaii. On the train from Chicago to Harrisburg, Pennsylvania, Joe Lockard learned quickly that there was a price to fame when a fellow passenger, recognizing the hero from Pearl Harbor, wouldn't let him out of his sight. He kept plying the new staff sergeant with sodas and candy. Lockard wasn't entirely sure what awaited him in his hometown of Williamsport, but the overly kind stranger annoyed him, keeping him from thinking about going home, seeing his family, and his girlfriend, Pauline Seidel, and depriving him of some much-needed rest. Finally the train pulled into the station at Harrisburg on Thursday, March 5th, where Joe, exhausted and feeling ill, was greeted on the nearly empty platform by his parents, sister, brother, and Pauline. He kissed his mother and greeted Pauline shyly. Then they all drove north along the banks of the Susquehanna River towards their home.

Lockard's hometown was gearing up for a celebration honoring their local hero, capped off by a testimonial in his honor at the Elks in Williamsport. He said later that couldn't understand why there was such as fuss, since his warning "didn't work anyway." Once home at his parents' he immediately went to bed and the doctor was summoned. The next morning, as dignitaries, friends, and reporters clamored for Lockard's attention, his mother fed reporters eggs and answered their questions as best she could. The next day Joe was feeling better and was able to go for a walk with his father.

Lockard was dazed by all the attention he got. "I'm 19 years old from a small town in Pennsylvania," he said. "All of a sudden it descends on me. I was wined and dined." He had left Williamsport only 20 months earlier with dreams of adventure in The Philippines and now returned a hero. During the excitement caused by his return home and the upcoming testimonial, Lockard slipped out of town and took Pauline on a quick trip to Winchester, Virginia to get married because the waiting period was shorter there than in Pennsylvania. They were married on March 10, 1942.

The testimonial was scheduled for the next day at the Elks Hall with Congressman Harness as the keynote speaker. Over 700 people crowded in to pay homage to the local hero; for four hours speaker after speaker told stories, read poems, held up Joe's devotion to duty as an example for all Americans to follow in this great war. Congressman Harness decried the unpreparedness of the government, labor, and industry, saying "If our responsible leaders had approached the vital, the imperative job of defending America in the Joe Lockard spirit, how much nearer do you believe we would be to final victory today?"[276] It was as if Joe Lockard were the new Paul Revere. They presented him with gifts. They even sang a new song for him: "Private Joe's on his Toes." Lockard, who had already wildly exceeded anybody's expectations, bafflingly told the crowd, "I will do all in my power to make all your expectations come true."[277] Later, he was honored with a plaque placed at his old school.

Also traveling cross country upon their arrival on the West Coast were Patsy Campbell and Eugenia Mandelkorn. When Patsy and her family arrived in Lawrence, Massachusetts in early February, still dressed in clothing too light for the weather, the people there looked at them like they were from Mars. But when Patsy told her class at her new school that she was at Pearl Harbor, "the kids were in awe." In Annapolis, Eugenia Mandelkorn's mother was upset when she saw her daughter because she didn't look well. A visit to the doctor revealed that she was pregnant, which explained why she was so uncharacteristically seasick during the Pacific crossing. The doctor's examination also revealed that the fetus was dead. She mourned the loss of her child, her only girl, conceived in the paradise of Hawaii, and she thought of her often throughout the subsequent years.

Eugenia Mandelkorn, Patsy Campbell, Doris Marze, Joe Lockard, Gail Moul, and hundreds like them were probably what Milton Silverman had in mind when he wrote in the *San Francisco Chronicle*, "... they were part of this new fierce breed of Americans – united, brave, baptised [sic] by fire and madder than blazes!"[278]

Chapter 13
"Each Family Should Decide for Itself"

Counting Evacuees

It is difficult to gauge how many civilians were evacuated in the first three convoys in December 1941. Each ship had a passenger list generated by the military government in Hawaii and sent on to the Red Cross on the West Coast, which Red Cross officials would crosscheck when a ship docked. Caseworker Anne Carter from Red Cross Disaster Service mentioned in her July 3rd report on dock activities that "There has been considerable discrepancy in those two lists which are now supposed to be pretty accurate."[279] If there were discrepancies in July when the convoys had become a matter of routine, little wonder there was confusion with totals for the first three convoys during the chaotic days of December, when convoy lists were completed at the last moment, and when the lines of authority had not yet been clearly established.

A comparison of Red Cross and Navy figures shows how difficult it is to get an exact number of evacuees. Harry Walden, Director of Military and Naval Welfare Service for the Pacific Branch of the Red Cross, sent these figures for the first three convoys from Honolulu to his national director in Washington:[280]

SHIP	ARRIVAL	MEN	WOMEN	CHILDREN*	PATIENTS	TOTAL
Scott	12–25-41	5	37	46	55	143
Coolidge	12–25-41	255**	184	21	125	585
Matsonia	12–31-41	249	495	93	0	837
Lurline	12–31-41	13	677	627	55	1372
Monterey	12–31-41	21	393	185	84	683
Bliss	1–6-42	5	75	93	0	173
Garfield	1–6-42	52	63	70	0	185
Harris***	1–6-42	0	120		40	160
TOTALS		600	2044	1135	359	4138

*Figures for children are estimates
**130 3rd Class passengers weren't classified by sex
***Docked at San Diego – women and children combined

According to these Red Cross figures, 4,138 people were aboard the first three convoys, 3,779 of them civilian and dependent evacuees. For the same month, the Commandant of the 14th Naval District at Pearl Harbor reported to the Chief of Naval Operations that in December 3,449 dependents and civilians were evacuated to the mainland, 330 fewer than what the Red Cross reported.[281] The Navy figures included 1,604 naval dependents, 1,011 Army dependents, and 834 civilians.

Those first three convoys hardly scratched the surface of the numbers of waiting evacuees in Oahu. As of January 18th, the Red Cross estimated that waiting to be evacuated were "Roughly twenty to twenty-five thousand Service families and in excess of ten thousand other civilians principally women and children during the next few months as transport available."[282] By the end of January, after nine convoys had departed for the West Coast since the beginning of the war, the 14th Naval District indicated there were still 9,255 Navy dependents, 2,415 Army dependents, and 13,750 civilians registered for evacuation.

But how many civilians and dependents were evacuated from Hawaii throughout the entire evacuation period? Gwenfread Allen in her exhaustive account of wartime Hawaii offers the figure of 30,000 for the total of civilians evacuated, 20,000 Army and Navy dependents and "10,000 Island women and children." While some native Islanders made the crossing, it seems that many of those 10,000 were mainlanders and tourists trying to get back home. Oddly, Allen discounted the intensity of the evacuation after May 1942, claiming that half of the still remaining 10,000 people in Hawaii waiting to be evacuated canceled their evacuation registration.[283] Yet, in late May, Frank Midkiff, visiting Washington, D.C., was concerned that there weren't enough ships to keep up with the demand of civilians on Oahu still registering for evacuation. He asked Admiral Greenslade, the new Commandant of the 12th Naval District, if some of the large ships returning to the mainland from the Pacific could be rerouted through Honolulu "to catch up with the demands for transportation."[284] Using rerouted ships meant that the accommodations would be "troop class," that is, the most Spartan of conditions, that some feared might be inappropriate for women and children.[285] Midkiff felt that troop class was appropriate under the circumstances and said so in letters to Clorinda Lucas, the Hawaiian socialite who assisted Green and Midkiff in the evacuation, and to Col. Jenna of the Office of Military Governor. He even wrote a draft of a letter intended for all registrants for transportation to the mainland asking them to avail themselves of this class of transportation as a means of getting home sooner, and pointing out the lack of luxuries this mode entailed. Admiral Greenslade wouldn't agree to rerouting ships, but did promise to add more ships to the "Hawaiian run."[286]

Red Cross figures show that in June more evacuees disembarked at West Coast ports than in any other month, accounting for over 25 percent of all evacuees arriving from Hawaii from December 1941 through July 1942. The following chart created by the Red Cross is very instructive; clearly showing that evacuation was significant even after the Battle of Midway (June 4–7, 1942) substantially lowered the risk that there would be another attack on Hawaii:[287]

	SF	SD	Seattle	LA
December	3200	4	1352	
January	3076	169	2089	
February	335	134	1593	
March	7883	92	1248	
April	6433	-	542	1350
May	1676	182	1824	24
June	8069	201	1327	
TOTAL	30,672	782	9,975	

=42,803

Most of the arrivals in the Seattle column probably were evacuees from Alaska, one of several areas from which naval and military dependents and civilians were ordered to evacuate on December 18, 1941.[288] Some were from Hawaii as well; at least one convoy from Hawaii landed at that port in

January 1941, and in March 1942, the War Department contacted the Seattle Children's Orthopedic Hospital Guilds to help find accommodation for an expected 3,000–6,000 evacuees from Hawaii due to arrive in Seattle soon.[289] In any event, the overwhelming number of Hawaii evacuees landed at San Francisco, Los Angeles (San Pedro), and San Diego.

Between June 5 and July 31, 1942, eleven convoys left Hawaii carrying evacuees, wounded servicemen, travelers, and cargo to the West Coast. However, the reasons for civilians leaving the Islands changed as 1942 wore on and the fear of another attack lessened. Native-born Hawaiian Ellenmerle Heiges from Hilo, for example, left Hawaii for the mainland in June 1942 to attend nursing school.[290] After the bombing, Ellenmerle got a job with the Army on the Big Island plotting the courses of incoming airplanes to determine whether or not they were friendly. After about six months she was approached by nursing recruiters who offered free nursing training on the mainland as part of the war effort. She also had been volunteering at a hospital in Hilo and liked medical work. Paying her own way to get from Hilo to Honolulu, she then spent a couple of nights in Honolulu before boarding a troopship for the crossing to San Francisco in June 1942. Blackout conditions and mandatory life vests were still the rule. Aboard the ship were other cadet nurses of all nationalities, including Japanese, and students going to college on the mainland.

Despite the changing status of some of the civilians being transported, evacuees still made up a significant part of the convoys after June 1942. Anne Carter of the Red Cross Disaster Service reported to DeWitt Smith at Red Cross National Headquarters "Most of the evacuees coming in to date [July 1942] have been women and children, the children ranging up to 16 years of age. With each boat, there are a few Social Security applicants, with the number increasing rather than decreasing..."[291]

One of those post-Midway convoys (#4115) arrived in San Francisco on June 29th, having left Honolulu on the 22nd and steaming at 12 knots. Seven vessels made up the convoy (the *Arthur Middleton, Alcoa Pennant, Republic, Etolin, President Grant, H.F. Alexander* and *Fort Royal*), five of which docked at Piers 2, 7, 35, 46, or 50. It is likely that not all of those ships in the convoy carried passengers, so that those without civilians, travelers or wounded might have docked elsewhere since they didn't require Red Cross assistance when landing. Of those getting off at San Francisco on the 29th, 1,265 were designated as civilians or Army dependents. A faster convoy, made up of the speedy *Lurline* and *Mount Vernon* left Honolulu on June 24 (#4132) traveling at 18.5 knots. The *Mount Vernon* docked at Pier 32 on the afternoon of the 30th with 382 civilians "and a large number of Navy personnel." Earlier that day an unnamed ship, most likely the *Lurline*, docked at Pier 30 carrying 1,384 civilians and 431 Army dependents. It is interesting to note that A.L Schafer, the Manager of the Pacific Area for the American Red Cross identified these evacuees as being from Hawaii "and other points 'down under,'" but if there were evacuees from other parts of the Pacific, they still would have to come through Hawaii.[292] But it is worth noting that on two successive June days in San Francisco seven vessels docked, unloading 3,462 civilians and military dependents.

After August 1942, requests for travel from the Islands were primarily businessmen, government employees, and people needing medical treatment or responding to emergencies, such as a death or illness in the family. By September, the Office of Military Governor declared, "the so-called period of evacuation ended during the month of September 1942."[293] Nevertheless, the policies regarding priorities and procedures stayed in place until August 1, 1943, when civilian transportation to the mainland became the responsibility of the War Shipping Administration.

"The Answer is Always No"

One thing that did not change about the evacuation despite the passage of time was the confusion experienced by potential evacuees. Even public officials in Hawaii were uncertain. In May, Ferris F. Laune, Secretary of the Hawaii Council for Social Agencies, wrote to Colonel Green, by now a general, asking if it was true that Hawaii-born (or brought-up) women married to military personnel were being evacuated to their husbands' families in the mainland. Green responded that each case was judged on its own merits and that there had been a misinterpretation of the Army's and Navy's "attitude – "...no person whose permanent home is or was in the Territory is presently requested to evacuate due to marriage to Military personnel." Even as late as June 29, 1942, a mother wrote to General Emmons asking whether she and her 12-year-old daughter could expect to be evacuated. Green replied, "All Army and Navy dependents not engaged in vital work in the Territory have been or are in the process of being evacuated to the mainland. In no case has any civilian other than dependents of Army or Navy personnel been ordered to leave ... it is a matter each family should decide for itself."[294]

Green faced evacuation pressures throughout 1942 from those wishing to leave the Islands and from those wishing to return. On September 11th, Green complained about the cases of people afraid of remaining in Hawaii and wishing to return to the mainland, but who weren't high on the priority list. "I am pestered with appeals of many others to go to the mainland because of fright. Some are important people. The answer is always No." On the other hand, he insisted on keeping out all but the most essential women wanting to return to the Islands, even well after Midway. And he expressed disdain for men on the mainland who wished to return to Hawaii, saying that many of them were cowards to have evacuated in the first place. Green complained there were hundreds of such cases of cowardice "some ... almost unbelievable."[295]

Many of those evacuees wanting desperately to go home to Hawaii were by no means cowards, but rather unfortunate Hawaiian residents trapped on the mainland when the Japanese attack occurred, and unlike their civilian counterparts on the Islands who were encouraged to evacuate to the mainland, the stranded Hawaiians faced a rigid bureaucracy forcing them to stay in place indefinitely. Many stranded Hawaiians in the San Francisco area organized regular "what's-new-at-home" meetings at the Western Women's Club to exchange news about home gathered from evacuees docking in San Francisco, and to provide mutual support during their ordeal of waiting. Among those wanting to go home was Mrs. Thelma Wicke, Director of Swimming at the Honolulu Recreation Department. Ironically, her counterpart from San Francisco was in Honolulu on December 7th. Not wanting to waste her time while waiting to go home (and knowing there was a temporary vacancy), Mrs. Wicke tried to apply for a job with the San Francisco Recreation Department, but was told she had to be a resident for a year before she would be eligible. Taking pity on her, Hazel Holly, a columnist for *The San Francisco Examiner*, noted the irony and wrote in mid-January, "Although both are good swimmers [Wickes and her counterpart], they don't think they're good enough to swim all the way home."[296]

The major obstacle preventing their return to the Islands was the naval and military establishment in Hawaii. The all-powerful General Green did not want any civilians to return to the Islands unless they were absolutely essential to prosecuting the war. In September 1942, an Office of Civilian Defense physician phoned Green saying all women and children should be kept from entering Hawaii, except those women "who are trained technicians and are necessary to the war effort." Green agreed. More women and children would burden territorial hospitals and would require "additional protection" that would draw from the already overtaxed military.[297]

Although the Navy determined which ships went from the mainland to Hawaii, the Military Governor had ultimate authority on who could be given permission to travel to the Islands, and as a result Green was frequently pressed with requests from Island residents for permission for family members or others to journey from the West Coast to Honolulu. One request illustrates the priority clearly. On July 27th, Dr. F.J. Pinkerton was denied permission to bring a woman from the mainland to assist him at the blood plasma bank. Yet at the same time, the doctor's request for permission to go to the mainland for a conference was granted. On October 15th, Green threw out most of the names on a long list of people desiring to return to Hawaii, writing, "...all persons who are too old, who are physically incapacitated and who have young children, should be kept on the Mainland..."[298]

The 12th Naval District in San Francisco didn't always see eye to eye with the naval and military leadership on the

Islands. E. A. Jackson, the Chief of Staff of the 12th, sent a message to the Commandant of the 14th at Pearl Harbor in September 1942 pointing out that "several dependents of Naval Personnel" either of Hawaiian blood or with official residences in Hawaii, and who were without relatives or friends on the mainland, had nowhere else to go but back home. Moreover, maintaining them on the West Coast was a burden on the Navy Relief Society. Jackson asked, on behalf of the Commandant of the 12th, that those responsible in Hawaii make sure that evacuees have places to stay on the mainland, and that those stranded there be allowed to return home.[299] The response from Jackson's counterpart, J.B. Earle, Chief of Staff of the 14th at Pearl Harbor, said that those without family who were evacuated to the mainland were probably among those who "were misled by announcements that special arrangements might be practicable for attractive low rent homes on the Coast."[300] Despite the strain on Navy Relief in San Francisco, the authorities in Hawaii were unsympathetic to Jackson's request. Earle insisted "that return of such persons to this area be controlled by reference of specific cases for the approval of the Military Governor..."[301]

Still people filtered through the screen. This was obvious when the fifth meeting of the "what's-new-at-home sessions" on January 13, 1942 reported lower attendance than previous meetings because 40 of its "members" were now back in Hawaii.[302] If indeed they were in Hawaii, they were probably getting in unofficially. In Honolulu, Green fretted that too many "undesirables" were still able to get into Hawaii under the present system, specifically citing "at least six prostitutes... and at various times persons of Japanese ancestry." By the Army's own admission, 1007 people, primarily Island residents and families, arrived in Hawaii in 1942, of which the Military Government had records of only about 400. In October, for example, a convoy carrying 300 or so unannounced and unapproved Island residents including women and children arrived in Honolulu.[303] Green blamed the Navy, the 12th District in particular, and insisted upon a new official policy that would give him more control.

But for the most part, those stranded on the West Coast lived months of frustrated waiting. In January 1942, the 12th Naval District indicated that about 300 Island residents on the mainland requested passage home. While some businessmen were allowed passage, by October not one civilian, non-essential woman or child had been given permission to return. The Interior Department pointed out that by this time (October, 1942) not only were there Island residents still trapped on the mainland since the Japanese attack, but now those civilians who were encouraged to evacuate from Hawaii, and the wives and children who did so at the insistence of the military and naval authorities, were anxious to return, especially in light of the improved security situation after Midway. Interior Secretary Ickes in a letter to Secretary of War Stimson wrote that morale on the Islands would improve considerably if wives and children were allowed to return.[304]

Month after dreary month went by with little relief. All the lonely Hawaiians could do was to notify the local Matson office of their names and addresses for when ships did become available to transport them home. The Matson Lines' assistant general manager was quick to note any returnees were limited to two handbags each and warned that cabins that used to contain two beds now might contain six to eight berths.[305]

Many of those stranded threw themselves wholeheartedly into helping others in the same predicament, or in helping evacuees from the Islands. By the end of January, Mrs. Frederick Wichman and Mrs. Samuel Damon, both stranded Hawaii residents, organized a Hawaiian Unit of the San Francisco Red Cross made up of 25 fellow "exiles" or former residents of Hawaii, to give aid to Hawaiian residents disembarking on evacuation ships. The impetus for forming the group came from the case of a young kamaaina woman, one born to the land, or a long-time resident of Hawaii, who after docking in San Francisco, was too shy to ask for a ride to the Red Cross Chapter House on Eddy Street, so walked all the way there, well over a mile away. Given situations like this, it was obvious that some Hawaiians needed help in navigating the complexities of mainland life and culture, so the Hawaiian Unit was formed.[306] Mrs. Damon was no stranger to Red Cross work, serving as vice chairman of volunteers for the Honolulu Chapter. And she was no stranger to the heartbreak felt by the "exiles;" her two young children and husband were on the Islands all the while she was trapped on the mainland.

On Hawaii, Frank Midkiff exerted as much pressure as he could to address the plight of the Hawaiians stranded on the West Coast. This was a personal matter for him because his wife was among those trying to get back. He probably was able to see her when he visited the mainland in July, but in September he asked General Green for permission to have his wife returned. Green, whose dislike for Midkiff has already been noted, and whose own wife was evacuated to the mainland in February, replied that under existing policy it would be permissible, but pointed out the embarrassment Midkiff should feel if, as the head of the evacuation committee, he permitted his wife to return.[307] Midkiff continued to press for a return of the stranded evacuees, seeking help from another enemy of Green's,

Pen Thoron, Director of the Interior Department's Office of Territories and Insular Possessions, and Secretary of the Interior Harold Ickes' special envoy to Hawaii. Green despised Thoron, who in February, at Ickes' insistence, had looked into financial irregularities within the Military Government. Midkiff asked "My dear Pen" to consider the needs of those Hawaiians stranded on the West Coast waiting to return to the Islands.[308]

Green's desire for more control, and the pressure from the Interior Department and the stranded Islanders themselves, led to the creation of a new joint Army-Navy policy in November.[309] The November policy ranked applicants seeking passage to Hawaii into five priority categories:

<u>Priority No. 1.</u>

a. Personnel of the Armed Service.
b. Male government employees, including male Civil Service employees.
c. Male civilian defense workers under contract.
d. Nurses and other female technicians.

<u>Priority No. 2.</u>

a. Female Civil Service Employees with no children who are married to Civil Service employees already in the Territory.
b. Business men and other male residents of Hawaii who have jobs or who are definitely employable.

<u>Priority No. 3.</u>

Other women without children who have contracts for employment which is essential to the war effort but who do not come with in (sic) priorities 1 and 2.

Priority No. 4.
Female Island residents who are employable but who also have children, or civilian defense workers.

Priority No. 5.
Women and children not dependents of service personnel or civilian defense workers, only when other priorities are completely exhausted.[310]

As part of this new policy "all applications for travel of civilian women to the Islands were submitted to the Military Governor" except those connected with the Navy.[311] The low priority granted for women and children allowed some to get passage, but, in effect, still kept hundreds waiting on the West Coast for months longer. Gwenfread Allen points out that between June and October 1943, 5,300 civilians were given passage to the Islands, yet the waiting list in San Francisco for that period grew from 1,367 to 3,185.[312]

Finally in April 1944, two hospital ships were assigned to take stranded Hawaiians and other civilians requesting passage back to Hawaii, completely clearing the waiting list after each made two round trips. By May 1944 space was made for 150 civilians per month to make the passage to Hawaii. This was eventually upped to 250.[313]

Chapter 14
"Madder Than Blazes..!"

For the first eight months after the United States' entry into World War II, approximately 30,000 civilian evacuees, about two thirds of them naval and military dependents, were convoyed from the Hawaiian war zone to the West Coast of the mainland. In that time, despite rough seas, overtaxed ships, inexperienced crews, and the threat of Japanese submarines, not one evacuee died as a result of the crossings.[314] My mother and sister were among those evacuees, departing on the second convoy leaving Honolulu on December 26, 1941 and arriving in San Francisco on New Year's Day.

Anybody paying attention throughout 1941 should have expected that war with Japan was inevitable. Local newspapers in Honolulu made this quite clear in their coverage of relations between Japan and the United States and in their stories about Japanese behavior in Asia. In the months before the attack, knowing that war was likely, territorial and military authorities designated residential areas around military installations as potentially "unsafe," and planned for the evacuation of civilians from those areas to so-called safe areas around Honolulu. In October 1941, the Territorial Office of Civilian Defense (OCD) completed a survey of houses in safe areas that could temporarily accommodate evacuees from unsafe areas in the event of attack. That pre-war planning paid off when after the attack hundreds of military and naval dependents, my mother and sister included, were efficiently evacuated to safe areas in Honolulu away from potential targets of further Japanese assaults.

The process of forming convoys showed the challenges the Army, Navy, and the remaining civilian government faced in their attempts to cooperate with one another. Both branches of the service demanded control over the evacuation of their personnel and dependents, at best creating confusion with the evacuees, and at worst causing duplication of effort, supplies, material, and men that the government could ill afford during that time of crisis. In order to reduce the confusion felt by the citizens of Hawaii, military and civilian authorities developed hierarchies for evacuees based on need. But it was never entirely clear to citizens whether the hierarchies referred only to civilian dependents of the Army and Navy, or to civilians in general. Despite rumors to the contrary, no civilians, unless they were military dependents, were forced to leave Hawaii against their will, even though the territory was under martial law from December 7th onwards.

The evacuation also highlighted glaring differences in evacuation philosophy between the Army and the Navy. From the very first days of the war, the Navy favored a cautious approach in the formation of convoys: over the vociferous arguments of the Army, the U.S. Navy insisted that all ships travel under naval escort between Hawaii and the West Coast. Army leaders, such as General Somervell on the mainland, and General Emmons on Hawaii, reasoned that fast ships capable of outrunning Japanese submarines didn't need an escort. To the Army the priority was to re-supply

Hawaii and get the wounded and dependent civilians out of the war zone as soon as possible. As a result of the Navy's caution, fast ships such as the *Lurline* and *Matsonia* bided their time in port at San Francisco for precious days after December 7th, waiting until the Navy found ships to escort them. As it was, the first convoy out of Hawaii carrying wounded and evacuees did not depart until December 19, 1941, twelve days after the bombing of Pearl Harbor. The fast ships idling in San Francisco were finally released on the 16th, and ten days later formed the second convoy of evacuees from Hawaii.

Even though the convoys forming in Hawaii for the transit to the mainland were military secrets, requiring that departure dates and destinations were revealed only at the last possible moment, the coverage of the arrival of these convoys to West Coast ports received considerable press attention, especially in the early days of the war. The arrival of wounded soldiers and sailors was a powerful physical confirmation of the casualties suffered during the Japanese attack. And the disembarking of American civilian refugees, many shocked, bewildered, grieving and cold, brought home the stunning reality that United States territory had been attacked by a powerful enemy.

That attack and its devastating effects made "this new fierce breed of Americans ... madder than blazes," as the *San Francisco Chronicle* put it. Angry indeed with the Japanese for launching the sneak attack, they were also incensed at the thought of being caught unawares, and those evacuees fed the anger on the mainland when they returned to tell their stories of that awful day. Somebody would have to pay – somebody was responsible. The Japanese would pay with their defeat, but those Americans responsible for letting down the nation's guard would pay, too. General Short and Admiral Kimmel, already found guilty of dereliction of duty by the Roberts Commission just weeks after the attack, were the first to feel the heat of the national anger. In the ensuing years, ten hearings, some secret, some public, were held assessing culpability for the attack; for the most part, Kimmel and Short and others were cited for acts of omission rather than commission for the lack of preparedness that allowed the Japanese to achieve such astonishing success on December 7th.

Even President Roosevelt didn't escape suspicion. Some in Congress, such as Representative Fred Crawford, a Republican from Michigan, wondered in early 1942 how much the president had known before the attack.[315] It even became a campaign issue during the election of 1944. Among those demanding a thorough public review of the events of December 1941 was Congressman Forest Harness of Indiana, Joe Lockard's champion, who called for a committee to investigate Roosevelt's role in the Pearl Harbor fiasco in order to determine if he was fit for re-election.[316] In later years, conspiracy theorists came to believe that the breaking of various Japanese codes before the war along with repeated warnings from Naval Intelligence about Japan's intentions should have been enough for the Roosevelt administration to at least have been better prepared for an attack on Hawaii. Statements from several high-ranking naval and government officials after the war, including Rear Admiral Robert Theobald, and even Kimmel himself, pointed the finger at Roosevelt. Conspiracy theorists, such as Robert Stinnett and John Toland, believed that Roosevelt's desire to get into the war led him to entice the Japanese into attacking United States' interests in Asia and the Pacific. Declaring war on Japan, so the theory goes, would get the United States into the wider war in Europe,

Roosevelt's aim all along. A Congressional Inquiry in 1945–46 found no evidence that President Roosevelt or any member of his administration enticed or coerced the Japanese into attacking Pearl Harbor, although a minority report to that inquiry charged the president and others with "failure to perform the responsibilities indispensably essential to the defense of Pearl Harbor ..."[317] Joe Lockard, politically no friend of Franklin Roosevelt, took exception to this latter view, saying years later, "It's hard for me to believe that any president would allow a bombing like that just to get the people all wound up ... I can't conceive he would allow that to happen."[318]

For the evacuees themselves, that voyage home, which so many made without knowing where they were docking until the last minute, represented the end of a way of life. Hawaii would never be the same; even if the evacuees returned to the Islands later in the war or waited until after the war was over, the society that they left behind no longer existed. The sleepy bucolic paradise so lovingly described by many evacuees would become more like the mainland; a special place still, but no longer quite so different.

Despite the efforts of Col. Green to have the evacuees share the burdens of the crossing equally, for some the journey across the ocean was without hardship and even pleasant, with spacious accommodations and plenty of food; it was like an adventure. For others it was forgettable, just another event sandwiched between the momentous day of the attack and arrival back home on the mainland. Many of the evacuees I spoke to, even those who were adults at the time, could provide very few details of what their crossings were like; they just couldn't remember. For others, though, it was an ordeal, the ships uncomfortable and overcrowded. Even those not grieving for the dead or worrying about the wounded, were leaving family members behind to the uncertainty of a war in which the Hawaiian Islands were likely to be invaded. Rough seas and the possibility of being sunk by enemy submarines left some evacuees paralyzed with fear, a fear shared by those left behind in Hawaii, who eagerly awaited word that their loved ones had docked safely on the mainland. Even the daily routine aboard ship brought home the sense of danger: life vests constantly worn, lifeboat drills, the tedious zigzag course, and total blackout conditions.

On the mainland, the returnees helped provide a rallying point for the war effort. The slogan "Remember Pearl Harbor" and the images widely available at that time showing the bombing and its effects, played a huge role in shaping public opinion. Local newspapers interviewed evacuees returning home, and they gave grim details of the air attack and its aftermath. Readers could get a sense of the swooping Japanese planes, exploding bombs, and machine gun fire; they could hear the blasts and feel the fear and confusion. Eyewitness accounts by the returnees detailed the heroic efforts to repel the attack and the terror of civilians dodging bullets, cowering in whatever shelters they could find.

Some of those evacuees, like my mother, Doris Marze, had their lives completely changed, tragically and irrevocably, by the events of December 7th. For them, the mood of the voyage home must have been foreboding, in addition to the grief they felt. What would their lives be like when they got back home? Many would have to pick up and start over. My mother's only choice was to return to her mother's crowded apartment in Salem, Massachusetts; with no other means of support, no job prospects, and no offers of help from her husband's family, she had nowhere else to go.

Other returnees had less traumatic experiences, but were returning to uncertainty, and to a mainland that had changed since December 7th almost as much as Hawaii had. On December 27th, the Willamette football team, Shirley McKay, and her father arrived in Salem, Oregon and were greeted by 1,000 joyous people lining the station platform when the 15-coach Southern Pacific train arrived from San Francisco. The team's homecoming was only one day later than the originally scheduled return date. Most of the team members soon enlisted in the service, and all but one of them survived the war.

Patsy Campbell's family didn't remain long in Lawrence, Massachusetts after they returned there in January 1942 to stay with her father's relations. A few months later they relocated to Navy housing at Long Beach, California and later to Tongue Point in Astoria, Oregon until they were reunited with their father sometime in 1944. Despite her miscarriage shortly after her return to the mainland, Eugenia Mandelkorn was glad to be home in Annapolis reunited with family and old friends. She took great joy in seeing that her parents and her son, Philip, so long separated because they had lived an ocean apart, took to each other at once. She faithfully wrote letters to her husband at sea, and yearned to be back in Hawaii, where she could at least see him when he came ashore. On March12, 1942, Joe Lockard was off to Washington to receive the Distinguished Service Medal from the undersecretary of war, and then ordered to report for officers' training at Fort Monmouth, New Jersey. One of the first American heroes of World War II, the Paul Revere of his day, Lockard would spend the rest of the war in North America reaching the rank of first lieutenant in the Signal Corps stationed in Alaska.

When General Green returned to the mainland for good in April 1943, he hoped for an assignment in the Mediterranean Theater of Operations. That didn't work out, and he was assigned to the Judge Advocate General's Corps, essentially the legal branch of the U.S. Army, as Assistant Judge Advocate General in Washington. One of the things that struck him on his return to Washington was that while people worked hard and diligently, it was not at the same pace and intensity as on Hawaii. Ironically, just three years earlier he had looked forward to the slower pace on the Islands. The war had changed everything.

In large part, the returnees' stories provided inspiration to the people at home, showing just what sacrifices some civilians had already made and what others might be called upon to make. Hundreds of the 2,340 servicemen killed at Pearl Harbor never made it home at all their remains forever laid to rest in Hawaii.[319] Andrew Marze was one of those. His remains were among the first 776 bodies transferred on January 25, 1949 from their temporary place of interment to the National Memorial Cemetery of the Pacific, located in the Punchbowl crater, just above Honolulu, where they remain today. The authorization for the inscription on the headstone was not filled out by his widow Doris, who by then was remarried, but by Andrew's father, Charles Marze. The official notification that the reburial had occurred was also sent to Charles Marze, rather than Doris. There could be no greater indication that her former life was over.

While my mother had no choice in the sacrifice she made, her dignity and grace and strength during those appalling early days, still can be an inspiration:

"You don't know what you can take until you have to take it."

Epilogue

By April 1943, well after the evacuations were over, it was General Thomas Green's turn to take passage across the Pacific: he was reassigned back home. Like so many of the evacuees before him, he was leaving the Islands aboard the *Lurline*, but unlike them, he noted that two things were different: there was no naval escort, and aboard the vessel were 2,800 Asian-American soldiers heading to Europe as replacements for the famous 442nd Infantry Battalion, which was made up primarily of Americans of Japanese ancestry. He looked back "over the ever-widening azure water" at Diamond Head, waved goodbye, and then did something that no evacuee could have done: he dropped a lei over the side.

Abbreviations

AFMP	U.S. Army Forces in the Middle Pacific
APL	American President Line
ARC	American Red Cross
BNP	Bureau of Naval Personnel
CINCPAC	Commander in Chief Pacific Fleet
CNO	Chief of Naval Operations
COM11	Commandant 11th Naval District
COM12	Commandant 12th Naval District
COM14	Commandant 14th Naval District
DAF	Director's Administrative Files
HAS	Hawaii State Archives
MGH	Military Government of Hawaii
NACP	National Archives College Park
NADC	National Archives, Washington, D.C.
NASF	National Archives, San Francisco
ND12	12th Naval District
ND14	14th Naval District
NHC	Naval Historical Center (Naval History and Heritage Command)
OCD	Office of Civilian Defense
OMG	Office of Military Governor
OPNAV	Chief of Naval Operations
RG	Record Group

SFMNHP	San Francisco Maritime National Historical Park
USAT	United States Armed Transport
USAMHI	United States Army Military History Institute
WD	War Diary
WD12	War Diary, 12th Naval District
WD14	War Diary, 14th Naval District

Bibliography

BOOKS

Allen, Gwenfread. *Hawaii's War Years: 1941–1945.* Honolulu: University of Hawaii Press, 1950.

Allen, Roy. *The Pan Am Clipper: The History of the Pan American Flying-Boats, 1931 to 1946.* New York: Barnes & Noble, 2000.

Anthony, J. Garner. *Hawaii Under Army Rule.* Stanford: Stanford U. Press, 1955.

Bailey, Beth L. and David Farber. *The First Strange Place: Race and Sex in World War II Hawaii.*

Baltimore: Johns Hopkins University Press, 1994, 26.

Bland, Larry I. and Sharon Ritenour Stevens, Eds. *The Papers of George Catlett Marshall vol. 3: "The Right Man for the Job, December 7, 1941- May 31, 1943."* Baltimore: Johns Hopkins U. Press, 1991.

Building the Navy's Bases in World War II, vol. 2. Washington, D.C.: U.S.G.P.O., 1947.

Bykofsky, Joseph and Harold Larson, *The U.S. Army in World War II. The Technical Services. The Transportation Corps: Operations Overseas.* Washington, DC: Center of Military History, United States Army, 2003.

Downing, David. *Sealing Their Fate: The Twenty-Two Days That Decided World War II.* Cambridge, MA: DeCapo Press. 2009.

Dyer, George C., Ed. *One the Treadmill to Pearl Harbor: The Memoirs of Admiral James O. Richardson, USN.* Washington, D.C. Department of the Navy, 1973.

Earle, Joan Zuber. *The Children of Battleship Row: Pearl Harbor 1940–41.* Oakland: RDR Books, 2002.

Jones, Wilbur D., Jr. and Carroll Robbins Jones. *Hawaii Goes to War: The Aftermath of Pearl Harbor.* Shippensburg, PA: White Mane Books, 2001.

Jones, Roger E., Ed. *History of the USS Phelps (DD-360): 1936–1945.* Annapolis, MD: United States Naval Institute, 1953.

Larson, Harold. *Water Transportation for the United States Army 1939–1942,* Monograph No. 5. Historical Unit, Office of the Chief of Transportation, Army Service Force, August 1944.

Miller, Edward S. *War Plan Orange: The U.S. Strategy to Defeat Japan, 1897–1945.* Annapolis: Naval Institute Press, 1991.

Mitchell, Donald W. *History of the Modern American Navy: From 1883 through Pearl Harbor.* New York: Alfred A. Knopf, 1946.

Morison, Samuel Eliot. *History of United States Naval Operations in World War II. V.3 The Rising Sun in the Pacific. 1931-April 1942.* Boston: Little, Brown, 1948.

Multiple authors. *These Are The Generals.* Alfred Knopf, New York, 1943.

Ohl, John Kennedy. *Supplying the Troops: General Somervell and American Logistics in WWII.* DeKalb: Northern Illinois University Press, 1994.

Prange, Gordon. *At Dawn We Slept: The Untold Story of Pearl Harbor.* New York: McGraw-Hill, 1981.

Prange, Gordon, et. al. *December 7, 1941: The Day the Japanese Attacked Pearl Harbor.* New York: McGraw-Hill, 1988.

—— *The Verdict of History: Pearl Harbor.* New York: Penguin, 1991.

The Public Papers and Addresses of Franklin D. Roosevelt: vol. X. The Call to Battle Stations 1941. New York: Russell & Russell.

Rodriggs, Lawrence. *We Remember Pearl Harbor: Honolulu Citizens Recall the War Years, 1941–1945.* Newark, CA: Communications Concepts, 1991.

Satterfield, Archie. *The Day the War Began.* Westport, CT: Praeger, 1992.

Sheehan, Ed. *Days of '41: Pearl Harbor Remembered.* Honolulu: Kapa Associates, Ltd., 1977.

Simpson, B. Mitchell III. *Admiral Harold. R. Stark: Architect of Victory, 1939–1945.* Columbia, SC: University of South Carolina Press, 1989.

Stillwell, Paul, ed. *Air Raid: Pearl Harbor!: Recollections of a Day of Infamy.* Annapolis: Naval Institute Press, 1981.

Stone, Peter. *The Lady and the President: The Life and Loss of the S.S. President Coolidge.* Yarram, Victoria, Australia: Oceans Enterprises, 1999.

Sweeney, Michael S. *Secrets of Victory: The Office of Censorship and the American Press and Radio in World War II.* Chapel Hill: The University of North Carolina Press, 2001.

Tuttle, William M. *Daddy's Gone to War: The Second World War in the Lives of America's Children.* New York and Oxford: Oxford University Press, 1993.

Wallin, Homer N. *Pearl Harbor: Why, How, Fleet Salvage and Final Appraisal.* Washington, D.C.: Naval History Division, 1968.

Wardlow, Chester. *The U.S. Army in World War II. The Technical Services. The Transportation Corps: Responsibilities Organization, and Operations.* Washington, DC: Office of the Chief of Military History, United States Army, 1951.

Weatherford, Doris. *American Women and World War II.* New York: Facts on File, 1990.

Wheeler, Gerald E.. *Prelude to Pearl Harbor: The United States Navy and the Far East, 1921–1931.* Columbia: University of Missouri Press, 1963.

Yellin, Emily. *Our Mothers' War: American Women at Home and at the Front During World War II.* New York: Free Press, 2004

ARTICLES

"Civilian Defense: The Ladies!" *Time Magazine,* 26 January 1942, 61–62.

Everson, Rosalie, "Lasting Memories: Pearl Harbor nurse recalls eerie quiet, chaos of Dec 7 attack," *Fort Lupton (Co) Press,* Jan. 5, 2010. Web.

Flanner, Janet. "Profiles: Ladies in Uniform." *The New Yorker,* 4 July 1942, 21.

Harsch, Joseph C., "A War Correspondent's Odyssey, in *Air Raid: Pearl Harbor! Recollections of a Day of Infamy.* Ed. Paul Stillwell (Annapolis: Naval Institute Press, 1981), 265.

Lewis, George H. "Beyond the Reef: Cultural Constructions of Hawaii in Mainland American, Australia and Japan," *Journal of Popular Culture* 30–2 (Fall 1996), 123–136.

Lockard, Joseph. "The SCR-270-B on Oahu, Hawaii, Reminiscences," *IEEE Aerospace and Electronic Systems Magazine,* no. 12 (December 1991), 8–9.

Mandelkorn, Eugenia, "View From Our Window," *Shipmate.* 29–10 (December 1966): 12–17.

John H. McGoran memoir. http://www.pearlharborsurvivors.homestead.com/McGoran2.html

Ramsey, Mary Ann, "Only Yesteryear," *Naval History*, Winter 1991, vol. 5, no. 4; online http://www.ussblockisland.org/Beta/V2Memories/Other_Memories_files/ONLY%20YESTERDAY%20by%20Mary%20Ann%20Ramsey.pdf

Riddell, Rhoda, "I'll Be Seeing You," *Modern Maturity*, November/December, 2001, 14.

Joan Martin Rodby in *We Remember Pearl Harbor: Honolulu Citizens Recall the War Years, 1941- 1945*, ed. Lawrence R. Rodriggs (Newark, CA: Communications Concepts, 1991).

Ryan, Peggy Hughes, "A Navy Bride Learns to Cope," in *Air Raid: Pearl Harbor!*, 235;

Sabin, L.S.. "Rising Suns Over Pearl." *Shipmate* 29.10 (December 1966): 7–11.

"The Wounded Return," *Time Magazine*, 5 January 1942, 15, 32.

UNPUBLISHED MANUSCRIPTS

Ginger's Diary, 1941, http://www.gingersdiary.com

Hammett, Mary Jo. "Pearl Harbor memories."

Kinkaid, Thomas. "Four Years of War in the Pacific: A Personal Narrative," at Operational Archives, Naval Historical Center, Washington, DC, 1951–52,

Lavering, Gordon, unpublished manuscript.

Rothlin, Carmel, unpublished diary.

Thompson, Pat, "A Day to Remember," unpublished manuscript.

PAPERS

Martial Law in Hawaii: Papers of Major General Thomas H. Green [microfilm]. Bethesda, MD: University Publications of America, 2003. U.S. Army Military History Institute (USAMHI), Carlisle, Pa. Original holdings in the Library of the Judge Advocate General's School, U.S. Army, Charlottesville, VA.

Martial Law in Hawaii, December 7, 1941 – April 4, 1943 [online]. Unpublished manuscript. Library of Congress (OCLC Number 461333055).

Papers of Rear Admiral Joseph W. Leverton, The Diary of Lt. J.W. Leverton. Naval Historical Center (NHC), Washington, D.C.

Papers of George C. Marshall: Selected World War II Correspondence [microfilm]. Bethesda, MD: University Publications of America, 1992. U.S. Army Military History Institute (USAMHI), Carlisle, Pa.

Papers of Admiral Harold R. Stark, Series II – Diaries & Journals, Diary 1941–42, Operations Archives, Naval Historical Center (NHC), Washington, D.C.

Pearl Harbor Game Collection. University Archives and Special Collections, Willamette University, Salem, Oregon.

GOVERNMENT DOCUMENTS

National Archives

Commandant's Coded Administrative Records, Records of the Naval Districts and Shore Establishments, 12th Naval District, Mare Island, San Francisco (ND 12), Record Group 181, NASF.

Deck Logs of U.S.S Louisville and U.S.S. St. Louis, Records of the Bureau of Naval Personnel (BNP), Record Group 24, NACP.

Evacuation of Military, Naval, and Civilian Personnel, Decimal File 1940–1942, Record Group 407, NACP.

Operations Division, Hawaii Dept., Records of the War Department, General and Special Staffs, Record Group 165, NACP.

Passenger Lists of Vessels Arriving in Honolulu, 1900–1953, Records of the Immigration and Naturalization Service, 1891–1957, Record Group 85, NADC.

Records of the Military Government of Hawaii (MGH); Records of the U.S. Army Forces in the Middle Pacific, 1939–47 (AFMP), Records of U.S. Army Forces in the Middle Pacific, World War II, Record Group 494, NACP.

Red Cross Central File 1935–46 (Group 3) (Red Cross File), Record Group 200, NACP. This Record Group number is no longer in use.

War Diaries for the Months of January and February 1942 WD 14; War Diaries of the 14th Naval District (WD 14), 7 December, 1941 to 1 January 1942; Brief of War Diaries for the Month of 8–31 December, 1941, WD 14, Records of the Office of the Chief of Naval Operations (CNO), Record Group 38, NACP.

OTHER GOVERNMENT DOCUMENTS

Guide to American President Line Records, 1871–1995, National Park Service, San Francisco Maritime National Historical Park, San Francisco, California.

HistoryLink.org. The Online Encyclopedia of Washington State History.

Log of the U.S.S. Wharton, http://usswharton.com/shipslog.html

Office of Civilian Defense (OCD), Evacuation Division reports – Oahu 1942, Progress Report

Territorial Office of Civilian Defense, April 1942, 16, Hawaii State Archives (HSA).

OCD, Director's Administrative Files (DAF), Evacuation Division to 6/1942, Correspondence, Maps, Plans 1941–42. HSA

OCD, Director's Administrative Files, Mainland Correspondence, 1942, HSA.

U.S. Bureau of Labor. *Wages in Boot and Shoe Industry*. Washington, D.C., U.S.G.P.O., 1913.

NEWSPAPERS

Atlanta Journal

Boston Daily Globe

Boston Globe

Boston Herald

Boston Post

Burlington (VT) Free Press

Galveston Daily News

Honolulu Advertiser

Honolulu Star-Bulletin

Kansas City Star

Laramie Republican Boomerang

Los Angeles Times

New York Times

North Platte (Neb) Daily Bulletin

North Platte (Neb) Daily Telegraph

Oakland Tribune

Ogden Standard-Examiner

Omaha Morning World Herald

Pittsburgh Post-Gazette
Pittsburgh Press
Reno Evening Gazette
Salem Evening News
San Diego Union
San Francisco Chronicle
San Francisco Examiner
Williamsport Sun
Wyoming Eagle

INTERVIEWEES

Dwight Agnew (evacuee)
Elsie (Huntress) Berman
Bob Briner (evacuee)
Theresa Fichtor
Peter Fullinwider (evacuee)
Shirley McKay Hadley (evacuee)
Jack Hammett
Ellenmerle Heiges
Nancy (Walbridge) Herzog (evacuee)
Everett Hyland
Sen. Daniel Inouye
Ken Jacobson (evacuee)
Willie Jarvis (evacuee)
Patricia (Bellinger) Kauffmann (evacuee)
Gordon Lavering (evacuee)
John Lee
Robert C. Lee
Joseph Lockard
Eugenia Mandelkorn (evacuee)
Jeffrey Maner
Andrea (Marze) Tonne (evacuee)
Beverly Moglich (evacuee)
Bob Moritz (evacuee)
Gail Moul (evacuee)
John O'Neill
Rosalie (Hutchison) Smith (evacuee)

Pat (Campbell) Thompson (evacuee)
Martha Toner (evacuee)
Joan Weller (evacuee)
Art Wells

Appendices

APPENDIX I - CONVOYS FROM HAWAII TO THE WEST COAST

Convoy Num	Depart Date	Arrival Date	Port of Arrival	Convoy List	Naval Escort
4024	12/19/41	12/25/41	SF	S.S. President Coolidge U.S.A.T. Scott	USS Detroit and Cummings
4032	12/26/41	12/31/41	SF	Lurline Matsonia Monterey	St. Louis Smith Preston
4033	12/30/41	1/6/42	SF/SD	Harris President Garfield Procyon Tasker Bliss	Task Group (T.G.) 15.7 Phoenix Perkins Aylwin
4034	1/4/42	1/14/42	SF/Sea	Diamond Head Explorer Makua Regulus Sepulga Vega	T.G. 15.3 New Orleans Reid
4035	1/6/42	1/13/42	?	Alcoa Pennant Aldebaran Hercules	T.G. 15.11 Helena Conyngham
4036	1/13/42	1/21/42	SF	Cuyama Etolin Henderson Japara Maui Pennant President Johnson President Taylor	USS Honolulu Farragut Cummings

4037	1/16/42	1/28/42	SF	Birmingham City Boreas Edna Hamakua Lumber Lady Lurline Burns Maunawili Phemius Roseville Sgt. Dodd Steelmaker	T.G. 15.8 Portland Benham Ellet
4051PE	1/23/42	1/29/42	SF	Garfield Harris Wharton	T.G. 15.17 Case Tucker
4052	1/23/42			(9 freighters) American Star Gibson Iowan Makiki Manoa Manukai Manulani Philippa, Steel Voyager	T.G. 15.2 Detroit Southard Chandler
4053PE	2/1/42	2/11/42	SF	Castor Crescent City Jos. Lykes	T.G. 15.7 Monaghan Flusser
4054PE	2/7/42	2/19/42	SF/SP	Arctic - SF Coast Merchant - SF Coast Miller - SF Eliza. Kellogg - SP H.T. Harper – SP Huguenot - SP J.A. Moffett – SP Lawrence Phillips – SF Makaweli – SF Montgomery City – SF North Haven – SF Pat Doheny – SP Pyro - SF Richmond – SP Victor H. Kelly – SP Wm. H. Point – SF	T.G. 15.18 Preston Cushing Smith
4055PE	2/10/42	2/17/42	SF/SD	Alcoa Pennant Aldebaran Hercules Poelau Laut Pres. Hayes	T.G. 15.19 Henley Helm Shaw

4056	2/13/42		SF	Adm. Nulton Arcata Chas. Christensen Coast Trader Dorothy Phillips El Capitan Kohala Liloa Ludington Maliko Maunlei Permanente Pt. San Pablo Steel Exporter Topila Waimea	T.G. 15.3 Cummings Farragut
4057	2/21/42		SF SP	Aquitania –SP Kitty Hawk Lurline Pres. Garfield US Grant Wharton	T.G. 15.16 Raleigh Tucker Conyngham
4058	2/24/42a 2/23/42b		SF SP	Cadaretta Diamond Head Ewa Henderson Kailua Lumberlady Lurline Burns Mahimahi Margaret Schafer Pomona Ponca City –SP R.D. Leonard –SP Santa Cruz Cement San Vicente Waipio	T.G. 15.17 Mustin
4070	3/6/42	3/11/42	SF	Pres. Monroe	
4071	3/8/42	3/15/42	SF SD	Calamares Hercules Jos. Lykes Pres. Hayes	T.G. 15.1 Detroit Case Reid

4072	3/10/42	3/22/42	SF SP	American Star Boreas El Cedro Gulfpoint – SP Hamakua Iowan Irving L. Hunt J.C. Fitzsimmons – SP Mamo Maunawili Muldova [?] Nira Luckenbach Phillipa Pres. Johnson Roanoke Samoa [?] Samuel L. Fuller – SP San Clemente Watertown – SP W.M. Irish – SP W.R. Gibson	T.G. 15.7 Flusser Aylwin
4073	3/19/42	3/24/42	SF	Aquitania Lurline	T.G. 15.2 St. Louis
4074	3/20/42	4/2/42	SF	Birmingham City Chas. Kurtz Coast Shipper DeRoche Huguenot J.C. Fremont Klamath Lawrence Phillips Manoa Mapele Muldova North Haven Paul Shoup Penmar P.S. Mitchie Richmond Samoa Solana Sirius Utacarbon Vega W.H. Point	T.G. 15.6 Blue Ralph Talbot

4075	3/22/42	3/29/42	SF	Alcoa Pennant Japara Pres. Grant Ranier Republic U.S. Grant Wharton	T.G. 15.8 Dunlop Craven
4076 Tanker Convoy	3/26/42		SP	Durago La Purrisima L.L. Abshire Ponca City Shenandoah W.F. Burdell	USS Porter Drayton
4077	4/1/42		SF/SP/SD	Adm. Chase Adm. Cole Arcata Arctic Chas. Christensen Coast Banker Coast Merchant Coast Miller Coast Trader Dorothy Phillips El Cedro Luddington Manulani Niagra – SD Permanente Point San Pablo Sartartia Steel Explorer Topilia – SP Tydolgas – SP Virginian Waimea	TG 15.9 Hull MacDonough
4078A	4/5/42	4/10/42	SP	Aquitania	Monaghan
4078B	4/6/42			Lurline	Detroit
4079	4/5/42		SP	Eliz. Kellogg Gulf Star Kanawha La Placentia Pat Doheny R.D. Leonard, W.C. Fairbanks	TG 15.4 Mahan Zane

4090	4/7/42		SF	Aldebaran Antigua Hercules Jos. Lykes Kittyhawk	TG 15.11 Patterson Jarvis
4091	4/10/42		SF	Desoto Kahala Liloa Makaweli Maliko Mary D. Maunalei, Montgomery City Nebraskan Santa Cruz Cement San Vincente W.S. Miller (from Hilo)	TG 15.17 Clark Cummings
4092	4/14	4/25	SF SP	D.G. Schofield Gulfpoint Maine S.L. Fuller Watertown W.M. Irish	Trevor Hopkins
4093	4/22	4/30 minus Nevadan	SF	Calamares Chaumont Hammondsport Henderson H.F. Alexander Maunawili Nevada[n] Pres. Grant Pyro Republic	San Francisco Case Reid
4094	4/19	4/30	SF SP	Alencon Cadretta Hamakua I.L. Hunt Iowan John Hancock Kailua Lurline Burns Manuel N. Luckenbaugh Roanoke Regulus Waipio Wm Luckenbaugh W.R. Gibson	TG 15.8 Craven Dunlap

4095	4/25	5/8	SF SP	Chas. Kurz – SP Deroche – SP Durango – SP Gulfwax – SP Kailua Larry Doheny – SP L.L. Ibshire – SP Ponca City – SP Pres. Johnson Richmond – SP Solana – SP Thom. Jefferson W.F. Burdell – SP	Ralph Talbot Blue
4096 8 knots	4/30	5/11 SF	SF SP	Adm. Nulton Boreas Chas. Kurz – SP Diamond Head J. Christensen J. Griffiths Klamath Makua, Manoa Mapele Penmar W.H. Point W.W. Dawes	TG 15.9 Hull MacDonough
4097 13.5 knots	5/5	5/11 SF	SF SD	Bliss Jos. Lykes Jupiter Maui Shasta Wharton – SD	TG 15.3 Detroit Grayson
No Number 18 knots	5/5	5/8	SF	Coolidge	St. Louis

4098 8 knots	5/11	5/21 SF	SF SP	Adm. Cole, Chas. Christenson, Coast Banker, Coast Merchant, Coast Miller, Coast Trader, Coast Slipper, E.B. Degolia – SP Ewa, Haoira, – SP Herman F. Whiton, H. L. Pratt, – SP J.A. Moffett, – SP Ludington, Mamo, (SF); Nevadan, Pat Doheny, – SP Permanente R.D. Leonard, – SP San Clemente, Steel Exporter, Topila, – SP Tydolgas, – SP Waimea,	TG 15.17 Dale Clark Avocet
4099 8.5 knots	5/20	5/31 SF	SF SP	Arcata, Arizonan Comet – SP Coos Bay D.G. Schofield – SP Gulf Queen – SP H.W. Longfellow, Kohala, Liloa, Makaweli Maliko Maunalei Nebraskan Santa Cruz Cement San Vicente Satartia Shenandoah – SP S. L. Fuller – SP Vermar Watertown – SP	TG 15.1 Southard Hovey

4110 11.5 knots	5/24	6/2 SF	SF	Alcoa Pennant Antiqua Etolin Henderson Hercules H.F. Alexander J.F. Bell J.W. Van Dyke Pres. Grant Pres. Polk Sinclair Rubilene Talamanaca	TG 15.8 Craven Dunlap
4110-A 9.5 knots	5/27		SP	Chas. Kurz, Deroche Durango Gulfwax J.C. Fitzsimons L.L. Abshire Ponca City Richmond Roanoke Solana Washington	Gamble Breese
4111 8.5 knots	5/31	6/9	SF	Aldebaran Anthony Wayne Arctic Cadaretta Chaumont Edgar A. Poe Hamakua Iowan Irving L. Hunt John Dickenson John Hancock Lurline Burns Maine Manulani Maunawili Montgomery City Phillipa Susanna Virginian	TG 15.7 Perry Wasmuch
4112 14.5 knots	6/5	6/12	SF	Hammondsport Kittyhawk Maui Pres. Johnson USS Jupiter (cargo ship) will join later)	TG 15.3 Detroit Ford Edwards

4113	6/8	6/19	SF	Adm. Nulton Desoto Diamond Head, District of Columbia James Christenson James Griffiths J.G. Whittier Kailua Penmar, Stanley A. Griffiths Waipio William Luckenbach, Nira Luckenbach dep PH to overtake 4113 (6/10)	TG 15.8 Whipple Alden
No Number	6/11	6/18	SF	Henry T. Allen (Navy troop transport)	TG 15.10 Clark
4114-A	6/13	6/23	West Coast (WC)	Gulfbird Gulfpoint Hahira J.A. Moffett Pyro W.M. Irish Calamares dep. PH to join 4114-A	TG 15.11 Lamson
4114-B 9 knots	6/19		WC	Absoroka Adm. Cole Barbara Olson Chester Sun Coast Banker Coast Miller Eastern Sun Ewa Ludington Manoa Mapele Nevadan, Pat Doheny Steel Exporter Teapa Waimea W.H. Point	TG 15.9 Conyngham, Hughes Parrott

4115 12 knots	6/22	6/30	SF	Alcoa Pennant Arthur Middleton Etolin Fort Royal H.F. Alexander, Pres. Grant Republic	TG 15.12 Paul Jones Bulmer
PE-4132 18.5 knots	6/24		SF	Lurline Mount Vernon	TG 15.3 Detroit; Lawrence dep SF to meet 4132 – Detroit leaves 4132 to search for lost plane
4133 8.5 knots	6/30	7/10	WC	Antigua Benj. Goodhue Cathwood Chas. Christenson Deroche Durango Eliz. Kellogg Frank G. Drum H.T. Harper Kohala Liloa L.L. Abshire Makaweli Maliko Manukai Nebraskan Paine Wingate Roanoke San Clemente Santa Cruz Cement San Vicente Solana W.B. Gibson W.C. Fairbanks Wm. Ellery Sirius dep. PH 7/2 to overtake convoy	TG 15.1 Long Chandler

4139 11.5 knots	7/8		SF SD	Bridge Henderson Kittyhawk Pres. Johnson Tangier Walter Vreden	TG 15.2 Mahan Smith
4150	7/10	7/20 SP	SF(8) SP(5)	Abraham Clark A.C. Bedford – SP Ardmore – SP H.L. Pratt – SP I.L. Hunt J.C. Fitzsimmons John Dickenson Maine Maunalei Maunawili Philippa Shenandoah – SP Western Sun – SP	TG 15.5 Edwards Ford
4154 9.5 knots	7/19	7/30 SP	WC	Camden D.G. Schofield – SP Diamond Head Dist. Of Columbia E.A. Poe Gulf of Venezuela – SP Gulfpoint – SP Hamakua Jane Christenson Kailua La Placentia – SP Manulani Permanente Topila Virginian W. M Irish – SP	TG 15.8 Whipple Alden
4155 12.5 knots	7/22	7/30 SP	WC	Alcoa Pennant Calamares Catawba Flagship Sinco – SP Republic Shasta Sinclair Rubiline – SP	TG 15.12 Bulmer Parrott

4157	7/30		WC	Boreas	TG 15.9
9 knots				Comet	Conyngham
				Dakotan	Preston
				Elihu Yale	
				Ewa	
				Gulfbird	
				Gulfwave	
				Irving MacDowell	
				John S. Ashe	
				Makiki	
				Mahimahi	
				Manoa	
				Nevadan	
				Stanley Griffiths	
				Waimea	
				Waipio	

Source: RG 38 Records of the Office of Chief of Naval Operations, War Diaries, 14th Naval District, and War Diaries CINCPAC, NACP.

SF = San Francisco

SD = San Diego

SP = San Pedro

Sea. = Seattle

WC = West Coast

APPENDIX - II LETTERS

A. From Citizens Concerned About the Evacuation:

1) Some citizens appealed to stay in Hawaii:

915 A-Alewa Dr.
Honolulu, T.H.
December 30, 1941

Commander J. A. (sic) Barrett
Overseas Transportation Office
Pearl Harbor, T.H.

Dear Commander Barrett:

If it would be at all possible to give me some information regarding my status as an evacuee I would be very grateful.

As my husband, Lt. j.g. K.L. Butler U.S.N.R. came on active duty from the mainland, his bona fide address is on the mainland: thus making it mine. However, I was raised here in Honolulu and my parents and family all make their homes here. Could you tell me what my chances are of remaining here with my family, which I would like very much to do.

Thank you.

Yours truly,
Mary Ella Butler
(Mrs. K.L. Butler)

RG 181, Records of the Naval Districts and Shore Establishments, 14th Naval District, Honolulu, Hawaii. Commandant's Coded Administrative Records 1940–1956, Folder 1942 A16–3/ND14 Evacuation Vol. 1 1942 to January 10, Box No. 0026, NASF.

Barrett's response – a form letter:

OFFICE OF THE COMMANDANT
FOURTEENTH NAVAL DISTRICT
AND
NAVY YARD, PEARL HARBOR, HAWAII, U.S.A.

January 9, 1942

Mrs. K.L. Butler
915 A-Alewa Drive,
Honolulu, T.H.

My dear Mrs. Butler:

Reference is made to your letter dated **30 December 1941.**

Present instructions require evacuation of all dependents of service personnel except those indicated:

(a) Dependents regularly domiciled in the Territory of Hawaii.
(b) Dependents employed in positions essential to national defense, as determined by the Commandant in each case.

These must file certificates in either case, copy of which is enclosed herewith.

Very truly yours,

J.B. Barrett,
Commander, U.S. Navy
Overseas Transportation Officer

RG 181, Evacuation, Vol. 1, NASF.

2) Some citizens were confused by evacuation policy and wanted clarification:

February 8, 1942

Lt. Col. Thomas H. Green, J.A.G.D.,
Office of the Military Governor,
Fort Shafter, T.H.

Honorable sir:

May I respectfully ask that you or the proper authorities in Hawaii clarify and make generally known the policy of the government in regard to civilian evacuation from Hawaii to the mainland. I do not have a personal ax to grind in this matter but see in it a means of generally improving morale.

As it appears now the families of army and navy personnel are being evacuated according to a priority plan as rapidly as facilities permit. This is perfectly reasonable and to be expected. However, as to the evacuation of civilians from Oahu and other islands, there seems to [be] no authentic information. The general impression (probably erroneous) is that civilian evacuation is conditioned by:

1. Having your job designated as a vital defense job.
2. "Pull" or knowing an Army or Navy family that will take your children up to the mainland with theirs.
3. Having enough money to pay "Clipper" or boat fares.
4. Whether one lives on Oahu or not.
6. (sic) Whether one is of Oriental ancestry or not.

If it is desirable to evacuate wives and children to the mainland it seems to me that "influence", money or racial background of citizens, should not be the basis. If we are following a democratic course, evacuation priorities should be decided on some such bases as nearness to dangerous areas, age and sex of children, health, age, and usefulness of adults, etc. The opportunity should be given citizens (children) of oriental ancestry and people in poor financial status to go to the mainland even if fares have to be paid and camps built to care for those who have no friends or relatives there.

Even though it may be months before such a policy could be out into operation, if it were publicized now it would be advantageous for morale. Above all it would assure us of the continued loyalty of the bulk of our Japanese citizens who are loyal but whose loyalty is now subject to strains and doubts as to whether we consider them Americans.

Possibly some such policy has already been enunciated by the authorities. If so may I suggest that it be given wider publicity. I know that you are overburdened with responsibilities in these difficult times but I presume to burden you with another problem because its clarification would do so much to bolster island unity and would be in line with our great American tradition of fair dealing.

Respectfully yours (sic)
Alfred M. Church

AMC:c

RG 494, Records of U.S. Armed Forces in the Middle Pac. 1941–45, Entry 346, Box 923, Binder #1, NACP.

3) Some civilians were desperate to leave Hawaii:

Lt. General Delos C. Emmons [No date]
Iolani Palace
Honolulu

My dear General Emmons:

In an article for the N.Y. Times, I remarked that martial law in Hawaii is giving us a fine demonstration of good government. I have considerable respect for your conduct of the civil and military affairs of our islands. The Army has been splendid in its relations with civilians.

There is one very striking exception to our confidence in the Army and I feel that you probably are not aware of it except in a very broad way. I refer to evacuation. Specifically, my complaints are:

1) That men are given relatively prompt transportation by the hundreds while women and children wait for months.
2) That families with no priority because of pregnancy, illness, age or other legitimate reasons are assigned accommodations while other families who registered much earlier are still here with no prospect of getting away.
3) That recent telephone calls were made to hundreds specifying the exact fare, the form in which such fare should be presented, the exact amount of luggage that should be taken, and the amount of notice that would be given, and that the status of these people who have not been called

again has not been clarified. In my own case, two calls to the Civilian Evacuation Committee brought forth these replies:

a) (On Friday, the 20th [1942]) "The Army assigned us more space and we thought we could take you but then they took priority on it. You can't go now and we don't know when you can go. Relax (sic!) because there's no chance of your being called."
b) (On Monday, the 23rd) "Why, that call didn't mean we expected to take you. The Army just called everyone so they'd be ready at any time. They wanted everyone to know that they are on 12 to 24-hour call."

4) That registered nurses with no reason to go but their own desire have left, while women and children who have been registered since December 19th are still here. This situation is acute. The morale of husbands is quite as low as that of wives, if not lower. We have all accepted the shortage of ships as part of the uncertainties of war, but we have no confidence that this problem is being handled intelligently and with fairness. We are, frankly, after more than two months of observation, without hope. Our situation grows worse, not better.

Missing words... merely that we cannot get him to Punahou. The nearest school is 2 1/2 miles from our house and we cannot even take him there. His education has stopped short.

My husband was on night duty (M.D. – He is a retired doctor.) following December 7th, leaving me alone on our hilltop with the two children. In case of another attack, this will doubtless be repeated. He worried so about us that he sent me on December 15th to make arrangements for evacuation. We have absolutely no on to call on here, and all our family is on the mainland. He was medical officer at U.S. Naval Air Base #1 at Dunquerque (sic) in the last war until he was captured, and he very likely saved the life of "Di" Gates, now Secretary of the Navy for Air, who got a terrific infection in an attempt to escape. Fortunately for Mr. Gates and possibly for our country, my husband's morale was splendid at that time because he knew his wife and child were being taken care of in safety. The way he feels now, I'm afraid he wouldn't be much help to Mr. Gates or anyone else.

We have a home and friends waiting in Vermont. Our income has not increased in recent years and we are faced with rising costs. We wonder whether we'll still have the fare if we ever do get called. I cannot get a job here because I am on the evacuation list, and because I have to take care of my boy. I could leave the children in Vermont and become a useful citizen again.

I appeal to you in the name of all those who are disheartened by the injustices of the evacuation system, and I appeal to you in my own name, because I still believe in democracy and the right to approach the head man when other approaches produce only bafflement.

Respectfully yours,

Barry F. Stevens
(Mrs. Albert Mason Stevens.)

> This letter would be better typed if I had not taken the second call so seriously. My own typewriter is in town. So is my toothbrush and I'm ready to brush my teeth on a wire-haired terrier.

RG 494, Records of U.S. Armed Forces in the Middle Pac. 1941–45, Entry 346, Box 923, Binder #1, NACP.

4) There were many reasons for wanting to evacuate, as this letter shows:

3472 Maunalei Ave.
Honolulu, T. H.
January 5, 1942

Commander Barrett
Pearl Harbor, T. H.

Dear Sir:

My husband, John Carman, Chief Storekeeper, U.S.S. Pennsylvania, was evacuated from Pearl Harbor Hospital to a mainland hospital nearly three weeks ago. At that time I registered in your office requesting transportation to the mainland and attached to that request was a letter from the doctor who handled my husband's case, recommending that I be sent as soon as possible. I am trying to be patient, but I appeal to you, Commander Barrett, to please endeavor to secure a passage for me aboard the next ship carrying an evacuation party to the coast.

Please forgive me for troubling you with this letter, but I feel confidant (sic) that you will appreciate my deep concern and my great desire to get to the bedside of my husband.

Thanking you for your kindness, I am,

Yours very truly,

Emma Carman
(Mrs. John Carman)

RG 181, Evacuation, Vol. 2, Jan. 11, 1942 – Feb. 15, 1942, NASF.

Barrett responded to Mrs. Carman:

January 12, 1942

Mr. (sic) John Carman,
3472 Maunalei Ave.,
Honolulu, T.H.

My dear Mrs. Carman:

Reference is made to your letter dated January 5, 1942.

A copy of the reference has been filed with your registration and every effort will be made to secure transportation for you when it becomes available. When it does become available, you will be notified promptly.

It is requested that you keep this office advised of any change of address or telephone number.

Very truly yours,

J. B. BARRETT
Commander, U.S. Navy,
Overseas Transportation Officer.

JBB:bcb

RG 181, Evacuation Vol. 2, NASF.

5) Barrett's response to a physician who had written to the Navy asking for a patent's exemption from the evacuation:

January 6, 1942

Mr. John W. Cooper, M.D.
353 Young Hotel Bldg.
Honolulu, T.H.

Dear Sir:

Your letter of December 27, 1941, addressed to Medical Department, Fort Shafter, regarding Mrs. Carolyn FitzGerald, Courtland Hotel, Honolulu, T.H., was forwarded to the Commandant, 14th Naval District and referred to me for reply.

Under existing instructions, dated December 31, 1941, "all dependents of service personnel of the Naval Establishment in the Territory of Hawaii, will be evacuated as transportation becomes available", unless exempted by reason of:-

(a) Regular domicile in the Territory of Hawaii.
(b) Employment in position essential to National Defense, as determined by the Commandant in each case.

If exemption claimed falls under either category, endorsed certificate should be executed and forwarded as indicated on the form used. Otherwise, no exemption is now authorized.

Yours truly,

J.B. Barrett,
Commander, U.S. Navy
Overseas Transportation Officer

c.c. Col. E. King, U.S.A.
Medical Department,
Fort Shafter, Oahu, T.H.
RG 181, Evacuation Vol. 1, NASF

6) Even Castle & Cooke needed clarification regarding evacuee status:

CASTLE & COOKE, LIMITED
General Agents
Matson Navigation Company
The Oceanic Steamship Company
Isthmian Steamship Company
Honolulu, Hawaii, U.S.A.
December 30, 1941
PC-P

Captain M.M. Frucht, USN (Ret)
U.S. Naval Representative of Evacuation
Castle & Cooke Building
Honolulu, Hawaii

Dear Captain Frucht:

Tourists, residents and visitors on other islands in the Hawaiian group [other] than Oahu, have been writing us and asking us regarding their status for evacuation.

We should appreciate your clarification as to what, if any, instructions we should give to people asking these questions.

Yours very truly,
Castle & Cooke, Limited
A.J. Pessel
General Passenger Agent

AJP:wp

RG 181, Evacuation, Vol. 2, NASF

Frucht referred the letter above to Admiral Bloch, who responded:

12 January 1942

Mr. A. J. Pessel
General Passenger Agent
Castle & Cooke, Limited
Honolulu, T. H.

My dear Mr. Pessel:

Referring to your letter of December 30, 1941, to Captain M. M. Frucht, USN, which has been referred to me for reply, so far as I know, there is no plan for the compulsory evacuation of civilians residing in the Hawaiian area.

From time to time as space is available, ships are allocated for the purpose of transporting civilians to the mainland; however, all of this transportation is on a voluntary basis.

As no one is in a position to predict when further ships will be available for passengers, it is impossible to arrange anything like a schedule.

Very truly yours,
C. C. Bloch
Rear Admiral, U.S. Navy
Commandant, Fourteenth Naval District.

RG 181, Evacuation, Vol. 2, NASF.

B. The Evacuation Form for civilians:

12/29/41

FORM: #100 Submitted to: <u>OFFICE OF CIVILIAN DEBARKATION AUTHORITY</u>

This form is to be used for Island Residents, Civilians and families, and civilian Defense Worker families for whom voluntary evacuation is requested.

Do not use this form for any government classifications.

<u>PLEASE PRINT ALL INFORMATION EXCEPT SIGNATURE</u>

I desire to purchase transportation to the mainland of the United States when facilities become available for the following memb<u>er</u>s of my immediate dependent family:

1. IMMEDIATE TRANSPORTATION /_/__________

(Give reason for immediate transportation)

2. DEFERRED TRANSPORTATION /_/__________

(Give reason for deferment and approximate date)

<u>SECTION 1</u>

<u>LAST NAME</u>	<u>FIRST NAME</u>	<u>SEX</u>	<u>RELATIONSHIP</u>	<u>PRESENT OCCUPATION</u>	<u>BIRTH DATE</u>	<u>PLACE OF BIRTH</u>
1.—						
2.—						
3.—						
4.—						
5.—						

Note 1: Include your own name in Section 1 if you desire transportation.

Note 2: Do not include anyone who is not a member of your immediate dependent family.

<u>SECTION 2</u>

Indicate the phone number and address where names listed in Section 1 may be quickly reached.
Phone number: ____________ Number & Street: ____________
SECTION 3: Indicate home or permanent address if different from that in Section 2.
Street & Number: _________City ________ State ____

SECTION 4: Indicate next of kin or closest friend other than those listed in Section 1.

____

(Name) (Relationship) (Street & Number) (City & state)

SECTION 5: Submitted By:

____

(Write Signature) (Occupation) (Employed By) (Employer's Address)

SECTION 6: Application Accepted By:

____

(Write Signature) (Office Accepting this Form) (Address)
Date Filed: _______________ Time Filed:

SECTION 7: DO NOT FILL IN THE FOLLOWING
Priority Rating: FIRST AVAILABLE DEFERRED TO _________ DEFEREED INDEFINITELY
(Check one) (Date)

____

(Signature Rating Officer)

SECTION 8: Passenger Notified of Priority Rating:
Date: ____________ Time: _________ Clerk: ___________________

SECTION 9: Passenger Notified to Secure Ticket:

____

(Name) (By Phone) (By Letter) (Date) (Time) (Clerk)
RG 181, Evacuation, Vol. 1, NASF.

C. Early references to the evacuation

1) Brief telephone communication between Col. Phillips (Short's) Chief of Staff, Hawaiian Department, Honolulu to Major Sexton for General Marshall – 10;15p.m. (Washington time) December 8, 1941:

"Desire authorization for evacuation of dependents at expense of government and for crating and shipping furniture."

RG 165, Records of the War Dept. General & Special Staffs, OPD 381, Hawaii Dept., NACP.

2) Admiral Bloch to Admiral Kimmel

15 December 1941

RESTRICTED
MEMORANDUM FOR:

The Commander in Chief [of the Pacific Fleet Admiral Kimmel]

I propose to immediately start to evacuate the dependents of Navy and Marine Corps personnel in Hawaii.

In order that I may have people to go on the first transportation available, I request that you take the necessary steps to have about 500 dependents of Navy and Marine Corps personnel attached to the Fleet register with the Transportation Office in the navy (sic) yard, giving their names, addresses, and other data that may be required in connection with this movement.

I suggest that the first ones taken be on a voluntary basis and that all notices put out be so communicated as not to cause panic among these dependents.

At a later date, I hope to get an office established up town so that this registration can take place up there. At the present time this seems to be impracticable.

C. C. BLOCH
Rear Admiral, U. S. Navy
Commandant, Fourteenth Naval District

Copy to:
Chief of Staff, 14th ND
Captain of the Yard
Transportation Officer

RG 181, Evacuation, Vol. 2, NASF

3) General Marshall to Major Winn [Marshall's son-in-law]:

To Major James J, Winn December 16, 1941
Personal and Confidential [Washington, D.C.]

Dear Jim: This is just a hasty note. Katherine [Marshall's wife] has been worrying about Molly [Marshall's daughter]. of course, reading of Panama black-outs and thinking about the feeding of the baby [M.'s grandson]. I merely want to tell you that if you think Molly and the baby should be gotten out of there, (sic) there is no problem here, only a possibly over (sic) enthusiastic welcome.

Of course, once Molly is up here she will not be allowed to go back [to Panama]. Also, and most confidentially, I do not know when we will start the evacuation of dependents from Panama; as yet General [Frank] Andrews has not made any recommendations. *We are of course starting the evacuation from Hawaii.* [author's emphasis]. It is quite possible that such action may be taken in Panama, though this is not certain.

I pass this all on for your own private information.

Faithfully yours

<u>The Papers of George Catlett Marshall: vol. 3,</u> p. 21

D. Red Cross Documents Pertaining to the Evacuation

1) Early Numbers on the Evacuees:

THE AMERICAN RED CROSS
PACIFIC BRANCH

Mr. Don C. Smith, Director DATE January 12, 1942
TO Military and Naval Welfare Service
Washington, D.C.

FROM Harry L. Walden SUBJECT Evacuees

Enclosed is the information which you requested in your letter of January 5th, regarding evacuation ships docking at San Francisco.

SHIP	ARRIVAL	MEN	WOMEN	CHILDREN	PATIENTS
U.S.S Scott	12–25-41	5	37	46	55
U.S.S. Coolidge	12–25-41	255	184	21	125
Third class 130 unclassified as to sex.					
U.S.S. Matsonia	12–31-41	249	495	93	--
U.S.S. Lurline	12–31-41	13	677	627	55
U.S.S. Monterey	12–31-41	21	393	185	84
U.S.S. Bliss	1–6-42	5	75	93	--
U.S.S. Garfield	1–6-42	52	63	70	--

The U.S.S. Harris docked at San Diego January 6, 1942 with 120 women and children and 40 patients.

The count on children is only an approximation as only one of the passenger lists designated children.

Harry L/ Walden
Director
Military and Naval Welfare Service

2) Agreement Outlining Red Cross Responsibilities:

OFFICE OF CIVILIAN DEFENSE
Ninth Regional Office
1355 Market St.
San Francisco, California
January 19, 1942

The following is a statement by the Office of Civilian Defense, The Office of Defense Health and Welfare Services and the American Red Cross of joint policies to be followed in handling of persons evacuated from territories and possessions of the United States to ports of the Ninth Civilian Defense Region.

"#1. The Office of Civilian Defense, working through its own facilities and those of the Office of Defense Health and Welfare Services and the American Red Cross, is recognized as general coordinator of evacuation services.

"2. Care of these persons evacuated due to war is a national responsibility. In order to coordinate all efforts and to provide properly for all contingencies, the Office of Civilian Defense, the Office of Defense Health and Welfare Services, and the Red Cross have, at the request of the Office of Civilian Defense, formed a joint regional committee. Handling of these evacuees is a matter of regional concern; therefore, the committee has set up the following regional plan:

A. Red Cross shall have nurses and social workers aboard evacuation ships for the welfare of the families and to expedite work at debarkation.
B. Social workers aboard shall register every family and interview these families needing help, determining their needs, formulating plans for assistance, and interpreting to evacuees services and facilities available.
C. On arrival at port of debarkation, the Red Cross shall be in charge of reception, intake services and interim care including provision of necessary food, shelter, clothing, medical aid and local transportation in cooperation with the Army and Navy. In providing these services such other organizations, facilities, and services as needed will be called upon.
D. In disbursal of evacuees the Red Cross will arrange for adequate transportation and will provide necessary assistance in transit.
E. Recognizing that the public and private agencies have facilities and responsibilities for continuing care, the Office of Defense Health and Welfare Services will arrange for utilization of such agencies in the provision of services for any continuing needs of the evacuees. The office of Defense Health and Welfare Services from records made by the Red Cross shall advise the proper public agencies at points of ultimate destination of the arrival of evacuee families, with notation of social problems, as known, and the American Red Cross will notify its local chapter."

(signed) Jack H. Helms, Acting Regional Director
Office of Civilian Defense

(signed) Richard N. Neustadt, Regional Director
Office of Defense Health and Welfare
Services
(signed) A. L. Schafer, Manager of Pacific Area
American Red Cross

3) The Red Cross and the situation on the docks at San Francisco

Mr. A. L. Schafer February 9, 1942

Mr. Fieser

Will you please send me as promptly as possible a memorandum summarizing the arrangements for handling of evacuees. The memorandum should include statements or copies of any agreements reached with other organizations such as the statement agreed upon jointly by you the OCD representative, and the federal Security representatives; the understanding with the American Women's Voluntary Services both in theory and in operations present arrangements with the Army and Navy; where responsibility is fixed for the operation, that is, whether under the control of the Pacific Area office or the Chapter concerned; the extent to which Volunteer Special Services in the Chapter operates independently; and the character of the Services given to evacuate and by whom.

Please indicate independently of this statement the extent to which the plans operated in handling the last ship.

James L. Fieser
Vice Chairman in Charge
of Domestic Operations

AMERICAN RED CROSS
Pacific Area
Civic Auditorium
San Francisco, California
February 14, 1942

Mr. James L Feiser (sic), Vice-Chairman
National Headquarters
American Red Cross
Washington, D. C.

My dear Mr. Feiser:

This will reply to your memorandum of February 9, 1942, in which you request a memorandum summarizing the arrangements for the handling of evacuees.

So far, this activities (sic) has involved three Chapters on the Pacific Coast, i.e., San Francisco, San Diego and Seattle. Approximately 5,000 evacuees have arrived in San Francisco, about 1,600 in Seattle, and approximately 1,000 in San Diego. The Chapters have done an excellent job in assuming responsibility for organizing and carrying of (sic) – activities necessary for such an operation. The Special Volunteer Services in each Chapter have been utilized to the fullest possible extent for the service to the evacuees. Canteens were established at the docks. Other volunteers were on hand with quantities of warm suitable clothing because many of the evacuees landed here with clothing suitable only for tropical and semi-tropical climates. Chapter Motor Corps provided transportation from the docks to central points which were known as "Reception Centers" at which Staff Assistants and others were on duty for registration purposes. Also, the Chapters' Home Service Staff, augmented where necessary by additional social workers from other agencies in the community, were assigned to these reception centers for the purpose of extending whatever service was necessary. Evacuees were then taken to local hotels for accommodations prior to their departure from the point of debarkation. Doctors and Nurses, selected by the Chapter concerned, were on the docks, available for any emergency service when the evacuees arrived. The local County Medical Associations and the Nurses' Associations gave excellent cooperation in this phase of the work.

Each of the three Chapters named above, at our request, designated a person to be in charge of the entire evacuation operations. In Seattle this person is Major C. C. Gill, Chairman of the Disaster Preparedness and Relief Committee; in San Francisco it is Mr. Robert S. Elliott, Executive Manager of the Chapter; and in San Diego it is Miss Edith Forrest, Executive Secretary of the Chapter.

Our Military and Naval welfare Field Directors stationed within the jurisdiction of these Chapters have served as liaison between the armed forces and the Red Cross. At the reception centers the Travelers' Aid Service was utilized to assist the evacuees with transportation problems from the port of debarkation to their home city. Representatives of commercial transportation organizations have also been available to serve evacuees desiring immediate transportation to the home city.

In the Area office the evacuation program has been under the general direction of our Disaster Relief Service.

On the whole, our relationships with the armed forces have been very harmonious, particularly in Seattle, San Diego, and with the Army officials here in San Francisco. They have been most cooperative. It happens, however, that here in San Francisco the Navy Relief Society had previously designated the local unit of the American Women's Voluntary Services as an auxiliary of the Navy Relief Society and, as such, requested it to provide transportation and some other services for wives of Navy personnel. As a result of this commitment on the part of the Navy Relief Society, which had the approval of the Commandant, Twelfth Naval District, a joint verbal decision was reached to permit the A. W. V. S. to share the work of volunteer motor transportation of the families of Navy personnel from the docks to the reception center, or a local hotel. This applies only to Navy personnel arriving in San Francisco.

Attached to this letter is copy of the agreement reached on the Regional level with the Regional Office of Civilian Defense, the Regional Office of Defense, Health and Welfare Services, and this office. We are also attaching copy of the Chapter Evacuation Report on which we are expecting Chapters to give us detail (sic) reports, with narrative data attached, at which time we shall be in a better position to give you more detailed information.

Very sincerely yours,
A. L. Schafer
Manager

SAN FRANCISCO CHAPTER
AMERICAN NATIONAL RED CROSS

March 23, 1942

Mr. A. L. Schafer, Manager
American Red Cross, Pacific Area
Civic Auditorium, Civic Center
San Francisco, California

Dear Mr. Schafer:

Referring to your letter of March 10, 1942, PCS 551 A 80 and to publicity recently given to the statement therein referred to, I must frankly state that in the light of the experience we have had here in this very important port of San Francisco, this was to me a most startling announcement.

I must refer to the correspondence that has passed between your office and mine and the discussions we have had regarding the difficulties our Chapter representatives have encountered in dealing with this evacuation problem.

There has been anything but the fullest measure of cooperation.

You will recall that when the reception of evacuees of this port was in prospect, you informed me that Secretary of the Navy Knox had conferred with Red Cross National Chairman Davis and had been assured by Chairman Davis that Red Cross was ready to take care of the evacuees. You asked me in my position as Chairman of the San Francisco Chapter if our Chapter would be prepared to perform its function in full in receiving and caring for the evacuees, and I stated definitely that we were so prepared.

We have been and are prepared to fully perform this function.

Caring for evacuees does not mean merely receiving them at the docks with canteen service and motor transportation to wherever they may desire to be transported locally, but the many other services that these evacuees require. I need not recount them all because you are thoroughly familiar with them, such things as proper medical attention, information service, careful routing to their ultimate destinations, and so on. In order to properly perform the full measure of service, it is essential that there be no interference with the Red Cross at any point of contact in the full performance of the Red Cross' very definite and inescapable obligation under its Congressional Charter and its obligation to the general public which so liberally provides the Red Cross with funds to enable it to render its services.

The Navy Relief Society here designated an outside competitive organization as its auxiliary, which organization has carried on a competitive, and in its effect, obstructive program ever since the Navy evacuees have been arriving, in spite of that organization's officials' very positive statements to the effect that they would undertake nothing of a competitive nature, both in local discussions and in what was presumed to be their understanding with the Chairman of our national organization. This has constituted an interference which has been disturbing not only to our Chapter in its effort to perform its duty, but to the public generally. It is a matter which should have been cleared in Washington, and as we see it, since our National Chairman sent the instructions through to our local Chapter to perform its function, it should have been just as definitely sent through from the head of the Navy to the Twelfth Naval District, to avoid confusion at the very start.

I feel, therefore, that in the light of the joint statement authorized by the Chairman of the American Red Cross, Mr. Norman H. Davis, and the President of the Navy Relief Society, Admiral Stark, the proper instructions should be given by them jointly to create the condition which will justify their statement.

Red Cross has a long, hard row ahead of it, and that is especially true of the Chapter here in the important port of San Francisco. The situation is so critical that every type of volunteer effort must be properly directed, and nothing of a competitive and obstructive character should be encouraged or even tolerated – and responsible authorities should see to it that such be not the case.

I have full sympathy with the work of the Navy Relief Society and shall contribute to its fund, but the Red Cross must of necessity be relied upon to carry on those indispensable services which are beyond the capacity of the Navy Relief Society to perform; and by the same token, the Navy Relief Society in all of its branches must emphatically, at such an important point as San Francisco, do everything to facilitate the work of the Red Cross

in the performance of its service.

It is a sad commentary that the Red Cross should have to plead for the opportunity of faithfully rendering the service which under its very Charter it is obliged to perform.

Our people have a right to expect that performance in the light of their very generous contribution to Red Cross.

I am expressing the opinion of our Chapter's Board of Directors, as well as my own personal feeling upon the subject.

Sincerely,

(Signed) Frederick J. Koster
American Red Cross
San Francisco Chapter

The American Red Cross
Pacific Area

TO Mr. James L. Fieser DATE March 25, 1942
National Headquarters

FROM Mr. A. L. Schafer SUBJECT

The statement of Mr. Davis and also the agreement worked out by Mr. (sic) and Mr. Bondy having to do with the cooperation of the Navy Relief Society resulted in the enclosed letter from Mr. Koster, Chairman of the San Francisco Chapter. This is being sent to you just for your information. Back of Mr. Koster's letter, primarily, is the evacuee program here in San Francisco According to Mr. Ernst, the O. C. D. in Washington requested the Red Cross to handle evacuees from Honolulu and not the Navy. Accordingly, the O. C. D. here have assumed primary responsibility and asked the Red Cross to handle the details of the program. though my original understanding by telephone conversation with Dewitt Smith was to the effect that the Navy itself had requested this service on the part of the Red Cross.

The Regional Office of the O. C. D. here had brought the A. W. V. S. in the picture, or at least, permitted them to remain in the picture with their Motor Transportation Service and Canteen. The A. W. V.S. here are a very aggressive group. Strange as it may seem, their leader, Mrs. Tucker, is a sister of Mrs. Cameron, Chairman of the Motor Corps Service of the Red Cross. I understand that these two women are not on speaking terms and that they are using these two organizations to express their own personal hostility to each other. The Chapter, particularly Mr. Koster, feels that the Red Cross should have the exclusive right on the matter of handling evacuees, which, of course, we cannot ask for yet from the O. C. D.

As further illustration of the activity of the A. W. C. (sic) S., we were advised two days ago that they were inaugurating a campaign in Oakland to get materials and money for the supplying of clothing, and principally layettes, to families among the evacuees from Honolulu. Their campaign was referred to the Chamber of Commerce in Oakland, which latter organization immediately communicated with the Oakland Chapter and the Oakland Chapter with this office, only to be advised that we have here in San Francisco a large stock of clothing including 4,400 layettes, which are being made available as needed in the handling of evacuees. With this information the Chamber of Commerce were loath to authorize a solicitation of funds by the A. W. V. S. in Oakland. Of course, as Mr. Koster indicates, the Navy itself has not been as cooperative as has the Army. As a matter of fact, I find now that the Navy were cognizant of and had encouraged the A. W. V. S. in Oakland to make available funds and materials for the purchase of layettes.

TO - Mr. Fieser -2- March 25, 1942

> We are just now taking on to the staff on a dollar a year basis a liaison man to represent this office in the Regional O. C. D. I think you know Mr. Gardner Bullis, a very prominent and successful attorney in Los Angeles and for many years a member of the Los Angeles Chapter Board. He has come to San Francisco to reside permanently and has been very keen to take on this liaison work with the O. C. D. we are looking to him to help in the straightening out of the relationship with this organization, though Mr. Shepard, the new Regional Director, is most cooperative and straight-forward.
>
> We are following up the matters referred to in Mr. Koster's communication and of course will keep in close touch with him relative thereto.
>
> A. L. Schafer
> Manager

RG 200, Red Cross documents and correspondence above from Red Cross Central File 1935–46 (Group 3), NACP.

4) A letter from an appreciative evacuee:

From Mrs. Alexander (Evelina) Rowell of Honolulu to her sister Mrs. Arthur Wentworth of Peabody, Mass., December 11, 1941.

> "I want to try to give you a little picture of what we went through. I imagine our letters are going to be heavily censored, so I will try to be very careful. I still can't believe that what has happened really occurred.

"We were all in bed at the time that the attack started. I heard the planes very clearly but thought nothing of it as we have planes soaring overhead most of the time. I heard bombs and anti-aircraft guns being fired, but still couldn't believe that it was anything serious.

"I got up and went out in the back yard and talked with neighbors who were also wondering. We could see many squadrons of five planes in 'V' formation, way up in the sky, but thought they were our own planes on maneuvers. We heard one flying quite low towards us and looked up expecting to see one of our bombers. And you can imagine how we felt when we saw the 'rising sun' on the wings.

"I couldn't move, I was so surprised. Evidently the old devil saw us and came back to finish us off but in the meantime we had gone. In our back yard we found numerous pieces of shrapnel and several machine gun (sic) bullets, and one big bullet, the next thing to a small cannon. They were all near where we had been standing. One piece went through our roof and landed in the bedroom but we were saved any harm by my neighbor's husband who rushed home from his defense work to take us all to where we spent the first night. We then went to a Red Cross evacuation center where we stayed until we returned to our homes Wednesday night (December 10).

"We were treated royally and let me tell you that any contributions from any source at all that could be

> sent directly to the Hawaiian branch of the American Red Cross could be used to good advantage as they are doing wonderful work. They clothed us, fed us, and entertained us and the children [Mrs. Rowell was accompanied by her two children] at absolutely no expense, with trained nurses, and workers on hand at all times. They even arranged for us to send cablegrams. I am so grateful to them I can't express it in words but I shall, in every act possible, from money to donations of clothes, etc.

Mrs. Rowell's husband, Alexander, was a naval officer. Their children were Shirley, 12 and Thomas, 4. Excerpts from the letter appeared in *The Salem Evening News,* December 23, 1941, 1, 10.

APPENDIX III - NEWSPAPER ARTICLES AND COLUMNS

Story of the Crossing: '**Blackouts... Lifebelts... and 'Always Rumors... but Morale Was High to the End'**
By Will Williams

(Williams a Honolulu newspaperman for five years, arrived in San Francisco yesterday morning with the islands' first group of civilian evacuees. He wrote the following account of the crossing exclusively for The Chronicle.)

War-struck evacuees from Honolulu stood on decks of ships yesterday awaiting their first glimpse of land "somewhere in California."

A few minutes later San Francisco's Golden Gate loomed before them - they were "home."

With tear filled eyes, they cheered in unison and their voices rolled across the water as the ships slid in beneath the Golden Gate Bridge.

They had completed a crossing which contrasted grimly with the usual effervescent "Aloha" spirit of peacetime travel between Hawaii California.

There were only traces of luxury in the evacuation voyage. Passengers were given as little as two hours sailing notice. Departure of the vessels was shrouded in secrecy.

They were all one-fare crossings and everything was "first class" if you thought of it that way. The frills of luxury were stripped from the vessels.

They are being operated now by Uncle Sam; and there's no room for nonsense.

Daily fire and boat drills, life preservers, enforced sobriety, blackouts, self-service were new experiences for tourists used to the light-hearted journeys of peace time.

Passengers slept on steel cots.

Throngs jammed the mess hall lines. The first-class dining rooms of peace were mess halls on this voyage.

An 18-man blackout patrol was recruited from passenger volunteers. All radios and liquor were kept in the purser's office.

Passengers had no doubt they were refugees. Room stewards, waiters and ships' personnel did their best, however, and morale aboard the ships was high.

There was an undercurrent of tenseness, especially at early dawn and just after dusk, the times when submarine attacks were most likely. During daytime the ships zigzagged.

At night, blacked out, the ships raced through the dark ocean at breakneck speed.

The destination was unknown. No passenger knew where the ships would land. The Navy guaranteed only to put them on American soil.

Arrival and departure times are war secrets. But the secret was over when the Golden Gate loomed up over the dawn gray ocean.

Church services were held aboard ship Sunday morning.

The Star Spangled Banner was sung many times on the way over, and "California Here I Come." Quiet little groups talked politics.

There were hundreds of rumors with nothing to verify them. Ships' officers did not know or weren't telling anything.

Aboard were many Kamaiinan, [unclear?] island residents, heartbroken at having to leave their homes in Hawaii. People in Hawaii feel they're all ready for 'em the next time the Japanese torpedo planes pay a visit. Their morale is high. But some had to leave.

"There may be plenty of trouble in Hawaii," said one, "but I'm going back just as soon as there is a ship to take me. And I can shoot, too!"

Women and children made up most of the passenger lists, and many were wives and families of navy (sic) personnel.

Bedroom stewards had to work overtime getting hot bottles of milk and buckets of fresh water. For baths and showers only salt water was available.

The passengers were glad to see that Golden Gate open up. They had a rough crossing, and a dangerous one, but their spirits were still high.

They know that Uncle Sam's navy is still keeping the sea lanes open for Americans!

San Francisco Chronicle, January 1, 1942, p. 6

Women Volunteers Greet Evacuees

Long Lines of Automobiles Await Ships Arriving From Islands

By Hazel Holly

THE TELEPHONE RANG early yesterday; sleepily, woman (sic) all over San Francisco groped for the phone.

A voice said, "Nine-thirty." Nothing more – just the time. From then on, the women knew exactly what to do. Asmembers of the Navy Wives' Emergency Service, the American Women's Voluntary Services and the Red Cross, these women have the job of transporting evacuees from arriving ships to their hotels and other destinations.

They were on the Embarcadero before 9:30, long lines of automobiles, each with their windshield stickers. And then the women waited – waited while the ships nosed up to the piers, while hawsers were stretched taut, and they looked up at the faces looking down. The faces were those of men, women and children who, on the last day of 1941, arrived safe on the mainland from the islands of war.

THERE WAS ONE man; he is a druggist and his wife a nurse. They went to the islands on a pleasure cruise, and remained long enough to help care for the wounded Sunday, December 7.

"I'm still listening for planes," he said. As for the trip, "It was pretty nervous, but most people behaved well."

"The worst moment came once when a wave hit the ship and the dishes fell off the tables. Everyone thought it was a torpedo. No, you don't sleep much with a lifebelt for a pillow.

"But this morning, when we came under the Golden Gate Bridge, everybody on the ship cheered and cheered and cheered."

THE LINES MOVED down the gangplanks and the piles of baggage, including tricycles, toys, baby buggies and dunnage bags spread farther and farther. Cars drove up, took on passengers, and were whisked away by the military police.

It was a motley crowd: there were women in fur coats with paper leis around their necks; there were hatless women in slacks; there was one young widow who carried a tiny baby; she didn't know where she was going.

THEY WERE ALL so very tired, so very glad to be safe ashore, and so appreciative that San Francisco women had come down to meet them, and to take them wherever they wanted to go.

But above all, they were all so very patient: they stood in lines waiting for telephones, for transportation, for hot coffee.

And when they left you, they said, **"Thank you, and a Happy New Year."**

The San Francisco Examiner, January 1, 1942, p. 15.

Honolulu Waterfront, Festooned With Barbed Wire, Busy As Ever

But You'd Never Know The Old 'Front Now

Warpaint, Barricades Alter Appearance

By LaSelle Gilman

If you are the type that likes to go about holding up skulls and musing, "Alas, poor Yorick! I knew him ..." you might try an afternoon stroll along the waterfront of Honolulu harbor. Because the center of the Pacific Crossroads has radically changed since war began, and you'd hardly know the old place now.

This reference to skulls does not mean that the harbor is dead and buried. Far from it. There's as much or more shipping and cargo handled in the port today as at any time in its colorful, bustling history. It's merely incommunicado, incognito, and wearing false whiskers.

The changeover was more gradual on the waterfront than in the city itself. When Dec. 7 arrived, Honolulu suddenly turned inside out and people who'd gone to bed in peace and risen in war hardly knew, from the looks of things, where they were. But down on the 'front, the handwriting had been up on the wall for months, and though martial law and other developments made some rapid changes there, the habitués were prepared for them.

Ships Disappeared

For a long time before the Pearl Harbor attack the waterfront had been getting ready. First, of course, many ships that once called here called no more after the outbreak of war in Europe. Then a lot of strange and curiously-laden craft began putting in and out as America's transpacific lifelines were established and supplies began rolling to the Orient. Ships coming through from the Far East brought thousands of evacuees, and those from the Antipodes were laden with British airmen; a steady stream of freighters was pouring emergency defense supplies from the Coast into Hawaii.

There was more hush-hush about shipping as time went on; nobody officially knew the names or schedules of vessels. On the docks vast piles of cargo began to accumulate, for materials were being sent here so fast than consignees couldn't take care of them. There were warlike activities on Sand Island and in the channel; and around the wharves. Offshore stood the guardian naval patrols. Passengers coming in from the Mainland had things to say about the mounting tension, the trend towards war.

Then the evacuees from the Far East started a new rush, and the Japanese liners abruptly stopped calling here, and went home. The ominous signs became so frequent that they were commonplace. And then Dec. 7 rolled around.

No More Smells

Today (and don't choose tonight or you might get shot) if you wander along the 'front, you'll see the same wharves and the same blue water, the little launches and tugs, the piles of cargo on the docks and the customs and coast guard officers, the stevedores and truck-drivers and all the familiar sights you used to see, and you'll hear the familiar sounds.

But you won't, for instance, smell the familiar odors: those exotic aromas of strange Far Eastern cargoes are absent, because ships no longer come here from the Orient or the South Seas.

And you'll see a lot more trucking – the streams of great trucks, piled high, are endless. From pier 2 to pier 34 and beyond they're busy moving freight. Down under Aloha Tower the cargo is stacked in little mountains. As for Aloha Tower itself – that clock face on the mauka side is blacked out, and the tower looks like a couple of barrels of paint had been poured over it. Because everything along the 'front – wharves and warehouses and other buildings – is camouflaged.

Irwin Park is a labyrinth of slit-trenches and public air raid shelters. Approaches to the waterfront are guarded by substantial sandbag barricades and plenty of barbed wire, and such approaches are closed after dark. Fire-hoses are laid out in new little rain-shelters, constructed near hydrants for quick use in an emergency. Likewise the harbor now has a fire boat on duty. Under the old cannon at Fort and Queen is a barricade, which seems to give the cannon a new lease on life.

Ships In Slips

There are soldiers everywhere along the waterfront. Sentries guard the wharves and roads, special police are there too. You'll get your pass worn out by looking, if you go far enough.

The ships are in the slips, working cargo; the big booms creak and groan under the weight. It's a new kind of cargo. One ship is unloading 1,000-pound aerial bombs, another rolls of barbed wire. These are the grey, anonymous ships of the long Pacific convoys. All are disguised under grey paint, the big and the little freighters, the ships that seem to have a familiar line but that are hard to recognize now. The seamen are hard at work aboard, sentries stand at the gangways. The stevedores are busy. And there are almost as many armed guards as longshoremen.

Where are the people? Well, the people are still there – the longshoremen gang foremen, the dock officers, the customs men. The customs men don't have as much to do now as before, but they're on the job. The coast guardsmen have more to do than ever. The immigration men are rarely around the waterfront now – few people come in from foreign lands these days.

The harbor is under naval supervision and the Navy is much in evidence there – more so than ever before. The Navy keeps watch, and direct (sic) the movements of ships. Everything that moves is under control of the district captain of the port office. Castle & Cooke's passenger department is no more – it's closed for the duration, as are many other offices around the 'front, and all steamer transportation between here and the Mainland is handled by the services. Reservations, space assignments, notification when to embark – these have become military matters, under military control.

Travelers – evacuees perhaps – leaving Hawaii move in accord with grave military tactics and their safe journey is a military success. Travelers thus serve in silence, and so does everyone else remotely connected with shipping in Honolulu. Details of voyages are military secrets, the ships in convoy move as units in a military campaign, and no one sails without military approvals. Ship names and sailing dates are not discussed.

Still, the waterfront is there, as always, and will be for a long time to come – long after the war is won and sandbags and barbed wire have been dragged away.

The Honolulu Advertiser, March 31, 1942, p. 3

The Home Front
By Tom Treanor

San Francisco, March 5. The extent to which the cold eclipse of total war has cast its night upon Honolulu is not generally realized in Los Angeles.

Our ties to the islands are neither so close nor so strong as San Francisco's. The war still seems so far away that we tend to believe that even there it really hasn't happened.

An occasional story is all we see of Honolulu in Los Angeles and some of these stories sound as if war life were all a bit of a picnic.

They tell of dinner parties with the guests invited to stay jollily (sic) all night because of the 8 o'clock curfew. But they don't say that these parties are a rarity and that of all the gayety (sic) which was once Hawaii's only a shred remains – if a shred.

THE ISLANDS ARE at war today and it's tough, tiresome, grim and depressing.

The women and children are gone or going. It's still optional for the civilians to decide whether they'll return to the mainland but the trend is to go.

There's a food shortage possible. The diet already isn't the best for children. Nor is the nerve strain.

The trip back is an ordeal. When the last load came in, the mothers, some of them with three and four children, looked blank with fatigue, worry and confusion.

A 13-year-old boy said: "There were more kids aboard than there were rivets." And he was just about right.

It was miserably crowded. The weather was rotten. Nearly everybody was sick at the same time. There weren't enough stewards to clean things up promptly. Many people had colds.

BECAUSE SALT WATER was used in the pipes it couldn't be heated to avoid corrosion.

To get hot water the passengers had to fill a bucket and take it to a steam pipe. They would put the pipe in the bucket and the steam would squirt in and be absorbed, heating it up.

There was a milk shortage, even for the babies.

And yet – the workers generally agree on this – there were no complaints. The evacuees were tired and bewildered, but they were taking it as war.

They're not to be pitied. They're lucky. They've already made their adjustment to the long struggle ahead.

THE RED CROSS here has a Hawaiian unit to take care of the evacuees. All of the members are women who once lived in Hawaii.

Their duties don't end with making the first arrangements for the newcomers as to housing.

In the dreary days to follow they will help them make an adjustment to a new life, which is full of worry about the men they left behind, and empty of all the familiar joys of the islands.

The first step in this direction will be a luncheon Tuesday, to which all evacuees will be invited, and at which will be read a digest of all the news that comes by letters.

There will also be suggestions as to luxuries which can be shipped to the men left behind.

And the women will be reminded not to mail their letters in lined envelopes. The linings have to be X-rayed, causing trouble to the censors and delay to the letter.

ON OAHU, THE principal island, the beaches are now covered with barbed wire.

Movies only run until 4 o'clock in the afternoon. In restaurants and clubs the evening meal must be concluded before 6:30. he blackout must be complete, a terrible discomfort in Honolulu because of the climate.

Food has gone up in price. There is only one restaurant where meals can be had for approximately the prewar amount. But this restaurant has been forced to sacrifice in quality. It is open only from 11 a.m. to 3 p.m. and is jammed.

THE MEN OVER there are anxious for magazines, for any kind of reading matter.

The public library has been put on wheels to do what it can to fill the need for reading matter, but large shipments are needed from the mainland.

It's good to send flashlights also. They can be shipped but passengers to the islands can't take them over in their luggage. The authorities are taking no chances of lights being flashed out of portholes to submarines.

EVERY MAN BETWEEN 18 and 60 has been put to some kind of work. If he hasn't a civilian job, he is given some kind of emergency duties.

The houses along the beach, which belonged to the wealthy seasonal visitors from the mainland, such as Doris Duke, have mostly been evacuated.

The old-time residents with their big places in the mountains have doubled up, taking in guests from below.

MRS. CHARLES GREGORY, born in Hawaii, a member of one of the old families, says that the discipline and the hardships are welcomed by the people.

They look on them as a means to win the war. They want them for that reason and they accept them uncomplainingly.

They have met their problem and are doing their best to conquer it. In the case of Honolulu this is more than a slight transition.

There was probably never a place in the world where life was easier, more carefree and more beautiful.

It has suddenly become ugly but there are no complaints. The reason may be that Hawaiians have a real love for Hawaii. They are not confused between their love for Hawaii and their habits of luxury.

Los Angeles Times, March 6, 1942, p. A. ProQuest Information and Learning Company.

Honolulu War Diary

By Leselle Gilman

The early evacuees from Hawaii have been arriving at various west coast centers and spreading east across the Mainland, and as they go, reports spread with them of life in wartime Hawaii. Such reports are most frequent in California cities, of course, where many evacuees are concentrated, and the newspapers have given them considerable prominence. Eventually the newspapers get back to Hawaii, the reports with them, and a variety of them is on hand.

Los Angeles newspapers have paid much attention to these travelers, and Tom Treanor, Times columnist (The Home Front), devoted a recent column to them. Most of the reports given to the papers are credible and comparatively factual - it is only the occasional evacuee, apparently, who gives out with a loud cry in public places, exaggerating his or her "adventures" and hardships. The Army and Navy wives and the local civilians stick pretty much to the truth.

Mostly it's the same old story–the events of Dec. 7 rehashed, the gas rationing, "fifth columnists," gas masks, defense work, raid shelters, food supplies, blackouts, shortened business hours. "It's an interesting place to be in just now," said one, "but Hawaii's no place to go for a vacation, even if you could."

A San Francisco headline: "Hawaii Paying 90 Cents for Dozen Eggs."

Of most interest in these clippings to us in Hawaii are the reports on the "trip back." According to Treanor's various interviews: it's an ordeal, and the travelers arrived "blank with fatigue, worry and confusion." Children predominated, the ships were crowded, the weather bad, most everyone had been seasick, there weren't enough stewards, most passengers had colds because of lack of steam heat aboard. "To get hot water the passengers had to fill a bucket and take it to a steam pipe. They would put the pipe in the bucket and the steam would squirt in and be absorbed, heating it up."

There was a milk shortage for the babies, he said. (Another traveler who left "on a British boat" said the ship hadn't been prepared for evacuees and hadn't restocked supplies in Honolulu, and no special baby food except English condensed and sweetened milk.) Passengers were eight to the cabin, husbands and wives separated. Ships, of course, traveled in convoys. One evacuee said their former liner, now a transport, could carry 2,600 passengers; bunks were taken out and hammocks hung; drinking water was rationed, bathing was in sea water.

"The Islands are at war today and it is tough, tiresome, grim and depressing," wrote Treanor. "...And yet there were no complaints. The evacuees were tired and bewildered, but they were

taking it as war. They're not to be pitied. They're lucky. They've already made their adjustment to the long struggle ahead..."

Evacuees said Honolulu shortages included magazines and flashlights. They were glad to meet the Red Cross Hawaiian unit, and after they got to the Coast they spent a lot of time getting together among themselves and wishing they were back in the Islands again.

"The discipline and hardships are welcomed by the people," Treanor quoted one kamaaina evacuee as saying. "They look on them as means to win the war. They want them for that reason and they accept them uncomplainingly. They have met their problem and they are doing their best to conquer it. In the case of Honolulu this is more than a slight transition. There was probably never a place in the world where life was easier, more carefree and more beautiful [several words had been omitted and phrases repeated; the sentence above is directly from Treanor's piece]. It has suddenly become ugly but there are no complaints. The reason may be that Hawaiians have a real love for Hawaii. They are not confused between their love of Hawaii and their habits of luxury."

Another West Coast columnist, Chapin Hall, looked over a recent edition of the Honolulu Advertiser and reported on it for his readers, pointing to the changes in Honolulu life which its columns reflect (evacuation mauka (sic), curfew, blackout, no tourists, censorship, high food prices, changes at Waikiki, bomb shelters, high rents, etc.)

"It obviously is not the Hawaii of yesterday," says Hall, but the Islands will come back, and so will the thousands of yearly visitors who once fell such willing victims to their charm."

The Honolulu Advertiser, April 4, 1942, p. 8

NAVY WIVES

By Helen Lamar

I have so much to write and I can't find a quiet spot in the entire building. Every room, every available space hums with activity. I am to have an office, but everyone is so busy there is scarcely a moment left for the janitor to make a room ready. I went to the assembly room first. It was early and not many men were in yet. But there I found a band preparing to practice. I sought the lounge. Here tables and chairs were piled higgledy- piggledy while a Chinese man swept up the debris of pop-corn cartons and yesterday's newspapers. (Men are so untidy.) I looked for an unused class-room. They were all busy, one had luncheon tables set up. Then I thought of the Chaplain's office. Perhaps he'd give me a corner.

It was there the war walked up and faced me squarely. I'll never forget what I saw in the Chaplain's office or outside the Chaplain's door. I'd like to call it the "March of the Pregnant Women." There they were lined up and waiting their turn to see the Chaplain about transportation home. Navy wives – with husbands gone, they had no idea where. They had heard no word for months, some of them. Their thoughts were mostly on home – home being the Mainland with their homefolks. Most of them had babies by the hand. I saw some little girls with soft flaxen ringlets clinging to their necks, little girls with no fear in their eyes – only trust that everything was all right with the world. The mothers didn't look very old either. Why does nature choose youth for the period of procreation? These girls had problems too big for them.

The Honolulu Advertiser, April 16, 1942, p. 10.

NOTES

1 *"Pandas: A Rare Gift is Sent...," San Francisco Chronicle*, December 27, 1941, 7.

2 Ruth Erickson telephone interviews, March 24, 30, April 6 and 12, 1994. Interviewed by Jan K. Herman, Office of the Historian, Bureau of Medicine and Surgery, U.S. Navy, Washington, DC.;
Pearl Harbor Survivors, John H. McGoran, http://pearlharborsurvivors.homestead.com/McGoran2.html.
"The Wounded Return," *Time Magazine*, 5 January 1942, 15, 32; John U. Terrell, "War Comes to the Coast," *San Francisco Chronicle*, December 26, 1941, 1B.

3 This quote is from a newspaper clipping dated January 10, 1942 in the possession of Phyllis Hansell, the daughter of Doris' sister, Elsie (Huntress) Berman. A search of all Boston, Lynn, Salem, and Haverhill newspapers at the Boston Public Library for the month of January 1942 failed to find which newspaper this clipping came from.

4 "Mrs. Toner Piled Pillows," *Boston Daily Globe*, January 7, 1942, 17; and Martha Toner phone interview, July 12, 2006.

5 David Downing. *Sealing Their Fate: The Twenty-Two Days That Decided World War II.* (Cambridge, MA: DeCapo, 2009), 172.

6 Ibid., 203.

7 Prange, et. al. *December 7*, 84–86.

8 Ibid.

9 Ibid., 93.

10 Gordon W. Prange, et. al. *December 7, 1941 The Day The Japanese Attacked Pearl Harbor* (New York: McGraw-Hill, 1988), 115.

11 Prange, et. al., *December* 7, 138.

12 Ibid., 140.

13 "Mrs. Marze, Widow of Pearl Harbor Victim, Returns to Live Here," *The Salem Evening News,* January 8, 1942, 4.

14 Ibid., 88.

15 The USS *Pennsylvania* Report of Pearl Harbor Attack. Department of the Navy, Naval History and Heritage Command website: http://www.history.navy.mil/docs/wwii/pearl/ph66.htm. The Report indicates the attack on the *Pennsylvania* was by high-level bombers flying at 10,000 to 12,000 feet. Prange describes the plane hitting the ship as a dive-bomber. See: Prange, *December 7,* 265.

16 Naval History and Heritage Command website: http://www.history.navy.mil/faqs/faq66–1.htm

17 George H. Lewis. "Beyond the Reef: Cultural Constructions of Hawaii in Mainland American, Australia and Japan," *Journal of Popular Culture* (Fall 1996), v. 30 (2). Online. http://proquest.umi.com.ezproxy.bucknell.edu/pqdweb?did=11323278&sid=1&Fmt=4&clientId=16987&RQT=309&VName=PQD

18 Beth L. Bailey and David Farber. *The First Strange Place: Race and Sex in World War II Hawaii* (Baltimore: Johns Hopkins University Press, 1994), 26.

19 Ed Sheehan. *Days of '41: Pearl Harbor Remembered* (Honolulu: Kapa Associates, Ltd. 1977), 37–38

20 Beverly Moglich, email message, August 14, 2001.

21 Joan Zuber Earle. *The Children of Battleship Row: Pearl Harbor 1940–41* (Oakland: RDR Books, 2002), 9–11.

22 Ibid., 14.

23 *Martial Law in Hawaii: Papers of Major General Thomas H. Green,* December 7, 1941- April 4, 1943 [online]. Chapter II, "Background." Unpublished manuscript. Library of Congress (OCLC Number 461333055). http://www.loc.gov/rr/frd/Military_Law/Martial-Law-Hawaii_Green.html Hereafter referred to as Green Online. Also available as *Martial Law in Hawaii: Papers of Major General Thomas H. Green* [microfilm]. (Bethesda, MD: University Publications of America, 2003). U.S. Army Military History Institute (USAMHI), Carlisle, Pa. (Green Papers). These papers also include ancillary works, including Green's daily diary for 1942 (Green Diary).

24 Prange, et.al., *Verdict,* 25–26.

The following anecdote illustrates how widespread the opposition to American policy was. My uncle (born 1923) and his grandfather were visiting his grandmother on December 7. When news of the attack came on the radio, my uncle's grandfather said, "I told you! I told you! I told you! That goddam Harry Collier selling scrap metal to the Japs." Collier owned a scrap metal yard in Salem, Mass., and evidently my great-grandfather believed he sold some of his material to the Japanese. My great-grandfather pointed to my uncle and said: "It's going to come back in bullets to you. One of them with your initials." John Lee, interview June 24, 2011.

25 Green online, Chapter IV, "Early Planning and the M Day Bill."

26 Joe Lockard interviews, 2007–2010.

27 "Antithetical to American interests," Gerald E. Wheeler. *Prelude to Pearl Harbor: The United States Navy and the Far East, 1921–31* (Columbia: University of Missouri Press, 1963), xii; "counter Japanese intentions," Samuel Eliot Morison. *History of United States Naval Operations in World War II. v.3 The Rising Sun in the Pacific. 1931-April 1942* (Boston: Little, Brown, 1948), 38; "back to Atlantic fleet," Gordon W. Prange, et. al. *The Verdict of History: Pearl Harbor* (New York: Penguin Books, 1991) 105; "over the objection," Edward S. Miller. *War Plan Orange: The U.S. Strategy to Defeat Japan. 1897–1945* (Annapolis: Naval Institute Press, 1991), 51; and Morison, 43; "This move," George C. Dyer, ed. *On the Treadmill to Pearl Harbor: The Memoirs of Admiral James O. Richardson, USN* (Washington, D.C.: Department of the Navy, 1973), 330; "difficult to defend," Prange, et. al., *Verdict,* 113; "Kimmel named," Prange, *At Dawn We Slept: The Untold Story of Pearl Harbor* (New York: McGraw-Hill, 1981), 52; and "despite protests," Morison, 47; and Homer N. Wallin. *Pearl Harbor: Why, How, Fleet Salvage and Final Appraisal* (Washington, D.C.: Naval History Division, 1968), 41–2.

28 Prange, et. al., *Verdict.*, 502.

29 "Increase the size," Donald W. Mitchell. *History of the Modern American Navy, From 1883 Through Pearl Harbor* (New York: Alfred A. Knopf, 1946), 379; and "Navy Language School," Morison, 30.

30 Morison, 47.

31 Dyer, ed., 328.

32 "Tough egg," Robert C. Lee, interview, August 10, 2001; "favorite uncle," Theresa Fichtor, phone interview, September 22, 2001; and "swell fellow," Llewellyn Huntress, letter fragment, no date, copy provided by Phyllis Hansell.

33 Roger E. Jones, ed. *History of the USS Phelps (DD-360); 1936–1945* (Annapolis, Md: United States Naval Institute, 1953), 35 (passim).

34 Details from Reverebeach.com.

35 Bob Upton, email message, July 1, 2004.

36 Passenger Lists of Vessels Arriving in Honolulu, 1900–1953, (microfilm), Roll 214, December 11, 1939 – January 17, 1940, Records of the Immigration and Naturalization Service, 1891–1957, Record Group 85 (RG 85), National Archives, Washington, D.C. (NADC).

37 Muster Rolls of Ship and Shore Establishments, Muster Rolls, 1860–1956, (microfilm) Reel #1358, Box 114, USS Dobbin, Records of the Bureau of Naval Personnel, Record Group 24 (RG 24), National Archives, College Park, Maryland (NACP).

38 The Seattle Public Library, utilizing *Polk-Husted Directories for Honolulu and Territory of Hawaii 1940–41* and 1941–42, confirms that Andrew Marze lived at 1653 N. King Street, Honolulu. As per phone conversation July 7, 2004. See also: *Building the Navy's Bases,* 136.

39 Pat Thompson, "A Day to Remember," unpublished manuscript. Also, interviews 2007–2010.

40 *Building the Navy's Bases in World War II,* v. II (Washington, D.C.: U.S.G.P.O., 1947), 136. Also, Pat Thompson email message, May 25, 2007.

41 Eugenia Mandelkorn, "View from Our Window," *Shipmate,* December 10, 1966, pp. 12–17. Also, interviews 2007–2009.

42 Mary Jo Hammett, "Pearl Harbor Memories." Unpublished manuscript.

43 Rents were so low, in fact, that Willie Jarvis' parents bought a small house in 1939 about three blocks from the beach near Royal Hawaiian Hotel for only $1200. Jarvis was 16 at the time of the bombing and father was in the Navy. Jarvis phone interview, May 29, 2007.

44 Sheehan, 22.

45 Ibid., 26, 31.

46 Ibid., 34 (passim).

47 The course of the S.S. *Coolidge* and details of events aboard ship during the crossing come from: S.S. *President Coolidge,* Deck Log Book, November 24, 1941 to December 24, 1941, and December 25, 1941 to January 8, 1942, Guide to APL Records, 1871–1995, National Park Service, San Francisco Maritime National Historical Park (SFMNHP), San Francisco, California. I am much indebted

to Edward LeBlanc, Archivist Specialist, Ted Miles, Reference Librarian, and William Kooiman, Reference Librarian, retired.

48 Information regarding the S.S. *Coolidge* comes from Stone, *The Lady and the President.*

49 The convoy to Manila docked on November 20, 1941. The *Louisville* spent several days in port taking on fresh water and other supplies. Then on the 25th she sailed to Tarakan, Borneo under CinPac orders. The *Louisville* refueled in Tarakan. See: Deck Logs of the U.S.S. *Louisville,* October to December, 1941, RG 24, NACP.

50 Lockard interviews. Also see: Joseph Lockard, "The SCR-270-B on Oahu, Hawaii, Reminiscences," *IEEE Aerospace and Electronic Systems Magazine,* no. 12 (December 1991), 8–9.

51 Thompson, "A Day to Remember," and interviews.

52 Hammett, "Pearl Harbor Memories."

53 Mandelkorn, "View from Our Window," and interviews.

54 Green online. Chapter IX, "The Blitz."

55 Hammett.

56 "Refugees from Hawaii Reach Pittsburgh Haven," *Pittsburgh Post-Gazette,* January 5, 1942.

57 "Pittsburgh Women Describe Jap Attack," *Pittsburgh Post-Gazette,* December 29, 1941, 9.

58 "Mrs Toner Piled Pillows," *The Boston Daily Globe,* January 7, 1942; and phone interview with the author, July 12, 2006.

59 Pat Thompson, "A Day to Remember," unpublished manuscript.

60 "Flier, Shot Down, Resumed Battle," *New York Times,* December 31, 1941, 5.

61 Gordon Lavering, phone interview, August 9, 2007; and email July 12, 2010.

62 From an excerpt of Carmel Rothlin's diary provided by Lee Anne Auerhan, her daughter.

63 See: Rosalie Everson, "Lasting Memories: Pearl Harbor nurse recalls eerie quiet, chaos of Dec 7 attack," *Fort Lupton (Co) Press,* Jan. 5, 2010. Web. www.ftluptonpress.com. Also see: www.womenofworldwariihawaii.com/2009/04/black-out-babies. Web. Accessed Sep 29, 2011. No longer accessible.

64 In her diary Rothlin describes him as a member of 'the legion of honor.' I have made the assumption that she meant the Territorial Guard, which was in large part made up of Japanese-Americans

from the University of Hawaii ROTC program. It was called out to duty on December 7th. The following month the military government disbanded it.

65 L.S. Sabin, "Rising Suns Over Pearl," *Shipmate* (December 1966), Vol. 29, No. 10, 7. Many thanks to Peter Fullinwider for presenting me with a copy of this publication.

66 Everett Hyland, phone interview, December 20, 2006.

67 Archie Satterfield. *The Day the War Began* (Westport, CT: Praeger, 1992), 31.

68 Art Wells email interview, Aug. 10, 2006.

69 USS *Dobbin*, Report of Pearl Harbor Attack, Naval History and Heritage Command, http://www.history.navy.mil/docs/wwii/pearl/ph39.htm.

70 Jeffrey Maner, telephone interview, December 13, 2005; Burton Williams, Oral History Interview, Pearl Harbor Navy Base archives, 4.

71 Green Online, Chapter IX, "The Blitz."

72 Hammett.

73 See the Green Papers, which provide a log of police calls during the night of December 8, for example.

74 Rosalie Hutchison Smith phone interviews, March 28, 31, and May 15, 2006.

75 U.S.S. *Louisville* Deck Logs do not show depth charges being released during this crossing. The cruiser did engage in anti-aircraft gunnery practice after December 7. It is possible that this is what Rosalie heard.

76 "Husband of Salem Girl Killed in Action During Jap Attack on Hawaii," *The Salem Evening News*, December 20, 1942, 1, 5.

77 From unknown newspaper (see note #3 above), January 10, 1942.

78 "Husband of Salem Girl," 1.

79 "One of the first things," Gwenfread Allen. *Hawaii's War Years*, (Honolulu: University of Hawaii Press, 1950), 35; "agreeing to martial law," Warner Gardner to Harold Ickes, December 10, 1942, qtd. in J. Garner Anthony. *Hawaii Under Army Rule*, (Stanford: Stanford University Press, 1955), 26, and "president responded," *Ibid.*, 127–28.

80 "Discussed the possibility," Mabel Boardman, Secretary of the American Red Cross to General Marshall, April 29, 1941, and Marshall to Boardman, April 30, 1941, The Papers of George C. Marshall [microfilm]: Selected World War II Correspondence.

Bethesda, MD: University Publications of America, 1992, reel 31; US Army Military History Institute (USAMHI), Carlisle, Pa.; "advisory board," Governor Poindexter to Admiral Bloch, October 22, 1941, Commandant's Coded Administrative Records, Records of the Naval Districts and Shore Establishments, Record Group 181 (RG 181),12th Naval District, Mare Island, San Francisco (ND 12), National Archives, San Francisco (NASF); and "his telephone operators," Scott to General Kimmel, December 5, 1941, RG 181, ND 12, NASF.

81 "Surveyed homes," Office of Civilian Defense (OCD), Evacuation Division reports – Oahu 1942, Progress Report Territorial Office of Civilian Defense, April 1942, 16, Hawaii State Archives (HSA); see also: "Hawaii: Excerpts from a Supplement to Locality Report for Period December 21, 1941-January 10, 1942," p.2, Red Cross Central File 1935–46 (Group 3) (Red Cross File), Record Group 200 (RG 200), National Archives, College Park, MD (NACP); see: "3,000 Civilians Moved By Hawaii Red Cross," *The Honolulu Advertiser*, December 14, 1941, 6.

82 Green Papers, Reel 11, Folder 2.

83 Qtd. in Gwenfread Allen, 35.

84 Ibid., 153.

85 "Supply Department Activities," 7 December, 1941 to 1 January 1942, WD 14, RG 38, NACP. See: Harold Larson. *Water Transportation for the United States Army 1939–1942*, Monograph No. 5. Historical Unit, Office of the Chief of Transportation, Army Service Force, August 1944, pp. 175–76.

86 Roosevelt to Stimson, December 8, 1941, cited in Chester Wardlow. *The U.S. Army in World War II. The Technical Services. The Transportation Corps: Responsibilities Organization, and Operations* (Washington, DC: Office of the Chief of Military History, United States Army, 1951), 44. The board was comprised of the Chairman of the Maritime Commission, the Army Chief of Staff, the Chief of Naval Operations, and Roosevelt's personal representative, Harry Hopkins.

87 *The Public Papers and Addresses of Franklin D. Roosevelt: vol. X The Call to Battle Stations 1941* (New York: Russell & Russell, 1969), 567.

88 *Ibid.*, 585–86.

89 Arrangements for Evacuation to the Mainland, Evacuees, Records of U.S. Army Forces in the Middle Pacific (World War II) (AFMP),

Records of U.S. Army Forces in the Middle Pacific, 1939–47, Record Group 494 (RG 494), NACP.

90 Gerald E. Wheeler. *Kinkaid of the Seventh Fleet: A Biography of Admiral Thomas C. Kinkaid, U.S. Navy* (Annapolis: Naval Institute Press, 1996), 136, 138.

91 Prange, *At Dawn*, 584

92 "on the mainland," COM 11 to COM 14, December 8, 1941; and "early date," OPNAV to CINCPAC, COM 14, December 8, 1941, WWII War Diaries (WD), Cinclant Nov-Dec 1945 to Cincpac Mar 1942, Brief of War Diaries, 8 December, 1941 and January 1942, Commander in Chief Pacific Fleet (WD CincPac), Records of Office of Chief of Naval Operations (CNO), Record Group 38 (RG 38), NACP.

93 B. Mitchell Simpson III. *Admiral Harold. R. Stark: Architect of Victory, 1939–1945* (Columbia, SC: University of South Carolina Press, 1989), 133. Stark noted in his Diary that Kewpie (Katherine's nickname) arrived home January 1st. See: *Papers of Admiral Harold R. Stark, Series II – Diaries & Journals*, Diary 1941–42, January 1, 1942, Operations Archives, Naval Historical Center (NHC), Washington, D.C.

94 "probable invasion," OPNAV to CINCPAC, December 10, 1941; and "Solace to West Coast," CINCPAC to OPNAV, December 11, 1941, WD CincPac, CNO, RG 38, NACP.

95 Peter Stone. *The Lady and the President: The Life and Loss of the S.S. President Coolidge* (Victoria, Australia: Oceans Enterprises, 1999), 29.

96 "In a tiffany box," John Kennedy Ohl. *Supplying the Troops: General Somervell and American Logistics in WWII* (DeKalb: Northern Illinois University Press, 1994), 11, 12; and "do the impossible," *These Are the Generals* (New York: Alfred Knopf, 1943), 183.

97 See: Larson, 161 and 175. However late from the Army's point of view, by December 18, three convoys were at sea (the one from Honolulu and the two from San Francisco), totaling at least 14 ships escorted by nine destroyers or light cruisers. By the end of December four more convoys, made up of 25 transports and nine Navy escorts, two heading eastward two westward, would cross the Pacific between Honolulu and San Francisco. Eventually the two services worked out their differences, and convoys from the West Coast to Hawaii settled into a pattern of about one every six days. See: Larson, 161.

98 WD CincPac, RG 38, NACP.

99 Larson, 153.

100 Ibid., 148–49 and 153.

101 See Joseph Bykofsky and Harold Larson. *The U.S. Army in World War II. The Technical Services. The Transportation Corps: Operations Overseas* (Washington, DC: Center of Military History, United States Army, 2003), 491, 492.

102 Ibid., 157.

103 Ibid., 493, 494.

104 OPNAV TO COM 14, December 12, 1941, WD CincPac, RG 38, NACP.

105 CINCPAC TO COM 14, January 3, 1942, War Diaries of the 14th Naval District (WD 14), War Diaries for the Months of January and February 1942, RG 38, NACP.

106 "Desire authorization," Colonel Phillips, Chief of Staff, Hawaiian Division, to Major Sexton for General Marshall, December 8, 1941, Operations Division, Hawaii Dept, Records of the War Department, General and Special Staffs, Record Group 165 (RG 165), NACP; "immediately start," Bloch to Kimmel, December 15, 1941, ND 12, RG 181, NASF; and "starting the evacuation," Marshall to Winn, December 16, 1941, Bland and Stevens, eds. *The Papers of George Catlett Marshall: vol. 3: "The Right Man for the Job, December 7, 1941-May 31, 1943"* (Baltimore: Johns Hopkins U. Press, 1991), 21.

107 Green Online, Chapter XI, Emergency Measures During First Ten Days.

108 "Ran the show," Green Diary, March 14, 1942; and "ourselves infallible," Green Diary, May 3, 1942, Reel 4, Folder 1.

109 "Green didn't like him," Green Diary, February 9, 1941, October 1, 1941; and "a legal basis," Gwenfread Allen, 166.

110 "A friend," Green Diary, April 9, 1942; and "see things their way," Green Diary, October 1, 1942.

111 Much information from Frucht's obituary, "Capt. Max Frucht Taken by Death," *San Diego Union*, May 11, 1951, A-10, and from Navy Department Press Release, July 17, 1941, Operational Archives, Naval Historical Center (NHC), Washington, D.C.

112 *The Honolulu Advertiser*, January 5, 1942, 1; January 15, 1942, 3; and January 31, 1942, 1.

113 Rear Admiral Yates Stirling, "Oahu Invasion Held Possible," *The Honolulu Advertiser*, February 22, 1942, 1.

114 COM 14 to OPNAV, January and February, 1942, WD 14, p. 4, RG 38, NACP.

115 Peggy Hughes Ryan, "A Navy Bride Learns to Cope," *Air Raid: Pearl Harbor!: Recollections of a Day of Infamy,* Paul Stillwell, ed. (Annapolis: Naval Institute Press, 1981), 234.

116 "Ration of beer," Ellenmerle Heiges interview, August 14, 2005; "silver buses," Laselle Gilman, "Honolulu War Diary," *The Honolulu Advertiser,* December 31, 1941, 10; and "dull under martial law," Gilman, "Honolulu's Once Gay Night Life Flickered Out With the Lights!" *The Honolulu Advertiser,* February 1, 1942, 1.

117 William M. Tuttle. *Daddy's Gone to War: The Second World War in the Lives of America's Children* (New York and Oxford: Oxford University Press, 1993), 8.

118 The Diary of Lt. J.W. Leverton (Leverton Diary), Papers of Rear Admiral Joseph W. Leverton, Naval Historical Center (NHC), Washington, D.C.

119 Gail Moul, telephone interview, December 23, 2006.

120 Nancy (Walbridge) Herzog, telephone interview, December 9, 2001.

121 Wilbur D. Jones, Jr. and Carroll Robbins Jones. *Hawaii Goes to War: The Aftermath of Pearl Harbor* (Shippensburg, PA: White Mane Books, 2001), 38.

122 Unpublished manuscript by Gordon Lavering and telephone interview, August 9, 2007.

123 "Experiences in Pearl Harbor Attack are Told by Refugees," *Oakland Tribune,* December 26, 1941, 16.

124 "Café Owner Sentenced to Five Years," *The Honolulu Advertiser,* January 4, 1942, 1, 10; and "Café Owners Draw Prison Terms, Fines," *The Honolulu Advertiser,* January 27, 1942, 1.

125 "Provost Court Meets in Country Districts," *The Honolulu Advertiser,* January 17, 1942, 5.

126 Senator Daniel Inouye, email interview, April 20, 2006.

127 "Defense Workers Get Stiff Sentences," *The Honolulu Advertiser,* January 15, 1942, 12; "Physician on Case Fined for Speeding," *The Honolulu Advertiser,* February 11, 1942, 3; and "Duke Reports Jail Filled to Overflowing," *The Honolulu Advertiser,* March 12, 1942, 1.

128 "Yankees Ask DiMaggio to Play for '41 Salary," *The Honolulu Advertiser,* March 6, 1942, 6.

129 "Well, Palooka and Joe Louis Aren't Kicking," *The Honolulu Advertiser*, March 7, 1942, 3.

130 "Williams to Enlist In Army is Boston Rumor," *The Honolulu Advertiser*, March 5, 1942, 8; and "Ted Wants 1 More Year," *The Honolulu Advertiser*, March 6, 1942, 6. The *Boston Post* ran a cartoon in the January 7, 1942 issue with the title "Teddy is Ready," showing two images of Williams, one holding his bat like a rifle and the other showing him in military uniform sighting down the barrel of a rifle. Two quotes in the cartoon say, "If Ted Williams is called to the colors he will make a mighty fine soldier!" attributed to Joe Cronin, and the other says "If Uncle Sam gives Ted a uniform th' guy'll certainly be dressed to kill." Two days later *Boston Herald* ran a front-page story saying Williams had passed his Army physical. See *Boston Herald*, January 9, 1942, 1.

131 "FDR Includes Sports in All Out War Effort," *The Honolulu Advertiser*, March 11, 1942, 8; and Red McQueen, "Hank Greenberg Predicts Tough, Hard, Long War," *The Honolulu Advertiser*, April 28, 1942, 6.

132 Shirley McKay Hadley, phone interview, May 24, 2010. Much of the information regarding the Willamette football teams comes from Pearl Harbor Game Collection, Willamette University Archives, University Archives and Special Collections. I am much indebted to Mary McKay, University Archivist.

133 Ken Jacobson, phone interview, May 28, 2010.

134 Bailey, 95, 109, and 112.

135 Green Papers, Provost Courts, Reel 1, Folder 4, Item 2

136 Green Diary, January 14, 1942.

137 "Not beaten up," Green Diary, January 25, 1942; "who are we?" May 2, 1942; "Oriental philosophy," March 4, 1942; and "permit the police," July 13, 1942.

138 Green Diary, July, 5, 9, and 13, 1942, and May 7, 1942. Corregidor, an island bastion in Manila Harbor, fell on May 6, 1942. The loss of Corregidor marked the fall of The Philippines.

139 Prostitutes to Green, September 9, 1942, Green Papers, Reel 1, Folder, 4, Item 3; and Green Diary, September 2, 1942.

140 Bailey, 124.

141 See: "Hawaii Social Workers Discuss War's Influences on Community," *Honolulu Advertiser*, April 12, 1942, 1, 13.

142 Laselle Gilman, "Honolulu War Diary," *The Honolulu Advertiser*, February 14, 1942, 10.

143 Erickson telephone interviews, March 24, 30, April 6 and 12, 1994.

144 Stone, 42, 43, and 195.

145 Exact figures are hard to come by. A Red Cross official gave a total of 858 passengers for the *Scott* and *Coolidge*. See: Harry Walden, Director Military and Naval Welfare Service, ARC Pacific Branch to Don C. Smith, Director Military and Naval Welfare Service, ARC, Washington, D.C., Jan. 12, 1942, Red Cross File. Two days earlier Walden had sent Smith a figure of 869.

146 The *Detroit* and *Cummings* would escort the convoy all the way to San Francisco, while the *Reid* accompanied them 500 miles out from Honolulu. WD14, RG 38, p. 86, NACP. Other ships may have been in this convoy for at least part of the crossing. The S.S. *Ramapo* and *Lake Francis* left Honolulu later that afternoon for the "Pacific Coast", while the *Montgomery City*, USAT *Irvin L. Hunt* and the *Mapele*, which had just arrived from New Zealand on the 18th, left the next day. Also leaving on the 18th were two ships bound for the "Pacific Coast" from Hilo. This would explain an observation by Nurse Erickson, who said there were "8 or 10 ships in the convoy." These other ships carried typical cargoes such as sugar, molasses, pineapples and cane to the West Coast, just as they had in pre-war days, but only the *Scott* and *Coolidge* arrived together at the Embarcadero on December 25. Port Director's Report, December 1941, p. 34, WD 14, RG 38, NACP; Randolph Sevier to Green, February 18, 1942; and Cargo and Passenger Control Report to Office of Military Governor, January 1 to June 30, 1942. Green Papers, Reel 2, Folder 4.

147 John H. McGoran memoir, http://pearlharborsurvivors.homestead.com/McGoran2.html

148 See: http://www.ssmaritime.com/malolo-matsonia.htm

149 "Its new career," OPNAV to CINCPAC and COM14, December 8, 1941, December Brief, p. 24, WD 14, RG 38, NACP; and "ahead of schedule," *San Francisco Examiner*, December 11, 1941, 5.

150 Gordon Lavering, unpublished manuscript, received August 13, 2007, and email August 20, 2007.

151 John O'Neill to author, email message, November 24, 2003.

152 "Convoy was back," St. Louis Deck Logs, p. 2556, RG 24, NACP; "were painted gray," Earle, 88; "reinforcements...correspondents," Joseph C. Harsch, "A War Correspondent's Odyssey," in *Air Raid: Pearl Harbor! Recollections of a Day of Infamy,* ed. Paul Stillwell (Annapolis: Naval Institute Press, 1981), 265; "workmen to help," War Diaries December 7–31, 1941, p. 23, WD 14, RG 38, NACP.

153 "Without any beds," Frucht to Bloch, December 22, 1941, ND 14, RG 181, NASF; "start boarding passengers," Frucht to Castle & Cooke, December 24, 1941, ND 14, RG 181, NASF.

154 Earle, 88, 89.

155 "Turkey in the bag," Dwight Agnew, phone interview, July 28, 2006.

156 Questions do arise from Mrs. Mandelkorn's recollections. In an email message dated August 12, 2007, Mrs. Mandelkorn identifies the friend as Mary Spear, whose husband, a submariner, was killed later in the war. I can find no reference to a Spear with a wife named Mary on the World War II casualty list maintained by the National Archives. It is possible that over the course of 60 years she may have confused that name with someone else's. Curiously, in a story written for *Shipmate* magazine in the 1950s, Mrs. Mandelkorn relates to the reader her actions during the bombing and the days thereafter, and mentions her friend Mary Bronson and five-year-old son Bobby, with whom she later was evacuated. Could she be mixing the two? At any rate, Mrs. Mandelkorn's descriptions of life aboard ship during the crossing and on the mainland upon arrival do ring true.

157 Earle, 91, 92.

158 Ibid., 92

159 Ibid, 92–94.

160 Log Books of the U.S.S. *St. Louis* (*St. Louis* Deck Logs), October 1, 1941 to May 31, 1942, pp. 2275, 2572, 2589, Records of the Bureau of Naval Personnel, Record Group 24, (RG 24), NACP.

161 Mandelkorn, email message, August 17, 2007.

162 Earle, 94

163 "One of three locations," Bloch to Commander in Chief, U.S. Fleet, December 23, 1941; "to relieve the pressure," Frucht to Commandant 14th· December 31, 1942, ND 12 RG 181, NASF. See also "Wounded Will be Evacuated," *The Honolulu Advertiser,* December 17, 1941, 1.

164 "Ordered all dependents," Bloch to Kimmel, December 23, 1941, ND 12 RG 181, NASF; and "contradictory orders," Gwenfread Allen, 167.

Allen gives a sense of the complexity of the evacuation process in a paragraph noting the different agencies and their responsibilities:

The evacuation unit of the Office of Civilian Defense consulted with the Army on policies; the Mainland evacuation unit of the territorial department of public welfare investigated each application and recommended priorities; the Army Transport Service made final determination of priorities and handled the actual sailings; the transpacific travel control bureau of the Office of the Military Governor was charged with maintaining control and surveillance over persons going to or from the Islands, and worked in cooperation with the Office of Military Intelligence, Office of Naval Intelligence, and the FBI; the Red Cross arranged for social workers to accompany the ships, and for the reception of evacuees in Mainland ports, and the Federal Social Security Board provided financial assistance. Later, an office of Island resident return was established in the Office of Civilian Defense to assist in setting priorities for returning evacuees. See: Gwenfread Allen, 108.

165 A.J. Pessel, General Passenger Agent for Castle & Cooke, to Frucht, December 30, 1941, and Bloch to Pessel, January 12, 1942, ND 12, RG 181, NASF.

166 Military Governor's Office to Green, December 30, 1941, AFMP, RG 494, NACP.

167 Butler to Barrett, December 30, 1941, ND 12, RG 181, NASF.

168 Roy Allen, *The Pan Am Clipper: the History of the Pan American Flying-Boats, 1931 to 1946* (New York: Barnes and Noble, 2000), 57, 59 and 87. The figure for the present-day dollar equivalent is http://www.dollartimes.com/calculators/inflation.htm.

169 See Roy Allen, 100–101; and "Clipper's Detour from War in the Pacific Brings it Home after 31,500 Miles," *The Pittsburgh Press*, January 8, 1942, 17.

170 Roy Allen, 100.

171 "Huge Clipper, Strafed by Japs, Safe in S.F.," *The San Francisco Examiner*, December 11, 1941, B.

172 "3rd Clipper Reaches S.F. From War Zone," *The San Francisco Examiner*, December 15, 1941, 6.

173 Mary Ann Ramsey, "Only Yesteryear," *Naval History*, Winter 1991, vol. 5, no. 4; online http://www.ussblockisland.org/Beta/Welcome.html

174 Patricia Bellinger Kauffmann, phone interview, May 7, 2014.

175 "Widow of Navy Hero Returns from Hawaii," *The San Francisco Examiner*, December 21, 1941, 9.

176 Naval Historical Center, online, http://www.history.navy.mil/photos/pers-us/uspers-j/hc-jones.htm

177 Green Papers, "Report to the Military Governor, January 1 to June 30, 1942," July 20, 1942, Restoration of Civilian Government, Reel 2 Folder 7.

The need for a Cargo and Passenger Control became apparent in December, given the number and differing speeds of vessels and escorts traveling both ways between Hawaii and the West Coast. For example, two convoys departed San Francisco on January 17 with the fast group (*Lurline, Matsonia* and *Monterey*) escorted by the USS *St Louis, Smith* and *Preston* arriving in Honolulu on December 21, making about 18 knots along the way. The slower group of vessels (*Aldebaran, Harris, Sabine, Tasker Bliss, Platte, President Garfield* and *Hercules*), escorted by the USS *Phoenix, Cushing* and *Perkins*, traveling at 14 knots, arrived at Pearl Harbor of the 24th. See WD 14, RG 38, NACP.

178 Pessel to Frucht, December 23, 1941, ND 12, RG 181, NASF.

179 "In mid-December," Frucht to Barrett, December 18, 1941, ND 12, RG 181, NASF; "structure didn't work," Bloch to Commander-in-Chief, Pacific Fleet, December 26, 1941, ND 12, RG 181, NASF; and "On February 13," "Army Announces Evacuation Priority List: Transport Service Takes Full Charge," *Honolulu Advertiser*, February 13, 1942, 4; "Castle & Cooke," "Castle & Cooke, Limited Announces" (advertisement), *Honolulu Advertiser*, February 13, 1942, 9.

180 Green Diary, February 10 and February 9, 1942.

181 "Control of the evacuation," Note in a Memorandum from Marshall to Adjutant General, March n.d., 1942, Records of the Adjutant General's Office, 1917–1958, RG 407, NACP; "pool the space," OPNAV to COM 14, December 12, 1941, Brief of War Diaries for the Month of 8–31 December, 1941, WD 14, RG 38, NACP.

182 "Navy's position," COM 14 to OPNAV, March 1, 1942, RG 407, NACP; "morale would suffer,' Emmons to Adjutant General, March 11, 1942, Memorandum for the Chief of Staff from Dwight Eisenhower, Assistant Chief of Staff, March 17, 1942, RG 407, NACP.

183 Frucht to Pessel, December 23, 1941; Pessel to Frucht, December 24, 1941; and Frucht to Castle & Cooke, December 24, 1941, ND 12, RG 181, NASF.

184 Midkiff to Locey, January 4, 1942; Midkiff to Green, January 3, 1942; Midkiff to Locey, Jan. 8, 1942; and Midkiff to Emmons, Jan. 5, 1942, OCD, Director's Administrative Files (DAF), Evacuation Division to 6/1942, Correspondence, Maps, Plans 1941–42, HSA; and Green Diary, January 22, 1942.

185 Midkiff to Green, January 3, 1941 (sic) AFMP, RG 494, NACP. Midkiff put the wrong year on the document.

186 Colonel Robert Dunlop, Adjutant General's Office, to Army Transport Service, Honolulu, February 8, 1942, AFMP, RG 494, NACP.

187 Midkiff to Emmons, February 22, 1942, AFMP, RG 494, NACP.

188 Green Papers, Reel 12, Folder 5. See also: Green Online, Chapter XVIII, "Evacuation of Women and Children."

189 Ibid.

190 Ibid., Green Online.

191 Irene Chilton in *We Remember Pearl Harbor*, 336–37.

192 Leverton Diary. Although that fear never materialized for Leverton and his family, it was precisely what happened to Bob Briner, then a 9-year-old, whose father, an officer on the USS *Pennsylvania*, greeted his arriving family's convoy at the docks in San Francisco on February 21. The *Pennsylvania*, the ship on which Andrew Marze was killed, had been sent for extensive repairs shortly after the December 7 attack. Bob Briner, phone interview, August 2, 2006.

193 Herzog, phone interview, December 9, 2001.

194 Rhoda Riddell, "I'll Be Seeing You," *Modern Maturity*, November/December, 2001, 14; Peggy Ryan, "A Navy Bride Learns to Cope," in *Air Raid: Pearl Harbor!*, 235; and Joan Martin Rodby in *We Remember Pearl Harbor*, 87.

195 Jeannette (Jay) Westin phone interviews, December 29, 31, 2008 and January 5, 2009.

196 Ginger's Diary, 1941, http://gingersdiary.com.

197 "Sister's...girlfriends," Peter Fullinwider, phone interview, August 1, 2006; "celebrated New Year's Eve," Joan Weller, phone interview, August 7, 2006; and 'in the drink," Bob Moritz interview, September 23, 2015.

198 Edna Reese, Recreation Report, March 1, 1942, OCD, DAF, Mainland Correspondence, 1942, HSA.

199 "Pineapples," from the Log of the USS *Wharton* http://usswharton.com/shipslog.html

200 Beverly Moglich, email message, July 14, 2002.

201 Jones and Jones, 115.

202 "Jittery Cats, Gun-Shy Dogs Arrive from Battle Zone," *Oakland Tribune*, April 23, 1942, 1.

203 Ryan, "A Navy Bride Learns to Cope," in *Air Raid: Pearl Harbor!*, 235–237.

204 Much of the detail of Ryan's description of her crossing can be verified by archival material. All of the ships she mentions in her story were indeed part of Convoy 4093 departing Honolulu on April 22 and arriving at San Francisco on the 30th. And the USS *San Francisco, Reid* and *Case* were the three warships providing escort. Even the fact that the *Nevada* left the convoy just before arriving on the West Coast is verified by CincPac records found in the National Archives in College Park. Ms. Ryan was obviously a very keen observer despite spending much of the voyage, as she says, "in my bunk."

205 "T.H. Wounded Reach W. Coast," *The Honolulu Advertiser*, January 1, 1942, 1; Mrs. Rothe, "An Inquiry from one who wants to help," *The Honolulu Advertiser*, January 7, 1942, 8; and *The Honolulu Advertiser*, February 21, 1942, 10.

206 *The Honolulu Advertiser*, February 1, 2, 14 and 15, 1942.

207 "A bargain price," Lawrence Rodriggs, *We Remember Pearl Harbor: Honolulu Citizens Recall the War Years, 1941–1945* (Newark, CA: Communications Concepts, 1991), 130–31. Rodriggs offers several more examples; and "two years earlier," Willie Jarvis, telephone interview, May 29, 2007.

208 Gilman, "Hawaii War Diary," *The Honolulu Advertiser*, February 14, 1942, 10.

209 Gilman, "Evacuees are packing," February 19, 1942, 10; "a mere trickle," March 13, 1942, 10; "trickle eastward,", April 23, 1942, 12; and "without military approvals," March 31, 1942, 3.

210 Gilman, "Those nasty newspapermen," March 9, 1942, 6; "lay it on thick," March 14, 1942, 10; and "another lecture", March 16, 1942, 8.

211 Gilman, "Hadn't returned," February 13, 1942, 12; and "in Honolulu several times," February 22, 1942, 24.

212 Gilman., March 14, 1942, 10.

213 Gilman., March 23, 1942, 8.

214 Gilman, April 4, 1942, 8.

215 "Do you know whether,", John U. Terrell, "War Comes to the Coast," *San Francisco Chronicle*, December 26, 1941, 1, 5; "boys with the burns," Dick Pearce, "More Hawaii Wounded Arrive," *The San Francisco Examiner*, January 1, 1942, 8; "Joe Louis punch," Ernest Lenn, "Ships With Hawaii Injured Reach S.F.," *The San Francisco Examiner*, December 26, 1941, B.

216 Hazel Holly, "Women Volunteers Greet Evacuees," *The San Francisco Examiner*, January 1, 1942, 15.

217 Zilfa Estcourt, "Women in War," *San Francisco Chronicle*, December 29, 1941, 6.

218 Ernie Pyle, "The Roving Reporter," *The Wyoming Eagle*, January 3, 1942, 23.

219 "The Hawaii Evacuees," *San Francisco Chronicle*, December 27, 1941, 7.

220 Evacuee Program, Red Cross File, NACP.

221 Hazel Holly, "Women Volunteers..." *The San Francisco Examiner*, December 27, 1941, 15; and Operations Report – Evacuee Program (Evacuee Program), December 25, 1941, Red Cross File, NACP.

222 Lenn, December 26, 1941, 1.

223 "My Husband is fighting," Terrell, *San Francisco Chronicle*, December 26, 1941, 5; "dry-cork life vest," Merle Williams, Jr., telephone interview, July 14, 2006.

224 "Daddy told us to run," Dick Pearce, "Young Evacuees Tell of Attack," *The San Francisco Examiner*, December 26, 1941, 1B; and "I didn't cry," "Children Tell More Details," *The San Francisco Examiner*, December 27, 1941, 5.

225 Pearce, "More Hawaii Wounded," *The San Francisco Examiner*, January 1, 1942, 1, 2

226 "The Pacific War: S.F. Doesn't Know," *San Francisco Chronicle*, December 27, 1941, 7.

227 Gilman, "Hawaii War Diary," *The Honolulu Advertiser*, April 4, 1942, 8, and March 14, 1942, 10.

228 President Roosevelt established the Office of Censorship with Executive Order No. 8985. The Office issued a voluntary censorship code on January 15, 1942. See: Michael S. Sweeney. *Secrets of Victory: The Office of Censorship and the American Press and Radio in World War II* (Chapel Hill: The University of North Carolina Press, 2001), 36, 41.

229 "Evacuees Picture Horror in Hawaii," *The San Francisco Examiner*, January 1, 1942, 8.

230 A note about January 6, 1942: The only major American author to witness the attack on Pearl Harbor was James Jones, whose masterpiece, *From Here to Eternity*, one of the only works of fiction to even mention the civilian evacuation, contains vivid descriptions of the attack and a realistic portrayal of Army life in Hawaii before World War II. In one aspect of his book, though, Jones got things completely wrong. The book ends with a meeting between the two main female characters departing on the *Lurline* on January 6th as a Navy band plays *Aloha Oe*, while waving passengers festooned with leis throw flowers and streamers to the people waving on the dock. Children run about playing and one of the characters throws a lei over the side. No one wears a life vest. The characters in the preceding pages bandy about the departure date of January 6th as the date they booked passage to go to the mainland. In reality, such dates were a military secret, accommodations were Spartan, and nothing was permitted to be thrown over the side because it could alert Japanese submarines that a ship was in the area. Moreover, the docks were off limits to civilians unless they held orders to evacuate. In reality, on January 6th the *Lurline* departed San Diego in a convoy headed to Pago Pago. See: War Diaries, January 1, 1942 to January 31, 1942, p. 26, WD 14, RG 38, NACP.

231 "Ship Reaches S.F.," *Oakland Tribune*, January 7, 1942, http://www.thepearlharborarchive.com.

232 Tom Treanor, "The Home Front," *Los Angeles Times,* March 6, 1942, A. ProQuest Historical Newspapers, online: http://proquest.umi.com.

233 A. L. Schafer, Manager, Pacific Area, to James L. Feiser, Vice-Chairman in Charge of Domestic Operations, National Headquarters, February 14, 1942, Red Cross File.

234 Adams to (General Emmons), Commanding General, Hawaiian Department, Paraphrase of Radiogram, December 15, 1941, Evacuation of Military, Naval, and Civilian Personnel, Decimal File 1940–1942, RG 407, NACP; "Evacuees With Tropical Garb," *The San Francisco Examiner,* January 2, 1942, 2.

235 Ferris F. Laune, Secretary of the Hawaiian Council for Social Agencies, to General Thomas Green, Executive Officer, Office of Military Governor, May 20, 1942, Correspondence: Evacuation of Civilians from Hawaii, 1941–1945, RG 494, NACP.

236 "Secured a room," Earle, 97; and "we waited for hours," Moglich, email interview..

237 Irene R. Chilton, in *We Remember Pearl Harbor,* 338–39.

238 Anne Carter, Disaster Service, to A.L. Schafer, Manager, Pacific Area, July 3, 1942, Red Cross File.

239 Marion McEniry, "Comfort, Aid Awaits Evacuees at Center," *The San Francisco Examiner,* January 17, 1942, B.

240 McEniry, "New Navy Organization Aids Its Own Evacuees," *The San Francisco Examiner,* January 8, 1942, 13.

241 "Official driving organization," Hazel Holly, "Mixup Mars Reception of Evacuees," *The San Francisco Examiner,* January 22, 1942, B; "ran classes," Zilfa Estcourt, "Women and War on Two Continents: This is as Much a Woman's Fight as a Man's Fight... The Energetic AWVS in San Francisco," *San Francisco Chronicle,* January 11, 1942, S1.

242 "Starting in a basement," Janet Flanner, "Profiles Ladies in Uniform," *The New Yorker,* July 4, 1942, 21; "claimed 350,000 members," Doris Weatherford. *American Women and World War II* (New York: Facts on File, 1990), 233; and "integrated units," Emily Yellin. *Our Mothers' War: American Women at Home and at the Front During World War II* (New York: Free Press, 2004), 210.

243 "Civilian Defense: The Ladies!" *Time,* January 26, 1942, 61–62.

244 Convoy 4036 consisted of the *President Taylor, President Johnson, Henderson, Cuyama, Etolin, Pennant, Maui* and *Japara,* a Dutch ship.

The USS Honolulu, Farragut and Cummings provided escort. See Appendix.

245 "A Red Cross car?" Holly, "Mixup Mars," B; "information card," "OCD Chief Backs Red Cross in Row," *San Francisco Examiner*, January 25, 1942, 7; and "wild confusion," Holly, "Mixup Mars," 1.

246 Office of Civilian Defense, Joint Statement, January 19, 1942, Red Cross File.

247 "The Red Cross Comes First," *San Francisco Chronicle*, January 24, 1942, 10.

248 "Women's Feud Over War Aid Settled," *The San Francisco Examiner*, January 27, 1942, 1, 7.

249 "Red Cross Group Will Go to 'Front,'" *San Francisco Chronicle*, January 26, 1942, 8.

250 "Red Cross Put in Charge of Evacuees," *San Francisco Chronicle*, January 25, 1942, 1, 17.

251 Consisting of the *U.S. Grant, Wharton, Kitty Hawk, Lurline* and *President Garfield* to San Francisco, and the *Aquitania* to San Pedro. Escort provided by the USS *Raleigh, Tucker* and *Conyngham*. See Appendix.

252 Hazel W. Gill to Honolulu Chapter, March 3, 1942. OCD Box 339/1 Director's Admin Files, Evacuation – Mainland Correspondence 1942, HSA.

253 Frederick J. Koster, San Francisco Chapter, American Red Cross, to Schafer, March 23, 1942, Red Cross File.

254 Schafer to Feiser, December 28, 1941, Red Cross File.

255 Stimson to Davis, January 27, 1942, Red Cross File.

256 Schafer to Feiser, March 25, 1942, Red Cross File.

257 Ibid.

258 Vincent to Hepner, May 20, 1942, Red Cross File.

259 Carter to Schafer, July 3, 1942, Red Cross File.

260 Ibid.

261 Schafer to DeWitt Smith, July 5, 1942, Red Cross File.

262 Gail Moul, phone interview, December 23, 2006.

263 Weather information comes from a variety of newspapers throughout the country, including: *Ogden Standard-Examiner*, January 2, 1942, 16; *Reno Evening Gazette*, January 5, 1942, 14; "Clicks from the Rails" column, *Ogden Standard-Examiner*, January 4, 1942, 6-A;

Laramie Republican Boomerang, Jan. 2, 1942, 2; *Omaha Morning World Herald*, Jan 2, 1942; and *Atlanta Journal*, Jan 12, 1942, 1

264 Mary B. Perry, Regional Child Consultant, to Richard N. Neustadt, Office of Defense Health and Welfare Services, January 9, 1942, Red Cross File.

265 Ibid. Cross-country rail travel remained challenging throughout the war. Describing her cross-country trip after arriving in San Francisco aboard the Lurline on March 1, 1942, Beverly Moglich noted that the train was crowded with troops, families of servicemen, and evacuees. The smoke from the coal-fired engine covered everything in a black dust and got into eyes, ears, and noses. There was water for the washbasins, but no showers during the five-day journey. After arriving at her destination, when she could finally wash her hair, the water turned black from the soot. See: Beverly Moglich, *Memoirs of a Navy Brat: A Girl's Adventure during the Depression and World War II,* Self-Published. Parker, Co: Outskirts Press, 2010, 139.

266 "Two trains," "Philippine Refugees Go Thru City," *North Platte (Neb.) Daily Bulletin*, January 3, 1942, 13; "Two days later," "Canteen Still Urges Donations," *North Platte (Neb.) Daily Telegraph,* January 5, 1942, 6; "husband was killed," "Appreciation of Canteen Expressed," *Daily Bulletin*, January 6, 1942, 6.

267 "Miss Wilson to write," "U.P. Donates Diningroom [ok] For Canteen," *Daily Bulletin*, January 1, 1942, 1; "4,700 soldiers", "Dining Room Donated for Canteen Use," *Daily Telegraph*, January 1, 1942, 10.

268 "The local chapter complied," C.W. Hendricks, Executive Director, El Paso Chapter, to Ruth Frederick, Administrative Assistant Chapter Service, May 14, 1942; "other chapters faced," H.F. Keisker [ok], Administrator, Services to the Armed Forces, Midwestern Area, to Robert E. Bondy, Administrator, Services to the Armed Forces, Washington, D.C. May 20, 1942; "nurses and social workers," Charles F. Ernst, Area Administrator, Services to the Armed Forces, to Bondy, June 16, 1942, Red Cross File.

269 A. L. Schafer, Manager, American Red Cross (ARC), Pacific Area, to F.A. Winfrey, ARC, National Headquarters, April 18, 1942, Red Cross File.

270 Bondy to Walter Marshall, ARC, Pacific Area, December 19, 1942, Red Cross File.

271 "Mrs. Doris Marzer (sic)...Unheard From at Honolulu," *Salem Evening News*, December 11, 1941, 2; and "Husband of Salem Girl Killed," *Salem Evening News*, December 20, 1941, 1; "Death of Petty Officer Cabled Salem Mother," *Boston Herald*, December 20, 1941, 24; and "Widow Returns," *Salem Evening News*, January 8, 1942.

272 "Widow's Brother Enlists," Unknown Newspaper, January 10, 1942. Seventeen-year-old Everett wanted to enlist too, but his mother wouldn't sign for him. She had lost too much already. He would have to wait until he turned 18, enlisting in the Navy in May, 1942.

273 "Pearl Harbor Premonition? Navy Man Killed in Action Gave Christmas Gifts Early Widow Reveals in Salem," *Boston Daily Globe*, January 10, 1942, 3.

274 "He's a Veteran at 10," *Kansas City Star*, February 6, 1942, 17, www/thepearlharborarchive.com.

275 Felix McGivney, "Galveston Students Who Had Narrow Escape," *Galveston Daily News*, 17 April 1942, 8, www/thepearlharborarchive.com.

276 "Pay Tribute to Lockard at Dinner," *The Williamsport Sun*, March 12, 1942, 1, 2.

277 "Lockard's Testimonial," *Ibid.*, 10.

278 Milton Silverman, "Isle Evacuees Mix Sorrow with Elation," *San Francisco Chronicle*, Dec. 26, 1941, 1.

279 Anne Carter, Caseworker, to A. L. Schafer, Manager of Pacific Area, American Red Cross, July 3, 1942, Red Cross File.

280 Harry L. Walden, Director, Military and Naval Welfare Service, Pacific Branch, to Don C. Smith, Director, Military and Naval Welfare, Washington, D.C., January 12, 1942, Red Cross File.

281 "War Diaries, January and February, 1942, p. 9, WD 14, RG 38, NACP.

282 "January evacuation figures," War Diaries, January and February, 1942, p. 9, WD 14, RG 38, NACP; and "even greater numbers," Schafer to Dewitt Smith, January 18, 1942, Red Cross File.

283 Gwenfread Allen, 107–08.

284 Midkiff to Greenslade, May 26, 1942, Commandant's Coded Administrative Records, Records of the Naval Districts and Shore Establishments, ND 12, RG 181, NASF.

285 To give an idea of what troop class might mean, consider that the SS Coolidge as a commercial passenger liner could carry about 980

passengers in all classes and 324 crew, but as a troop carrier over 5,000 soldiers.

286 Midkiff to Lucas; Midkiff to Jenna, May 26, 1942; Midkiff to All Registrants, June 1, 1942; and Greenslade to Midkiff, June 2, 1942, ND 12, RG 181, NASF.

287 Schafer to L.M. Mitchell, ARC National Headquarters, Washington, D.C., October 15, 1942, Red Cross File.

288 For example, 65 wives and children of servicemen arrived in Seattle on January 7, 1942 from Alaska, where "evacuations are being made in order to prevent a housing shortage, and the [sic] provide more cargo space for military supplies." See: "Evacuees Tell of Jap Raid." *The Oregonian* [Portland, Oregon] 8 Jan. 1942, 3. Readex: America's Historical Newspapers. Web. 26 Sep. 2011.

289 See: David Wilma, "War Department asks Children's Orthopedic Hospital Guilds to assist secret movement of Hawaii evacuees on March 29, 1942," HistroyLink.org, February 25, 2004. The Red Cross table shows that far fewer evacuees arrived in Seattle in March and April, although it is possible that evacuees were rerouted to Seattle after landing in San Francisco, which received over 6,000 evacuees in April alone.

290 Ellenmerle Heiges interview, August 14, 2005.

291 Schafer to Dewitt Smith, July 5, 1942, report from Anne Carter enclosed, Red Cross File.

292 "Of those getting off," Carter to Schafer, July 3, 1942; and "from other parts," Schafer to Dewitt Smith, July 5, 1942, Red Cross File.

293 Green Papers, Wartime Security Controls in Hawaii, Part 7 - Conservation and Utilization of Transportation Facilities, pp. 34, 37, Reel 19. In a radiogram to an unknown recipient on October 2, 1942, Emmons says that the evacuation of Army and Navy dependents "and other Caucasians" is "near completion." See: Evacuation of Dependents of Military, Naval, and Civilian Personnel, Records of the Adjutant General's Office, Records Group 407 (RG 407), NACP.

294 Ferris F. Laune, Secretary of the Hawaii Council for Social Agencies, to Green, May 20, 1942, and Green to Laune, June 8, 1942, MGH, RG 494, NACP; and Green to Mrs. Walter C. Grace, June 29, 1942, Correspondence re: to Evacuation of Civilians from Hawaii, 1941–45, MGH, RG 494, NACP.

295 Green Diary, September 11 and 12, 1942, Reel 4, Folder 1.

296 Hazel Holly, "Group From Islands Seeks Ship Home," *San Francisco Examiner*, January 14, 1942, 15.

297 Green Diary, September 12, 1942, USMHI.

298 Ibid., July 27, 1942 and October 15, 1942.

299 Jackson to Commandant, 14th Naval District, September 26, 1942, ND 12, RG 181, NASF.

300 Such a story appeared in the January 20, 1942 issue of *Honolulu Advertiser*, attributed to the Army. The story, couched in vague terms (families "may find," etc.), said that a limited supply of such housing, ranging in price from $13.50 to $28.50 a month, located in several sites in San Francisco, could be available for families of non-commissioned Army personnel and low-income civilian evacuee families.

301 Earle to Commandant, 12th Naval District, October 12, 1942, ND 12, RG 181, NASF.

302 "News From Home: Stranded Hawaiians Learn of Island Price Control, Blackouts," *San Francisco Chronicle*, January 14, 1942, 13.

303 Green Papers, Miscellaneous Writings – OMG Activity Reports, Passenger Transportation 7 Dec. 41 through 31 Dec. 42, Reel 14, USMHI.

304 Ibid.; and Green Papers, Wartime Security Controls in Hawaii: 1941–1945 (cont'd), Part 7: Conservation and Utilization of Transportation Facilities (Transportation Facilities), Reel 19, p. 47.

305 "News From Home," 13.

306 "Honolulu Women Here Will Assist Evacuees," *The San Francisco Examiner*, January 30, 1942, 15; and Zilfa Estcourt, "Women in War: New Red Cross Unit to Aid Stranded Islanders," *San Francisco Chronicle*, January 30, 1942, 12.

307 Green Diary, September 22, 1942, Reel 4, Folder 1.

308 Green Papers, Frank Midkiff to P. Thoron, Director of Territories and Insular Possessions, Dept. Of Interior, December 2, 1942, Martial Law – 1941–1943, Reel 1.

309 Green Papers, Wartime Security Controls in Hawaii: 1941–1945 (Cont'd), Part 7: Conservation and Utilization of Transportation Facilities, pp. 43–45, Reel 19.

310 Ibid., 48

311 Ibid.

312 Gwenfread Allen, 347.

313 *Ibid.*, 347, 348.

314 This does not included wounded servicemen who may have died during the crossing. For example, one sailor did succumb to his injuries just before the first convoy docked at San Francisco.

315 Quoted in Prange, *At Dawn*, 602.

316 Ibid., 631.

317 Quoted in Ibid., 724.

318 Interview with Joe Lockard, November 20, 2009.

319 National Park Service figures.

END